Advancing Grounded Theory with Mixed Methods

This groundbreaking book introduces an innovative new perspective on mixed method grounded theory methodology (MM-GTM) by conceptualizing it holistically as a distinct, qualitatively driven methodology that appreciates the integrity of each of the methods it embraces. This practical and accessible text advocates for using MM-GTM in a way that promote meaningful interaction between qualitative and quantitative data during analysis. Its principal contribution is to provide a set of research tools to develop or refine a multi-faceted analytical framework in applied fields in the social and behavioral sciences, including nursing.

Used as either a resource or a textbook in a survey course about research methods, the text references dozens of examples about how a dialectical exchange between different sources of data can be built into core grounded theory procedures, including theoretical sampling, coding, case-based memoing, and integrated visual displays. With a whole chapter devoted to reporting, the book also considers the way that indexes of quality that extend beyond methodological transparency can be used to evaluate research that partners mixed methods with grounded theory and other qualitative methods.

Featuring student-friendly pedagogy throughout, including self-assessment questions, a glossary, and a framework that summarizes key points, this text is an essential read for all research methods students or early career researchers ambitious to develop a theoretical perspective with qualitative, mixed methods, or evaluation.

Elizabeth G. Creamer is professor emerita of educational research and evaluation in the School of Education in the Virginia Tech College of Liberal Arts and Human Sciences. She is the author, co-author, or editor of more than more than 7 books, and nearly 200 peer-reviewed journal articles, book chapters, and reviews. Her most recent book is *An Introduction to Fully Integrated Mixed Methods Research* (SAGE, 2018).

Advancing Grounded Theory with Mixed Methods

Elizabeth G. Creamer

LONDON AND NEW YORK

First published 2022
by Routledge
2 Park Square, Milton Park, Abingdon, Oxon OX14 4RN

and by Routledge
605 Third Avenue, New York, NY 10158

Routledge is an imprint of the Taylor & Francis Group, an informa business

© 2022 Elizabeth G. Creamer

The right of Elizabeth G. Creamer to be identified as author of this work has been asserted by her in accordance with sections 77 and 78 of the Copyright, Designs and Patents Act 1988.

All rights reserved. No part of this book may be reprinted or reproduced or utilised in any form or by any electronic, mechanical, or other means, now known or hereafter invented, including photocopying and recording, or in any information storage or retrieval system, without permission in writing from the publishers.

Trademark notice: Product or corporate names may be trademarks or registered trademarks, and are used only for identification and explanation without intent to infringe.

British Library Cataloguing-in-Publication Data
A catalogue record for this book is available from the British Library

Library of Congress Cataloging-in-Publication Data
A catalog record for this book has been requested

ISBN: 978-0-367-17479-8 (hbk)
ISBN: 978-0-367-17480-4 (pbk)
ISBN: 978-0-429-05700-7 (ebk)

Typeset in Bembo MT Pro
by Apex CoVantage, LLC

Dedication

This book is dedicated to my older sister, born Linda Lee Greene, who died of leukemia just a few weeks before the COVID outbreak was officially acknowledged in the United States. She was an indefatigable champion of my turn to textbook writing and the audience of emerging scholars across the world it addresses.

Abbreviated table of contents

Preface		*xvii*
1	**Definitions**	**1**
2	**Variety**	**26**
3	**Process**	**46**
4	**Visualization**	**72**
5	**Dissonance**	**93**
6	**Reporting**	**119**
Appendices		*147*
Index		*168*

Annotated table of contents

1   Establishing language and purpose   1

This chapter builds an argument for the creative potential of partnering mixed methods with grounded theory for purposes of advancing analytical insight and developing an explanatory framework. It MM-GTM as a distinct methodology and creates a platform for dialog across disciplines by introducing key terminology.

2   Varied approaches to using mixed methods with theoretical frameworks   26

The chapter provides a glimpse of the range of ways that mixed methods has been paired with grounded theory and how it can serve as an integrative framework at the onset of a study, offer interpretive insight as a study is underway, and/or stand as its principal outcome.

3   Mixed methods and the process of theorizing   46

This chapter is about the procedures that advance theorizing, including how qualitative and quantitative data can be integrated through theoretical coding, analytical memo writing, case-based analysis, and theoretical sampling.

4   Advancing theoretical reasoning with visualizations   72

This chapter considers the ways that in empirical research, visual displays represent ideas at the same time they generate them. The chapter introduces creative approaches to integrating different sources of data in visual displays to advance theoretical reasoning. These include mapping, timelining, and variations of cluster mapping.

5   Leveraging dissonance to advance theoretical reasoning   93

The opportunity to engage dissonance and incongruities in the results emerging from different methods is a unique benefit of a mixed methods approach. When pursued systematically, these often generate original insight.

6   **Highlighting quality through reporting**   119

A specific research design or method is no guarantee that a study is scientific or that the results are credible or useful. This chapter considers different strategies that can be used to gauge the quality of MM-GTM research, including in the ways that research procedures or a final theoretical framework can be visualized effectively in a table or figure. A list of indicators of quality is discussed that extends beyond a singular reliance on transparency about research methods during reporting.

Detailed contents

List of tables, figures, and boxes	xiii
Preface	xvii
Purpose	xviii
Goals	xviii
Audience	xix
The author's qualifications and positionality	xx
Pedagogical features	xxi
1 Establishing language and purpose	**1**
Introduction	1
Various ways of defining theory and its purpose	3
Conceptualizing MM-GTM as a methodology	14
Distinguishing exemplars of an integrated approach to MM-GTM	20
Conclusions	23
2 Varied approaches to using mixed methods with theoretical frameworks	**26**
Introduction	26
Implications of the word "design"	28
Methodological adaptability of grounded theory	33
Consulting the literature throughout the research process	34
Demonstrating variability in MM-GTM with a group of exemplars	35
Conclusions	42
3 Mixed methods and the process of theorizing	**46**
Introduction	46
Integrated analysis using abduction	48
Introducing examples in this chapter	51
Singling out core grounded theory procedures	54

	Theoretical coding	*58*
	Mixed analysis through integrated case-based memos	*62*
	Theoretical sampling	*65*
	Conclusions	*69*
4	**Advancing theoretical reasoning with visualizations**	**72**
	Introduction	*72*
	Joint and integrative visual displays	*74*
	Different types of integrative displays	*77*
	Exploring examples of mixed methods used with a visual display to generate analytical insight	*78*
	Timelining as a visualization strategy that enables integration of different types of data	*81*
	Conclusions	*89*
5	**Leveraging dissonance to advance theoretical reasoning**	**93**
	Introduction	*93*
	Different perspectives about the centrality of dissonance to the research process	*96*
	Potential sources of dissonance that emerge over the life of a research project	*98*
	Designing for dissonance	*101*
	The chapter exemplars	*102*
	Exploring dissonance with a case-based approach in MM-GTM	*105*
	Warranting inferences through visual displays	*113*
	Conclusions	*116*
6	**Highlighting quality through reporting**	**119**
	Introduction	*119*
	Considering the variety evident in the chapter exemplars	*121*
	Articulating a methodological rationale for MM-GTM	*123*
	Visualizing a theoretical model developed with MM-GTM	*125*
	Wrestling with ways to gauge quality in MM-GTM	*130*
	Challenges faced by investigators using MM-GTM	*136*
	Conclusions	*139*
Glossary		*143*
Appendices		*147*
	Appendix A: List of exemplars by chapter	*149*
	Appendix B: List of examples of MM-GTM	*151*
	Appendix C: Summary by chapter and cross-cutting theme	*153*
References		*156*
Index		*168*

Tables, figures, and boxes

TABLES

1.1	Overview of Steps in the Process of Analyzing Multiple Sources of Data in MM-GTM Through an Abductive Process	18
1.2	List of Chapter Exemplars, Field, and Distinguishing Features	22
1.3	Linking Key Points from Chapter 1 with the Cross-Cutting Themes	24
2.1	Example Developed from Evans et al. (2011): Framing Multi-Dimensional Research Questions in Ways that Promote Integration	33
2.2	Contribution of the Literature to Theoretical Reasoning Throughout the Research Process	35
2.3	Innovative Features of the Three Exemplars of MM-GT from Chapter 2	36
2.4	Core Elements of a Formal Grounded Theory, Their Definition, and Key Components of the Catallo et al. Grounded Theory Model to Explain the Intimate Abuse Disclosure	40
2.5	Linking Chapter 2 to Cross-Cutting Themes	44
3.1	Innovative Features of the Four Examples of MM-GTM from Chapter 3	52
3.2	Illustrative Example of a Data Display from Multiple Sources of Data	54
3.3	Core Grounded Theory Procedures and Definitions	55
3.4	Priority Awarded to Core Grounded Theory Procedures by Schools of Thought	56
3.5	Frequency of the Use of Core Grounded Theory Procedures in an Analysis from a Systematic Review of 64 MM-GT Articles by Guetterman et al. (2017)	56
3.6	Illustrating Causal Pathways in the Grounded Theory Model Produced by Bussing et al. (2012)	61
3.7	Linking Key Themes from Chapter 3 to Cross-Cutting Themes	70
4.1	Purposes of Integrative Visual Displays in MM-GTM, by Phase	76
4.2	Definitions of Different Types of Visual Displays in MM-GTM	77
4.3	Examples of Visual Displays, by Field, Type, Purpose, and Stage of the Research Process	78

4.4	Davis and Baulch's (2011) Visual Depiction of Common Life Trajectories	84
4.5	Illustrative Joint Display Linking Qualitative and Quantitative Data from the Data Matrix from the Forest Example	88
4.6	Linking Key Themes from Chapter 4 to Cross-Cutting Themes	90
5.1	Varying Points of View about Exceptions, Dissonance, and the Need for Verification in Grounded Theory and the Implications for Mixed Method Designs, by School of Thought	98
5.2	Procedures that Leverage Dissonance in Ways that Advance Theoretical Reasoning	101
5.3	Innovative Features of the Chapter Exemplars	102
5.4	Example of Data for a Case-Based Analysis with Visual Components	106
5.5	Shell of a Concordance Table Illustrating a Way to Document Strength of Support Across Cases	114
5.6	Excerpt from a Joint Display from Castro et al. (2010) that Reveals a Clear Pattern	115
5.7	Documenting the Systematic Testing of Alternative Explanations from the Hypothetical Collaborative Space Study	116
5.8	Additions from Chapter 5 to the Architecture of the Cross-Cutting Themes	117
6.1	Documenting the Contribution of Selected Theoretical Propositions from a Grounded Theory Model: A Hypothetical Example	136

FIGURES

1.1	Final Composite Model from Kawamura et al. (2009)	13
1.2	The Link Between Mixed Methods, Grounded Theory Methods, and Theory Building	15
1.3	Overlap Between the Analytic Logic and Procedures of Grounded Theory and Mixed Methods	20
2.1	Framing a Research Problem in a Multi-Dimensional Way	30
2.2	A Multi-Level Conceptual Model from Evans et al. (2011, p. 280)	32
3.1	An Inductive–Deductive–Abductive Analytical Cycle: Integrative MMR-GTM	50
3.2	Conceptual Model from Bussing et al. (2012)	60
3.3	A Facsimile of the Timeline Completed by Participants in the Study About War-Related Trauma	69
4.1	Example of a Case-Based Timeline	83
4.2	Generating Analytical Insight from a Matrix-Mapping Activity	86
4.3	Procedural Diagram of the Design of Matrix-Mapping Activity	87
5.1	Potential Sources of Dissonance in a MM-GTM Study	100
5.2	Embodying a Stair-Step Process to Develop Theory from a Mixed Method Case-Based Analysis	110
6.1	A Final Composite Grounded Theory Model from Shim et al. (2017)	129
6.2	Wesely's (2010) Procedural Diagram Showing in Interactive Design	133

BOXES

1.1	Kawamura et al.'s (2009) Study of the Impact of a Health Intervention	11
2.1	Evans et al.'s (2009, 2011) Adaptation of a Life Course Perspective	37
2.2	Catallo et al.'s (2013) Use of MM-GTM to Understand Paradox in a Randomized Control Trial	39
2.3	Westhues et al.'s (2008) Study About Mental Health Services for Immigrant Populations in Canada	41
3.1	Jone's and Kafetsios's (2005) Study About War-Related Childhood Trauma	67
5.1	Exploring Group Differences in a Study About the Implementation of Management Software by Kaplan and Duchon (1988)	104
5.2	Using Mixed Method Case Studies to Theorize Public Space in London by Carmona (2015)	107
5.3	An Exploration of the Link Between Motivation and Persistence in a Language Immersion Program by Wesely (2010)	112
6.1	Shim et al.'s (2017) MM-GTM Study About a Health Intervention	127

Preface

Leading experts in the development of grounded theory have long expressed support for the potential to consider multiple sources of data in service of using a qualitative approach to develop or refine an explanatory framework. Those endorsing the idea of utilizing quantitative data along with qualitative data in grounded theory have not considered the impact this could have on research procedures like theoretical sampling. Despite this long-standing endorsement of the benefits of collecting both qualitative and quantitative data and evidence that this has been done with some frequency in practice, no one to date has dedicated the type of attention that is needed to create an intellectual framework for how mixed methods and grounded theory can be paired in ways that respect the integrity of each.

Both mixed methods and grounded theory have proven themselves to be methodologies that are adaptable to diverse circumstances and philosophical paradigms (Sebastian, 2019; Urquhart, 2013). This groundbreaking book introduces an innovative perspective on mixed method grounded theory methodology (MM-GTM) by conceptualizing it holistically as a distinct, qualitatively robust method and methodology that retains the integrity each of the methodologies it embraces. The methodology builds on the multiple areas of overlap between the methodological assumptions of grounded theory and mixed methods, while at the same time recognizing that each has a unique contribution to make. MM-GTM takes advantage of the strengths of each method. The methodological framework presented is not positioned as a critique of grounded theory, but an expansion of the ways it can be used in conjunction with different types of data.

Advancing Grounded Theory with Mixed Methods illustrates ways that the interest in diverse perspectives embedded in a dialectical logic that includes abduction can reframe core grounded theory procedures, like coding and theoretical sampling, as mixed method procedures. This approach disrupts the notion that using mixed methods with grounded theory is accomplished simply by the addition of quantitative data or analytical procedures. It also contests the assumption that the main reason for pairing mixed methods with grounded theory is to add a quantitative stage whose purpose is to confirm the qualitative findings. Instead, it proposes a methodological framework that maintains the integrity of both the method and methodology of grounded theory, while demonstrating ways they can be used in tandem with other methods to generate new analytical and theoretical insight that is useful in applied fields.

Academic fields differ in the priority awarded to research that has a theoretical foundation. It is mandatory for research in some fields, like experimental psychology, where an investigator is expected to deploy a formal theory that has demonstrated reliability in multiple settings. The role of an off-the-shelf theory as an indicator of quality is less apparent in fields that have a distinctly applied focus, including nursing and education where grounded theory has been used most widely. In those settings, a theoretical framework is sometimes consulted later in the research process to explain unexpected findings. A methodologist well known in the community of nursing scholars and among mixed methodologists, Margarite Sandelowski (1993) maintains, stated or not, theoretical understanding is always implicit in the way a problem is conceived.

The framework I present in this book develops the idea of MM-GTM as both a method and a methodology. It foregrounds an iterative and interactive approach to data analysis by overlaying an abductive logic where a back and forth exchange between different types of data is embedded in the core set of grounded theory procedures.

PURPOSE

The aim of this practical text is to serve as both a resource and an instructional tool to advance the use of qualitative and mixed method procedures in the development and refinement of evidence-based explanatory frameworks in education, health sciences, and other applied fields. I use the expression "explanatory framework" as an umbrella term that includes a grounded theory, a conceptual framework developed from the literature, and a theoretical framework that is developed through the systematic empirical procedures. I build on the argument that "Qualitative research can be prominent in mixed methods research rather than compromised by it" (Creswell, Shope, Plano Clark, & Green, 2006, p. 1).

This text opens the door to a conversation between qualitative and mixed methods research by presenting MM-GTM as a type of integration at the methodological level where both methods make a substantive contribution to explanatory insight. This book is not the resource to consult for a detailed dissection of differences between the ways that the founders, Glaser and Strauss, approached grounded theory. Nor does it provide a painstaking historical review about the ways their thinking evolved over time that already has been well-documented. Although I take pains to recognize that there are differences between grounded theory approached with a post-positivist, pragmatist, constructivist, interpretive, or postmodern framework on such issues as the role of literature, I do this principally to emphasize the dynamism of the methodology and the ways it has been adapted in practice.

GOALS

This book aims to arm an investigator new to mixed methods and/or grounded theory with the practical tools necessary to execute MM-GTM, without the suggestion that it uses a "cookbook" or "one-size-fits-all" approach. Each chapter has a one- or two-word title that zeroes in on its purpose. The topics addressed in each chapter are listed as follows.

1. **Chapter 1: Definitions.** This chapter builds an argument for the creative potential of partnering mixed methods with grounded theory for purposes of advancing analytical

insight and developing an explanatory framework. It presents MM-GTM as a distinct methodology and creates a platform for dialog across disciplines by introducing key terminology.
2. **Chapter 2: Variety.** This chapter provides a glimpse of the range of ways that mixed methods has been paired with grounded theory and how it can serve as an integrative framework at the onset of a study, offer interpretive insight as a study is underway, and/or stand as its principal outcome.
3. **Chapter 3: Process.** This chapter is about the procedures that advance theorizing, including how qualitative and quantitative data can be integrated through theoretical coding, analytical memo writing, case-based analysis, and theoretical sampling.
4. **Chapter 4: Visual Displays**. This chapter considers ways that in empirical research, visual displays represent ideas at the same time they generate them. The chapter introduces creative approaches to integrating different sources of data in visual displays to advance theoretical reasoning. These include mapping, timelining, and variations of cluster mapping.
5. **Chapter 5: Dissonance.** This chapter explores how the opportunity to engage dissonance and incongruities in the results emerging from different methods is a unique benefit of a mixed methods approach. When pursued systematically, these are often generate original insight.
6. **Chapter 6: Reporting.** This chapter considers different strategies that can be used to gauge the quality of MM-GTM research, including in the ways that research procedures or a final theoretical framework can be visualized effectively in a table or figure. A list of indicators of quality is discussed that extend beyond a singular reliance on transparency about research methods during reporting.

AUDIENCE

Grounded theory has become a dominant data-analytic technique in a wide variety of academic disciplines, including sociology, anthropology, social work, education, information, management, nursing, and other fields related to health (Timmermans & Tavory, 2012). In addition to this list, the book is a resource for early career researchers across the world in other applied fields, including child development, counseling, criminology, business and management, human geography, gerontology, and instructional technology. A set of exemplars is featured that were produced by researchers in diverse fields. The fact that the selection includes several exemplars that were launched during doctoral research is meant to underscore that combining mixed methods and grounded theory is not an inordinately ambitious goal for a doctoral student. Added to that is the conviction that building or refining a theoretical framework is critical to the skill set of novice researchers with an ambition to publish.

The textbook will advance the skills of undergraduate and graduate students enrolled in a research methods course in qualitative, mixed methods, or evaluation. Its most likely home is a course about qualitative research methods where it would serve as an effective companion to classic texts about qualitative research by Merriam and Tisdell (2016) or Patton (2002) that introduce students to a generic set of qualitative analytical procedures. *Advancing Grounded Theory with Mixed Methods* is compatible for pairing with books about grounded theory, including those by Corbin and Strauss (2008) and Charmaz (2006, 2014a). In an evaluation course, this text could be used to guide a content analysis designed to construct a contextually nuanced conceptual framework to guide data collection and analysis. The text will extend a mixed methods research course designed to provide students the skills necessary to write an effective grant proposal. The insight offered by the text could be leveraged by an assignment to build and refine a conceptual framework from the literature and, subsequently, to use it as a guide for developing an interview or observation protocol.

THE AUTHOR'S QUALIFICATIONS AND POSITIONALITY

My qualifications for authoring this textbook are related to my experience as a researcher, teacher, and writer. For the majority of my career, my research. I taught doctoral level methods courses in both qualitative research and mixed methods research at a research university in the United States for over 20 years. An experience developing the modules for my first online course in mixed method research approaches provided a springboard for the publication of my 2018 textbook, *An Introduction to Fully Integrated Mixed Methods Research*. In that book, I introduced a framework that reflects a conviction of the power of embedding the intention to integrate data sources throughout all phases of the research process and the phrase coined by Jennifer Greene in 2007, a mixed method way of thinking. I join her and another esteemed colleague, Pat Bazeley (2018a), to emphasize the potential gain to conceptual and theoretical insight when different sources of data are integrated during analysis.

The analytical procedures I propose in this textbook reflect my affinity for the groundbreaking work of Kathy Charmaz (2014a) and her constructivist approach to grounded theory. With the foundational view that knowledge is constructed, rather than discovered, and the acknowledgment that more than one empirically grounded interpretation is not only possible but likely, I find that the constructivist paradigm is closer to my own views about the nature of knowledge and how it is constructed than other approaches to grounded theory. I join Charmaz in avoiding discussions of causality that are associated with a realist perspective. I waiver from Charmaz's constructivist approach in that I am not a relativist. I am more compelled than Charmaz was to pursue differences between the perspectives of participants, not for purposes of reconciling them, but to get a better glimpse at the social forces that might lie underneath.

This textbook is aimed at an international audience. The framing of mixed methods in this textbook is influenced by writers in the United States, the United Kingdom, and from the growing group of researchers interested in mixed methods that I have met from Australia, China, Europe, Japan, New Zealand, the Philippines, and South America. My approach to mixed methods reflects an offshoot of constructivism referred to as dialectical pluralism (Johnson, 2012; Johnson & Schoonenboom, 2015). The principal reason for this is my fascination with the contribution of dissonance, incongruities, and contradiction between results from the analysis of different types and sources of data to explanatory insight (Creamer & Edwards, 2019).

My interest in polyvocality in the representation of authors' voices (Creamer, 2011), resistance to formulaic approaches, and awe about research in the face of so much complexity inches my views closer to the postmodern camp. I am persuaded that there is much to be gained by designing a research project to purposefully leverage different viewpoints and perspectives. I present MM-GTM in a practical way, but not in a way that suggests it is a recipe or rule book that should be slavishly followed, but as a platform, like a diving board, for the generation of innovative new perspectives, methods, and methodological combinations. The perspective underscores the important role that creativity, persistence, and intense curiosity can play in producing research that impacts practice.

Most MM-GTM is complex and likely to unfold across multiple phases and in ways that are not entirely predictable (Johnson & Walsh, 2019). Joining Mertens (2015) in prioritizing the complexity of mixed method research, as Canadian scholar Cheryl Poth does (2018a, 2018b), introduces tensions with the naming systems associated with mixed method and with research conducted in two phases with distinct qualitative and quantitative strands. A scholar from the United Kingdom Nigel Fielding made a similar observation, writing: "Following textbook prescriptions laying down approved research designs may be a necessary rite of passage, but the benefits of mixing methods flow from creative innovation and conceptualizing rather than a pragmatic approach" (2012, p. 126).

I depart from many of my US-based colleagues and the preoccupation with classifying and naming study mixed methods designs based on the timing and sequence of data collection and analysis. The complexity of the research designs evident in practice and the fact that no two studies are alike is one explanation for why I cannot center research design in the discussion of mixed methods that appears in this text. The increasing frequency of practice that foregoes data collection by using existing databases also negates the usefulness of defining research design by the timing of data collection and analysis. I do not categorize the studies I incorporate in this text with the common terminology used in mixed methods about basic designs, believing it would be too cumbersome and potentially alienating for the cross-disciplinary audience that is my target.

PEDAGOGICAL FEATURES

Several features incorporated in this textbook are designed to facilitate instruction and ease the process for the reader to distill key points. These are:

- The text has an architecture or infrastructure that is built around a set of three cross-cutting themes. The link between the discussion and each of the cross-cutting themes is summarized in each chapter. Appendix C provides a comprehensive table that identifies key points from each chapter, organized by cross-cutting theme.
- Key features of the design of each of the chapter exemplars are summarized in a text box.
- Quotes from methodological leaders in mixed methods and/or qualitative research are set aside in the text. Reading these before launching into the full chapter is one way to get a handle on the key arguments presented in each chapter.
- A set of self-assessment review questions appear at the end of each chapter.

- Suggestions for supplemental activities are listed at the end of each chapter.
- Key terms that are used across chapters are listed in a glossary of terms. Each glossary term is highlighted in bold in the text the first time it is used with an accompanying definition in italics.
- There are two appendices for those looking for more examples. Citation information about each of the exemplars I singled out in the text is listed in Appendix A. A list of additional reputable examples of MM-GTM appears in Appendix B.

CHAPTER 1

Establishing language and purpose

This chapter builds an argument for the creative potential of partnering mixed methods with grounded theory for purposes of advancing analytical insight and developing an explanatory framework. It MM-GTM as a distinct methodology and creates a platform for dialog across disciplines by introducing key terminology.

TERMS INTRODUCED IN THIS CHAPTER

- Abduction
- Analytic density
- Conceptual framework
- Constant comparative method
- Fully integrated mixed methods research (FIMMR)
- Fully integrated mixed method grounded theory methodology (FIMM-GTM)
- Grounded theory
- Mixed method research
- Mixed method grounded theory methodology (MM-GTM)
- Multi-method research
- Theory

INTRODUCTION

Since it first began to ferment as a movement with its own set of methodological gurus, mixed method approaches have continually demonstrated adaptability to diverse problems and disciplinary contexts. Its astonishingly broad cross-disciplinary appeal may be unique in that there are thousands of examples of empirical publications and an expansive body of methodological literature supporting the creativity and ingenuity in which it has been applied in practice. Emerging at the same time as the movement toward interdisciplinary team-centered research, the span of the usefulness of approaches that combine methods in practice can be seen by the application of mixed methods to study topics as diverse as poverty in Bangladesh, climate change in

Siberia, police practices in Canada, managing the growth in urban locations, and safe drinking water in rural Aboriginal communities. One reason for the adaptability of mixed methods is that it shares, along with multi-method research, the bedrock assumption of the contribution to quality of consulting multiple sources of data that is an ontological assumption endorsed by virtually all social and behavioral researchers. What distinguishes mixed method from **multi-method research** is the priority awarded to integrating information from multiple sources of data. *Multi-method research incorporates multiple sources of data and/or methods but does not integrate them in a substantive way.*

At the core of the logic of mixed methods is a commitment to the purposeful engagement of diverse sources of data, analytical procedures, methods, and perspectives in pursuit of greater understanding of the complex interplay between individual and social phenomenon and the natural environment. The most common form of mixing is at the methodological level (Sandelowski, 2014). Its wide adoption across fields of inquiry invites the kind of cross-method conversations that are evident in integrated methodological approaches, like mixed methods approaches to grounded theory (Creamer, 2018a), case study (Cook & Kamalodeen, 2020; Guetterman & Fetters, 2018), participatory action research (Ivankova, 2015; Ivankova & Wingo, 2018), and visual methods (Shannon-Baker & Edwards, 2018). Such partnering challenges us to reconsider the long-standing notion that in today's rapidly changing world that a researcher can afford to narrowly identify his or her expertise as either qualitative or quantitative. Addressing multi-dimensional topics like those related to poverty, health inequality, immigration, violence, or sustainability requires expertise in a variety of domains. Every researcher needs the skills to be adept at using more than one method to contribute to cutting-edge research.

> In the social sciences, we are better scholars, more able to contribute to social inquiry at large, if we develop expertise in a variety of approaches.
>
> (Pearce, 2015, p. 54)

There are many different ways to build a theoretical component in a research study, including by integrating findings from multiple sources of data to build and test a grounded theory or to refine or debunk a long-standing one that has been validated in other settings. Approaches vary as a researcher might initiate a study with a theoretical orientation, find themselves in a position to see the merits in more than one theoretical orientation, or unexpectedly find the need to reach out to the literature to find an explanation for a paradoxical finding. Each of these different approaches to theory construction or refinement underscores a commitment to the contribution to quality of diverse research practices and approaches.

Purpose and contribution

The text offers insight about the research methods and methodology of designing and doing research that integrates a mixed methods and grounded theory. The purpose of this text is to provide an instructional tool that advances the use of qualitative and mixed method procedures in the development and refinement of evidence-based explanatory models in education, health sciences, management, information, and other applied fields in the human and behavioral sciences. The text will fit well in a graduate level research method training course or seminar that begins with a review of grounded theory methods and then shifts to how these can be extended through mixed methods.

One of the aims of this chapter is to open the door for ongoing, cross-disciplinary dialog between qualitative and mixed methods researchers by presenting mixed method grounded theory methodology (MM-GTM) as a type of integrated methodology. A methodology is a specialized type of theory that provides a logic that links procedures. An integrated methodology links one or more methods that are epistemologically compatible. The methodology is not presented as a critique of grounded theory, but as an expansion of the ways it can be used in research in the social and human sciences.

The first chapter introduces some of the key terminology and many of the key themes that will be developed throughout the subsequent five chapters. It builds an argument for MM-GTM as an integrated methodology. The cross-cutting themes weave in and out of every chapter, re-surfacing in each to be further developed and elaborated.

Three principal ideas are at the center of this chapter:

1 The methodological literature, if not necessarily what is evident in practice, has narrowly framed the use of mixed methods with grounded theory in ways that preserve the distinctions between the qualitative and quantitative strands where one phase devoted to developing theory using grounded theory methods and a second that is used to refine or test it using quantitative methods.
2 A MM-GTM approach can also be used to develop or refine an explanatory framework in ways that embed the logic of mixed method in grounded theory analytical procedures.
3 Unexpected findings that emerge from comparing and integrating different sources of data are a major source of innovation and theoretical insights.

Organization of the chapter

The chapter begins by introducing different terms associated with both grounded theory and mixed methods, including by making a distinction between a theoretical (explanatory) and a conceptual framework and between mixed method and multi-method research. It then moves to pointing to evidence of the prevalence of MM-GTM. The next section singles out an exemplar of fully integrated MM-GTM in a way that recognizes its complexity. Next, we consider MM-GTM as a distinct methodology that embeds an abductive logic and a back-and-forth exchange between data from different sources in the constant comparative method and to the analytical procedures like theoretical sampling so central to grounded theory. The use of examples and exemplars is discussed next, with an explanation of the distinction I make between the two. The chapter concludes by linking the key themes from this chapter to the wider set of cross-cutting themes.

VARIOUS WAYS OF DEFINING THEORY AND ITS PURPOSE

Theory construction is at the heart of the scientific process (Jaccard & Jacoby, 2010) and evidence-based practice. A methodologist well known in the community of nursing scholars and among mixed methodologists, Margarite Sandelowski (1993) maintains, stated or not, theoretical understanding is always implicit in the way a problem is conceived. Understood in everyday conversation as a hunch or supposition (Weick, 1995), a theory can be viewed simply as an explanation for the way things work (Collins & Stockton, 2018). In the context of empirical research, a **theory** *is a cohesive explanatory framework generated through a systematic set of empirical procedures*. In empirical research where theory is constructed from data, a theoretical framework offers an explanation for a complex phenomenon without erasing the variability in the way it is experienced. Expanding on the relationship between theory and the way research is executed, Agerfalk (2014) wrote: "Theories help to organize our thoughts, explain phenomena, ensure consistent explanations, improve our predictions, and inform design" (p. 594).

In the context of the social and human sciences, the type of theory produced through MM-GTM is not an abstraction with limited practical utility. A theory can provide an explanation or multiple explanations not only about *what* is happening in a setting, but also *why* and *how* that might be the case. Its practical utility to evidence-based policy and practices lies in offering a better understanding of the "why" and "how" of observed effects (Burch & Henrich, 2017). This kind of reasoning is essential to justify an intervention designed to improve learning, health, or well-being. Without a theoretical basis, an intervention is an expensive version of trial and error (Eccles, Grimshaw, Walker, Johnston,& Pitts, 2005). Using multiple methods and multiple frameworks creates the best context for generating novel ideas and new insight (Jaccard & Jacoby, 2010).

> Theories help to organize our thoughts, explain phenomena, ensure consistent explanations, improve our predictions, and inform design.
>
> (Agerfalk, 2014, p. 594)

No matter how well substantiated, many widely cited theories about human behavior, such as those about learning or motivation or rational choice, are shaped by the socio-cultural climate at the time they were first conceived and validated. They can be a poor fit to guide investigations of dynamic environments like schools, hospitals, or for-profit or not-for-profit organization and the diverse clientele they serve. In a multi-cultural society, for example, it seems antiquated to assume a perspective developed in the 1950s that an immigrant's acculturation to a new society requires the abandonment of one's home culture, foods, and holiday practices. We can yearn for the seeming certainty offered by a well-established theory and validated instruments, but one of the principal conclusions drawn by researchers struggling to explain dissonance between the results suggested by their qualitative and quantitative data is that the phenomenon they studied were far more complex and multi-faceted than initially conceived (Creamer, 2018c).

Grounded theory

There are multiple prominent schools of thought about grounded theory and what constitutes its core principles. The method, according to Charmaz and Thornberg (2020), is often mistakingly treated as a "mechanical application of procedures" (p. 7). **Grounded theory** *is first and foremost a methodology that provides a comprehensive approach to generate a theoretical framework inductively from data*. "The very purpose of grounded theory research is to produce theory," Sandelowski maintains

(1993, p. 214). The aim of grounded theory is to develop an abstract explanation, not prediction (Charmaz, 2017a). Although approached in many different ways, grounded theory is conventionally conceived as a systematic inductive or emergent approach to understand basic social psychological processes and the ways individuals, groups, or organizations change over time (Benoliel, 1996). According to Glaser, grounded theory is "the systematic generation of theory from data that has itself been systematically obtained" (1978a, p. 2). Although arguably in can never be entirely so, an inductive or emergent approach is used both to build and refine theory. Grounded theory makes the critical distinction between the process of discovery associated with an inductive mindset and theory generation and the confirmatory mindset and deductive reasoning associated with hypotheses testing. Theory building, not verification, is the aim of grounded theory (Urquhart, Lehmann, & Myers 2010).

The very purpose of grounded theory research is to produce theory.
(Sandelowski, 1993, p. 214)

Although it is not something most grounded theorists write about, a **conceptual framework** is one of many variants of the way that theorizing can be approached in a research study. This type of explanatory framework is a critical step in the process of constructing the design of a study because it can provide a logical coherence that links across of phases of the research process (Creswell & Plano, 2011; Maxwell & Loomis, 2003). *A conceptual framework offers a tentative explanatory framework that is based on a synthesis of related literature and what is known in a practical way about a phenomenon.* It is assembled by the researcher to map how all the literature works together in a study (Collins & Stockton, 2018). It reflects assumptions about the phenomenon being studied (Maxwell, 2012). A conceptual framework often integrates more than one theoretical perspective. Conflicting explanations evident in the literature can offer a convenient and elegant way to frame the need for a study.

Although the terms are often used interchangeably, a theoretical (analytical or explanatory framework) and a conceptual framework differ in the source on which they are based. A theoretical framework is empirical; it emerges from a systematic and, hopefully, through analysis of data. Although this point is controversial among grounded theory experts, a conceptual framework is structured through preliminary engagement with the literature. Likely to undergo many revisions over the course of a study, a conceptual framework serves multiple functions. These include (a) to identify a tentative set of core constructs, (b) to structure data collection instruments, and (c) to create a tentative, initial coding scheme. Viewing it as tentative and eminently revisable is one way to avoid "forcing" it on the interpretation of the data. It is helpful to maintain a stance where, as Gorard characterizes it, theory is always partial, tentative, and waiting to be replaced by a better explanation (Gorard, 2004).

The role of preconceptions and the literature at the onset of a grounded theory study remains a hotly contested one among grounded theory practitioners, as does the discussion about how much the literature can be engaged at the onset of a study without unduly biasing the researcher. I address both are issues in Chapter 2. The invitation and the challenge in grounded theory is to maintain the type of exploratory stance that invites discovery and new insight.

One of the methodological drives of grounded theory is as a data-driven way to understand basic social-psychological processes that involve change over time (Benoliel, 1996).

Social-psychological processes are temporal in that they involve change over time. Charmaz describes a temporal process as having "clear beginnings and endings, and benchmarks in between" (2006, p. 10). This temporality is linked to a process that leads to change (Charmaz, 2006).

Glaser (1978a) observed that research about basic social-psychological process can be based on the individual as the unit of analysis. A study about the development of identity as a scientist, engineer, or medical practitioner, for example, uses the individual as the unit of analysis. On the other hand, a study of teams might use the group as the unit of analysis. Understanding underlying processes that shape a phenomenon is not simply about validating knowledge but developing explanations that point to connections and relationships that have not been observed before (Van Maanen, Sorensen, & Mitchell, 2007). It requires knowledge of interactions within a context (Irwin, 2008) and considering those contexts as multiple and multi-faceted (Charmaz, 2017a).

Attending to social processes can offset the tendency in qualitative research, particularly in the Western world, to frame our questions and analysis at the level of the individual (Charmaz, 2017a). The potential to think theoretically about a phenomenon is vastly expanded when we step back from a singular focus on individual experiences, to one that considers these in terms of multiple, intersecting contextual influences. This might be how relationships, familial units, neighborhoods, communities, organizations, and culture can influence individual perceptions and experience.

Examples of social-psychological process that might be the basis of a MM-GTM study are nearly endless. Some examples of social-psychological processes appear in the following:

- Recovering from trauma
- Becoming environmentally conscious
- Re-acclimating after immersion in another culture
- Withdrawing from an abusive relationship
- Developing inclusive leadership practices
- Navigating infertility
- Learning a new technology
- Living single
- Embracing spirituality
- Seeking help to enhance well-being
- Evolving personal, sexual, or professional identity
- Developing complex reasoning skills
- Navigating a new culture
- Developing corporate culture in an open building environment
- Adapting to a new technological innovation

Change rarely occurs in a linear or predictable way (Mason, 2006). Individuals, groups, or organizations are likely to vary in the paths they travel to accomplish change.

Mixed methods and grounded theory

A number of leading figures in the development of grounded theory as a methodology have pointed to, but not pursued, the potential that is inherent in either a multi-method or a mixed methods approach to develop an explanatory framework. Most of these figures have framed their endorsement in terms of the value of the multiple sources of data, including using quantitative data, in grounded theory procedures. Glaser (1978a), for example, famously argued "all is data" when he extolled the value of taking advantage of a full range of different types and sources of data. This vantage point is also evident in a statement by Holton and Walsh (2017) who endorsed the inclusion of quantitative data in grounded theory, without pursuing it further by suggesting ways that might be accomplished. Authors of a textbook about classic grounded theory, Holton and Walsh noted: "For grounded theorists, using both qualitative and quantitative data opens a vast realm of additional empirical possibilities for generating theory" (2017, p. 11).

Others have made a more obvert connection between mixed methods and grounded theory by suggesting it can involve not only different sources of qualitative and quantitative data, but also analytical procedures. This viewpoint is evident, for example, in a statement by Kathy Charmaz, an influential spokesperson for a constructivist approach to grounded theory, when she wrote but did not further pursue the idea that "an emerging grounded theory can indicate needing more than one type of data and can incorporate more than one type of analysis" (2014a, p. 323). Isabelle Walsh offered an expansive point of view of the way integration can occur that goes beyond just data. She wrote: "A [grounded theory] may thus be generated using qualitative and/or quantitative data, methods, and techniques" (2015, p. 536).

The contribution of dissonance, ambiguity, and paradox is so central to my view of mixed methods and what Jennifer Greene (2007) refers to as a "mixed method way of thinking" that it is explicitly referenced in my working definition of **mixed method research**:

> A systematic approach to data collection and analysis that combines different sources of data and quantitative and qualitative analytical procedures **with the intention to engage multiple perspectives** in order to more fully understand complex social phenomenon.

Dissonance between the results supported by analyses of different or integrated sources of data often can be the first clear indication that a phenomenon is more complex and multi-faceted than initially conceived (Creamer, 2018c).

Mixed method grounded theory methodology (MM-GTM) *is a methodology that embeds a dialectical logic in the constant comparative method and grounded theory procedures to develop a mid-level theoretical framework or to elaborate an existing one.* MM-GTM studies that demonstrate more than a cursory familiarity with grounded theory as a method and methodology often award more priority to the qualitative research methods than to mixed methods. In the notation system that serves as a shorthand among methodologists with expertise in mixed methods, the double capitalizing is intended to communicate an equal partnership where neither mixed methods nor grounded theory is demoted to a secondary position during data collection and analysis. The fact the mixed methods appears first in this abbreviation is more a reflection of my own interests and expertise than it is a statement that one methodology is more important than the other.

Fully integrated mixed method research

Fully integrated mixed method research (FIMMR) *is an approach to mixed methods research where integration of qualitative and quantitative data and/or analytical procedures is embedded throughout the research process; from the formulation of research questions, to data collection and sampling, during analysis, and during the process of drawing of conclusions* (Burch & Heinrich, 2017; Creamer, 2018a; Nastasi, Hitchcock, & Brown, 2010; Tashakkori, 2003). As compared to an equal priority mixed method design where the strands are compartmentalized but no one method is subordinated, results that emerge from integrated analytical procedures, it is best described as reflecting a mixed priority (Creamer, 2018a).

FIMMR was first described as the "most advanced, and most dynamic of all mixed model designs" (Tashakkori & Teddlie, 2003, p. 689). Contemporary views of this design frame it as one that is highly compatible with research launched with the purpose to better understand the complex interplay between micro- (i.e., individual) and macro- (i.e., historical, political, organizational, interactional) that is so characteristic of multi-level mixed methods research (Creamer, 2018a). The word "dynamic" reflects how fully integrated research often has to adapt not only to changes in the research environment or among a research team, but also to the unexpected detours introduced when data and methods are thoroughly integrated.

Fully integrated mixed method grounded theory methodology (FIMM-GTM) uses grounded theory procedures and strategies to integrate different sources of data throughout the research process, including during data analyses, to produce and sometimes to test a theoretical framework.

Indications of the prevalence of MM-GTM

Guetterman, Babchuck, Howell Smith, and Stevens (2017) were the first set of authors to offer some indication of the prevalence of MM-GTM. They located 61 MM-GTM articles using conventional search terms and the procedures of a systematic review. Their search procedures pulled in articles that included the use both the words "qualitative" and "quantitative" in the title or abstract but did not necessarily incorporate a reference to either mixed method or multi-method. It is possible that the search terms may have contributed to the disappointing results that emerged from their cataloging of the features of these studies. Only about one-third of the publications provided any evidence of employing or producing a theoretical framework. Most fell far short of using the full complement of grounded theory procedures. These authors were no doubt disappointed to conclude: "Researcher employing grounded theory in mixed methods research rarely drew upon all or even most of the features of grounded theory" (p. 10).

A count of the appearance of in doctoral dissertations offers a second indicator of the prevalence of MM-GTM. Howell Smith et al. (2019) executed a systematic search of doctoral dissertations where the words "grounded theory" and "mixed methods" appeared anywhere in the text. Their electronic search revealed that mixed methods and grounded theory have been paired in doctoral research for quite some time. They located 482 dissertations, with an average of 48 dissertations appearing between 2011 and 2017. The number of dissertations increased steadily from 2001 through 2016, followed by a decline in number in 2016 and 2017. Now readily accessible through online repositories, doctoral dissertations are likely the best prognosticator that the idea of pairing mixed methods with grounded theory.

A "classic" approach to MM-GTM

Well known among the community of scholars who have built an argument for the epistemological foundations of mixed methods in dialectical pluralism, R. Burke Johnson joined two other colleagues to introduce the idea that MM-GTM is a distinct methodological approach (see Johnson, McGowan, & Turner, 2010). Johnson et al. coined the expression mixed method grounded theory (MM-GT). They pointed to a way that mixed methods can leverage the idea first articulated by Glaser and Strauss (1967) that grounded theories can be constructed from both qualitative and quantitative data.

Facing a climate when there were still heated debates about the compatibility between qualitative and quantitative methods, Johnson et al. (2010) conceptualized MM-GTM in ways I do not. They framed it as mixing two dramatically different sets of philosophical assumptions about how knowledge is constructed. They argued that "MM-GTM as articulated here offers a creative and dynamic combination of objectivist and constructivist grounded theory" (p. 74). Objectivist believe in a singular reality that can be captured objectively, while constructivists highlight that reality is often multiple and everyone experiences it in different ways. Johnson et al. (2010) positioned MM-GTM as an opportunity to fuse the "conflicting demands" (p. 72) of generating nomothetic (i.e., law-like, generalizable) knowledge with particularistic, local, and contextual ideographic knowledge. The separation that is maintained between the qualitative and quantitative phases in this approach to MM-GTM makes it possible to accommodate two different paradigmatic perspectives.

Johnson et al. (2010) offered a view of MM-GTM that clearly differentiates the purpose and methods used in the qualitative and quantitative strands of a study. Greene (2007) refers to this type of approach as a component design. This conceptualization matches the foundational categorization of mixed methods designs as primarily either concurrent (data collection and analysis occur separately) or sequential (one phase precedes, and is dependent, on another). Johnson et al. (2010) prioritized triangulation, rather than analytical insight, as the principal reason for using mixed methods.

The logic of component design is evident in the way that Johnson et al. (2010) distinguished different purposes for the qualitative and quantitative strands of a study. This same logic, cast at the project rather than study level, is evident in the impressive body of work produced by Judith Wuest about a two-decade-long project to develop a theory about family caregiving that used MM-GTM (Wuest & Hodgins, 2011). The qualitative and quantitative phases served a distinct purpose. The initial phase was a qualitative one. It used grounded theory procedures to identify a core construct and to pose hypotheses about the relationships between constructs for the purpose of developing a theoretical framework. A quantitative phase followed the initial qualitative one. Its role was statistically to test the reliability of the constructs and the significance of the paths that linked them.

Johnson et al. (2010) viewed MM-GTM in a complementary way in that qualitative and quantitative data are collected about different constructs and for different purposes. Qualitative analysis, for example, can provide an indication of an underlying causal mechanism while quantitative data more readily identifies both anticipated and unanticipated outcomes. Emerging so recently after the emergence of mixed methods as a distinct methodology in the late 1980s, the timeframe Johnson and colleagues were operating in may have made it difficult for them to envision the possibility that qualitative and quantitative data could be collected about the same constructs.

The logic of a classic approach to MM-GTM introduced by Johnson et al. (2010) extends to one its first formal manifestations in reporting that emerged from a dissertation completed by Minjung Shim (Shim et al., 2017) that is discussed in greater detail in the final chapter. R. B. Johnson was a member of the doctoral committee. The committee also contained a member widely recognized for her expertise in grounded theory. Shim described her research as employing a multi-phase mixed methods research design. Shim declared that the purpose of her research was to build and confirm a grounded theory model. In reality, like virtually all MM-GTM research with this aim, she achieved more than a single purpose. She confirmed parts of the preliminary model developed from the literature and interviews, while simultaneously elaborating it by removing and adding constructs and hypothesized paths that linked them.

Prioritizing the role of mixed methods in building explanatory power

A number of methodologists writing about mixed methods have prioritized the purposes it can serve in MM-GTM in ways that extend beyond the classic purpose identified by Johnson et al. (2010) in the first discussion about it to appear in print. Members of this group have showcased the potential contribution of mixed methods in a way that is compatible to the purpose of grounded theory to assist with the process of theorizing. Writing from the field of information systems, Isabelle Walsh (2015), for example, highlights the role of integrating different types of data for purposes above and beyond triangulation: "The purpose is not to test or correct what has been found previously, but to extend understanding of the phenomenon under scrutiny and the scope of the emerging theory" (2015, p. 550).

One of the most compelling arguments for the use of mixed methods is the potential to promote sophisticated analytical conceptualizations (Fielding, 2009, 2012). Fielding (2012) maintains the "radical potential" of mixed methods is not in terms of confirmation and a search for the "right answer" but "to build prismatic understanding of social phenomenon and the potential to promote analytical density" meaning the potential for "sophisticated analytical conceptualization" (p. 125). Fielding advocates for recognizing the value-added of mixed methods in creating inferences or a conceptual explanation with greater **analytic density** or conceptual richness (2009). Analytic density refers to the potential to build the type of multi-dimensional conceptual understanding of social phenomenon that is essential to the iterative process of building knowledge in a scientific way (Fielding, 2012). *Associated with validity, analytical density refers to envisioning constructs in a multi-dimensional way or to developing or elaborating an explanatory framework in a way that adds conceptual nuance or richness.* Analytic density can be achieved by strategies that integrate findings from different methods in ways that create the opportunity to discern patterns, detect relationships between constructs, identify conditions that influence the outcome, and that recognize the multi-dimensionality of core constructs (Creamer, 2021). The opposite of analytical density, according to Fielding (2009), is the type of tunnel vision that leads an investigator to refuse to engage a hypothesis or theoretical proposition because it is incompatible with his or her preconceptions.

> The radical potential of mixed methods is not in terms of confirmation but to build prismatic understanding of phenomenon and the potential to promote analytical density.
> (Fielding, 2012, p. 125)

Similarly, in writing about the link between thinking of research problems in a multi-dimensional way, Jennifer Mason (2006), a sociologist, mounted an argument for putting explanation at the center of our social research inquiry. She wrote: "Placing explanation at the center of enquiry reflects an interest in the complexities of how and why things change and work as they do in certain contexts and circumstances" (Mason, 2006, p. 19).

An exemplar of MM-GTM

Research driven by the purpose of integrating mixed methods with grounded theory to develop a more nuanced and comprehensive understanding is evident in the research Kawamura undertook for her dissertation, under the supervision of a leader in the mixed methods world, Nataliya Ivankova (i.e., Kawamura, Ivankova, Kohler, & Purumean-Chaney, 2009). From the field of public health, her dissertation produced results that suggested that a sense of identification with a popular media figure can promote behavioral change among patients with hypertension. The fixing drive of a conventional parallel/concurrent mixed methods design accounts for why these authors chose to postpone integration of the results of the qualitative and quantitative data until the penultimate point of bringing the results together at the inference stage.

Box 1.1 summarizes key features of the Kawamura et al. (2009), including its purpose, the way it was designed, how integration was achieved, strategies used to navigate dissonance, and the theory produced.

BOX 1.1

Kawamura et al.'s (2009) Study of the Impact of a Health Intervention

Purpose: Kawamura et al. (2009) achieved a good deal more than they set out to in this complex multi-layered study from the field of public health that was framed to develop an integrated grounded theory model using mixed methods to explore how a sense of identification with a media figure in radio program might impact levels of activity among patients with cardiovascular disease.

Design: Referred to as a concurrent or parallel mixed method design because the qualitative and quantitative data were collected, analyzed, and reported separately. The instruments were designed to expand understanding of a conceptual model developed from the literature. The sample of participants for both strands overlapped.

Integration: Integration occurred at the final inference stage when the theoretical framework developed from quantitative analysis and the grounded theory produced from the qualitative phase. The interweaving of qualitative and quantitative constructs produced a composite grounded theory model with a more multi-faceted set of positive and negative consequences of the program than was initially conceived. It also identified a set of mediating factors that influenced the process.

Unexpected findings: Because integration did not occur until the final stage of drawing the composite model, inconsistencies between findings from the qualitative and quantitative strands were not pursued.

Theory produced: These authors developed a final composite model that has all the components of classic grounded theory. At the center of the model is a three-stage temporal sequence that begins with identified similarity with the media figure, moves to emotional involvement, and advances to gains in motivation, attitude, and practice. The composite model is unique because proposed paths (relationships between constructs) were generated from both the qualitative and quantitative analysis. Some constructs and paths in the model were derived from both qualitative and quantitative sources.

The authors use language about the value-added of a mixed methods approach to the development of a grounded theory that highlights its link to complexity. The authors observe:

> Neither a quantitative nor a qualitative study by itself would explain the degree and complexity of [parasocial] impact on physical activity and self-efficacy and practices in the context of this study. Integrating the two models developed from the analysis of quantitative and qualitative study strands provided both the level of detail and comprehensiveness needed to understand this complex social phenomenon and its roles in promoting health behavior among its participants.
>
> (Kawamura et al., 2009, p. 100)

The reference to "comprehensiveness" points to the complementarity rationale for using mixed methods where the principal outcome is to produce a more comprehensive, multi-layered, and nuanced explanation.

The composite model produced by Kawamura et al. (2009) is essentially a multi-layered, holistic meta-inference that combines qualitatively and quantitatively derived constructs and paths. An innovative feature of this article is the way the theoretical framework is visualized.

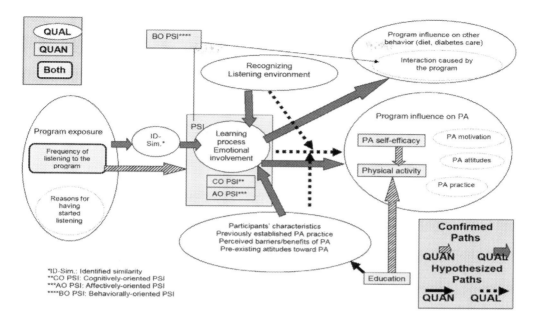

FIGURE 1.1 Final Composite Model from Kawamura et al. (2009)

Graphics that depict interrelationships (paths) between constructs derived from both qualitative and quantitative procedures is another innovative feature of this visualization. Different shading techniques are used to identify qualitatively and quantitatively derived outcomes, paths, and mediating factors. Although it only applies in one case, a different box shape designates constructs in the model that are supported by both qualitative and quantitative data. The uses of different types of visual symbols and its acknowledgment of both convergence and divergence are the two principal reasons I reproduce their Figure 4 here with copyright permission as Figure 1.1.

The fact that qualitative and quantitative data were collected and analyzed separately (a concurrent, parallel design) accounts Kawamura et al.'s (2009) approach to navigating the inconsistencies between qualitative and quantitative findings that emerged once they were considered together as an integrated whole. The authors commented on the inconsistencies, which were substantial, but reported no steps to reconcile them. Labeling their findings as contradictory, Kawamura et al. observed: "Four of the five features [of the model] were identified as contradictory across the findings of the qualitative and quantitative analysis" (p. 96). Framing that the results of the quantitative and qualitatively derived grounded theory models as complementary by virtue of addressing different research questions, these authors sidestepped further analysis but chose to embellish their initial conceptual model with some additional constructs that emerged over the course of the analyses.

MM-GTM as an invitation to leverage dissonance and paradox

A process that is deliberate about engaging the dissonance and paradox often introduced by diverse viewpoints among collaborators or between findings from different analytical procedures is the hinge that links mixed methods, grounded theory, and complexity. Rather than being framed as a problem or a by-product that signals a weakness in the methods, dissonance, and the uncertainty associated with it is prized in a dialectical perspective for its potential to generate innovative insight. The potential for dissonance and the contribution of a dialectical stance to innovative insight is a theme that connects this and my first textbook (Creamer, 2018a). Jennifer Greene, an influential figure in the formalization of mixed methods as a methodology, is often quoted for her description of a dialectical stance. She writes, a dialectical stance "seeks not so much convergence as insight . . . the generation of important understanding through the juxtaposition of different lenses, perspectives, and stances" (Greene, 2005, p. 208). Dissonance is not an apologetic footnote to research in mixed methods: it is a player at the center of the stage.

A mixed method way of thinking actively engages with difference and diversity.

(Greene, 2005, p. 208)

The role of seemingly stark differences between preliminary findings emerging from qualitative and quantitative analytical procedures and the contribution of unexpected sources of data is evident in two of the exemplars I feature in this textbook. As she navigated the complexities of her dissertation research, findings that countered the intent of her randomized control study (RCT) led Christina Catallo to take an unexpected detour. She diagrammed an individual change map for each participant to pinpoint the key decision points of a group of women who scored high on a survey about intimate partner violence, but nevertheless chose not to disclose it to emergency room personnel (i.e., Catallo, Jack, Ciliska, & MacMillan, 2013). Catallo et al.'s research is discussed in greater detail in the next chapter.

Although mixed methods and grounded theory have been paired productively and innovative ways for quite some time, particularly in applied fields like education and nursing, a philosophical foundation for this argument has not previously been developed. I explore this task in some detail in the next section of the chapter.

CONCEPTUALIZING MM-GTM AS A METHODOLOGY

Both mixed methods and grounded theory have been characterized as methodologies that are adaptable to diverse circumstances and priorities. Innovative applications of each continue to emerge. Highlighting the ways researchers adapt grounded theory to diverse circumstances, Seidel and Urquhart (2013, p. 237) observed: "Grounded theory method (GTM) is an evolving method that is subject to idiosyncratic interpretation and flexible deployment." Reiterating the idiosyncratic way grounded theory has been deployed, Morse and Niehaus (2009) maintain that "All types of grounded theory are individual methods in their own right" (Morse & Niehaus, 2009, p. 95). The way an investigator deploys a methodology is an expression of his or her ontological and epistemological perspective and the wider social and intellection strains of thought that influence a time period (Ralph, Birks, & Chapman, 2015).

There are multiple areas of the overlap between the methodological assumptions of grounded theory and mixed methods. The areas where there is an overlap in the methodological assumptions provide the groundwork for the argument of MM-GTM as a distinct

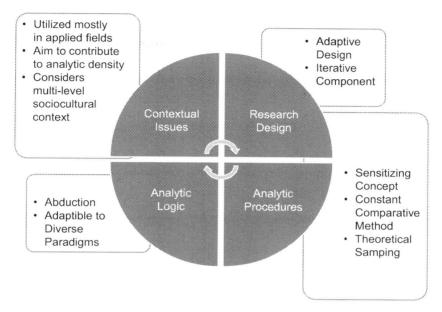

FIGURE 1.2 The Link Between Mixed Methods, Grounded Theory Methods, and Theory Building

methodology if not a meta-methodology. As a distinct methodology, MM-GTM has own rationale for linking a set of core procedures and using them in a systematic way.

Principal areas of methodological compatibility between mixed methods and grounded theory include the following:

1. The aim is to develop analytic density.
2. Adaptable to diverse philosophical positions and paradigms.
3. Both adapts and generates complexity.
4. An iterative approach to both data collection and analysis.
5. Abduction as one of the analytical logics that can be used with the constant comparative method and theoretical sampling.
6. Abduction powers theoretical sampling.

Figure 1.2 summarizes key areas of overlap between the methodological framework of grounded theory and mixed methods. Four areas are highlighted: contextual issues, research design, analytic logic, and analytic procedures. The contextual overlap between grounded theory and mixed methods includes (a) an emphasis on developing analytical density, (b) that both methods are used most frequently in applied fields, (c) compatibility with diverse philosophical paradigms, and (d) that research questions are constructed in a multi-dimensional way that recognizes a multi-layered social-cultural context.

A second area of overlap shown in Figure 1.2 relates to an adaptive design (Poth, 2020) that both recognizes and generates complexity. An iterative component fueled by the constant comparative method is a second feature of the design.

The analytic logic recognized in Figure 1.2 highlights abduction as part of both the constant comparative method and theoretical sampling. The final section of Figure 1.2 recognizes analytical procedures that can accommodate many types of approaches, including mixed methods. This applies to theoretical sampling, developing a coding system, and the role of the literature and other theories in serving as sensitizing concepts and to explain unexpected findings that emerge during the coding process.

The methodological assumptions of most approaches to grounded theory and mixed methods might seem to differ in terms of the appreciation for the contribution of dissonance to generating theoretical insight. This is related to the role of verification and the treatment of exceptions. Very little space is awarded to these topics in most textbooks about grounded theory. The act of engaging or integrating findings from different sources of data that occurs in mixed methods allows for confirmation, but at the same time recognizes the disconnects that generate topics for further exploration.

We further explore some of the major areas of overlap between mixed methods and grounded theory in the next section.

Compatibility with multiple paradigms

A fourth way that the methodological grounding of mixed methods and grounded theory is compatible is that both have proven accommodating of diverse perspectives. Both grounded theory and mixed methods have been adapted by investigators operating from diverse epistemological paradigms. Urquhart made this point by observing, for example, that grounded theory can be "appropriated by researchers with different assumptions about knowledge and how it can be obtained" (2013, p. 36). Grounded theory has been approached from diverse paradigmatic perspectives that include post-positivism, interpretivism, constructivism, postmodernism, critical inquiry (Mills, Bonner, & Francis, 2006; Sebastian, 2019), and pragmatism (Morgan, 2014).

Morgan has taken the controversial position that a pragmatic approach guides most social science research methodology, including mixed methods (2013, 2014) and grounded theory (2020). Without overlooking its link to a pragmatic grounding, others writing about mixed methods affiliate with the lens of dialectical pluralism as a guide for investigators committed to the exploration of diverse perspectives (e.g., Johnson, 2012) or a commitment to social justice that is associated with a transformative research agenda. Researchers joining interdisciplinary endeavors are likely to need competencies in more than one method and to recognize the legitimacy of more than one paradigm.

The iterative exchange embedded in the constant comparative method

One of the principal arguments for the compatibility between the mixed methods and grounded theory derives from an endorsement voiced by the founders of grounded theory, now more than 50 years ago. The **constant comparative method** is an approach to analysis conventionally framed to mean that data analysis and data collection co-occur. *It is an analytical strategy where data, and eventually emerging constructs and themes, are continuously compared and contrasted as data collection and analysis unfolds*. Whether you are in the field, collecting data or using a secondary data set, analysis begins as the first unit of data is encountered.

Walsh (2014) used language that suggests a link between mixed methods and the constant comparative method. "Data are continuously compared to previously collected and analyzed data, looking for similarities and differences to help toward conceptualizing and theory building," Walsh wrote (2014). She added: "The use of mixed methods can feed into the cycles of inductive analysis and constant comparison required by the grounded theory method" (2014 p. 13). In a study with a strong mixed methods orientation, Gasson and Waters (2013) also referred to the analytical process they employed in ways that link mixed methods, grounded theory, and the constant comparative method: "Qualitative and quantitative analyses where embedded, and our results emerged through constant iterations between qualitative and quantitative data as they were collected and thru the analyses of all our data as one set" (p. 154), they noted.

MM-GTM is adaptable for use with an existing data set. This could be the case, for example, with a study involving social media posts or a body of documents like case notes or memos, where analysis could be launched with a small a subset of the data. In this scenario, theoretical sampling might involve dipping back into a data set to target the selection of cases to further elaborate the properties of a core construct.

Linking the constant comparative method to an abductive logic

Other authors have pointed to the same type of iterative cycle during analysis that Walsh (2014) linked to the constant comparative method but identify it as an approach to analysis that has roots in American pragmatism. It is referred to as **abduction**. Abduction is one of three approaches to reasoning that include induction (generalizing from the specific to the general) and deduction (generalizing from the general to the specific) (Locke, Golden-Biddle, & Feldman, 2008). *Understood in a generic way, it is the process of generating multiple possible explanations for an unexpected or surprising finding* (Charmaz, 2019; Locke et al., 2008), treating these as tentative hypotheses or theoretical propositions. Abduction is recognized as analytic induction in some approaches to grounded theory (Suddaby, 2006). Because it involves engagement with prior knowledge it is not compatible with Glaserian or classic grounded theory (Morgan, 2020). The act of abduction is akin to a detective generating multiple possible explanations for something that might seem subtly off kilter in a crime scene. Obtaining additional data to rule out competing hypotheses is linked to internal validity (Johnson & Schoonenboom, 2015).

In an article provocatively titled "What Grounded Theory is Not," Roy Suddaby of the University of Alberta in Canada characterized abduction in a way that directly links it to the constant comparative method. Suddaby, writing from the field of management, characterizes abduction as "a process by which a researcher moves between induction and deduction while practicing the constant comparative method" (2006, p. 639). Although the line between the two is not hard and fast, induction is considered exploratory and has long been associated with a qualitative approach. It is the line of reasoning so central to grounded theory that begins with observations about data and moves to more abstract generalizations. Deduction, on the other hand, is most frequently associated with hypotheses or theory testing and quantitative approaches. It is the process of testing how well a generalization fits data. Grounded theory requires the interplay between induction and deduction (Strauss & Corbin, 1998). Because it involves the process of generating multiple possible explanations, particularly when those are heterogeneous, it is argued that abduction is the only approach to reasoning that can lead to original insight and introduce new conceptual views of a phenomenon (Locke et al., 2008; Weick, 1989).

An abductive approach to analysis introduces a level of complexity by introducing doubt and uncertainty during the research process. In making a case for its centrality to original insight, Locke et al. (2008) highlight the pivotal role that doubt or uncertainty play in the process of theorizing. Doubt can initiate an inquiry, as when a researcher finds competing explanations for a phenomenon, none of which resonates with her experience. Locke et al. vividly capture the process that might ensue when preliminary analysis yields dissonance in that the results are completely at odds with what was anticipated:

> Doubt is the engine of abduction. The living state of doubt drives and energizes us to generate possibilities, try them out, modify, transform, or abandon them, try again, and so on, until new concepts or patters are generated that productively satisfy our doubt. From this perspective, doubt is essential, not aberrant, part of the research process: The question is not whether, but *how* to engage doubt [emphasis theirs].
>
> (p. 908)

These authors highlight the inventiveness that is required to work your way through these kinds of "empirical conundrums."

An abductive process is particularly useful in light of unexpected research findings (Timmermans & Tavory, 2012). It is probably very compatible with a team setting where collaborators work in a very interactive style and feel free to bat about very different ideas about how to explain paradoxical findings. In an abductive approach, intriguing findings can generate a very tentative hypothesis (if–then types of statements generally referred to as propositions in grounded theory research) that are weighed deductively, and then further excavated by additional data analyses and often data collection.

Table 1.1 provides an overview of the steps in an analytical process for MM-GTM that is iterative and includes an inductive, deductive, and abductive logic during analysis. The table highlights integration by adding a center column that is absent from more conventional depictions of the research process in mixed methods research.

TABLE 1.1 Overview of Steps in the Process of Analyzing Multiple Sources of Data in MM-GTM Through an Abductive Process*

Steps	Qualitatively Analyzed Data	Integration	Quantitatively Analyzed Data
Step 1	Initial analysis		Initial analysis
Step 2		Preliminary inferences compared with a combination of induction and deduction; some confirmed.	
Step 3		Alternative explanations generated.	
Step 4	Revisit initial analysis; new analysis; additional data sought.		Revisit initial analysis; new analysis; additional data sought.
Step 5		Compare new round of tentative inferences; draft or refine a theoretical model.	

* To be read from the top down.

Table 1.1 depicts an analytical process that begins with the separate analysis of qualitative and quantitative data that can occur in concurrently or sequentially. Then it shifts to a more integrated approach where there is a type of cycling between induction and deduction to generate hypotheses and then to move on to explore them further through additional data collection and analysis (Thomas, 2010). Rather than the view emerging from the first and second generation of methodological textbooks about mixed methods that frame inferences and meta-inferences as only occurring at the final stage of the analytical process, Table 1.1 depicts a process where interpretation and inferences are drawn throughout the research process.

The type of active dialog depicted in Table 1.1 between findings emerging from different sources of data requires both creativity and insight into its potential implications that can only come from being embedded in the literature. One who argues that regardless of paradigm all research involves interpretation, Bazeley writes: "Researchers move routinely between deductive and inductive thinking about their topic as they consider what is known and puzzle about what they are finding out in an iterative cycle of developing and testing ideas from and with data" (2018b, pp. 335–336). I explore the process of abduction further in Chapter 3 about how a mixed methods approach can be embedded in grounded theory procedures.

The link to complexity

The complex nature of individual actions and interactions within multi-layered socio-cultural context is a third rationale for the compatibility between mixed methods and grounded theory (Guetterman et al., 2017; Johnson et al., 2010). "We believe that the human world is especially rich and complex, and that MM-GTM can offer an important method for understanding complexity," Johnson et al. observed (2010, p. 72). Complexity requires a dynamic research design that can accommodate changes in the research environment and navigate empirical findings that do not always cohere in expected ways (Poth, 2018a). A telltale sign of complexity is when researchers end an investigation realizing that the phenomenon they studied is far more complex than they initially understood.

Mixed methods research projects almost always involve complex study designs (Saint Arnault & Fetters, 2011). There are multiple signals that a research design is complex. Three signatures of a complex research design include: (a) when the core construct is multi-dimensional and framed as embedded in a socio-cultural context, (b) data are collected from multiple levels of an organization, or (c) when participants are distributed across geographically diverse settings (Poth, 2018b). In a school setting, for example, this might include teachers, parents, students, and administrators in multiple different settings. Diversity among collaborators is another dimension of complexity (Poth, 2018b). Saturation of the properties of all categories can be an elusive standard to achieve in a complex research design.

Contributions of each method

That both mixed methods and grounded theory make a distinct contribution is an additional dimension of the argument for distinguishing MM-GTM as a distinct methodology. For grounded theory, this includes assurances that there will be a genuine exploratory or inductive phase that resists the logic of hypotheses testing. An additional contribution is that it offers a

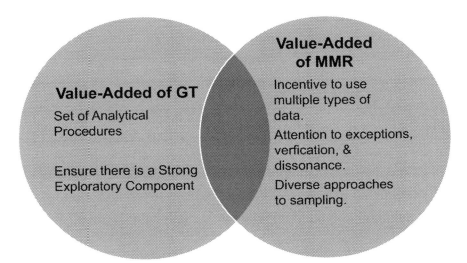

FIGURE 1.3 Overlap Between the Analytic Logic and Procedures of Grounded Theory and Mixed Methods

set of procedures for data collection and analysis that are absent from mixed methods. Both of these can offset an inclination to downplay the qualitative portion of MM-GTM. The unique contribution of mixed methods includes a push to be inclusive of different types of data, a logic that justifies attention to dissonance, and more options for sampling, verification, and weighing exceptions.

Figure 1.3 uses a Venn diagram to depict the unique contributions of grounded theory and of mixed methods as research methods used in a MM-GTM project.

The topics of verification or confirmation and the treatment of exceptions are two areas where it is possible to pinpoint what can be gained through the pairing of mixed methods and grounded theory. Leading voices in the different approaches to grounded theory, including its founders, do not award much attention to procedures that contribute to verification, seeing the purpose of grounded theory as developing theory rather than verifying it (Dey, 1999). The same ambivalence extends to exceptions and outliers. Charmaz acknowledges the role of confirming hunches and promising leads but resists the idea of systematic attempts at verification in grounded theory (Morgan, 2020). There is little justification for verification in constructivism because all truth claims are equally valid (Bryant, 2009). Similarly, dissonance is only prioritized as a source of original insight in postmodern approaches to grounded theory (Apramian, Cristancho, Watling, & Lingard, 2017).

DISTINGUISHING EXEMPLARS OF AN INTEGRATED APPROACH TO MM-GTM

For me, insight about the ways mixed methods is used in practice has been propelled less by a prescription derived from a textbook, but from attention to dissecting how it has been reported in empirical publications. When it is driven by curiosity and the quest to find innovative examples, the scope of the search for exemplars profits by a purposeful strategy to expand the reach of the mainstream journals, like the *Journal of Mixed Method Research* or the *International Journal of Multiple Research Approaches*, which have made such an impact on the field. These are by no means the only sources of creative examples of mixed methods research. Appearance of good examples in a wide range of disciplinary venues that extend beyond those in health sciences and education attest not only to the breadth of the use of mixed approaches and its acceptance in many publication venues, but also can be seen as one way that mixed methods promotes conversations that cross disciplines. I have been very purposeful in my selection of examples and exemplars in this text to present an expansive view of the way that mixed methods and grounded theory methods have been combined to communicate its wide use across multiple disciplinary venues. For the sake of simplicity, I refer to them all as MM-GTM even though it would be more accurate to describe the examples as MM-GT.

My own search to locate every possible article I could lay my hands on that include the terms "grounded theory" and "mixed methods" in the title or abstract, has brought me to a more positive impression than Guetterman et al. (2017) were able to extract from their cataloging of the way grounded theory procedures was implemented. On scrutiny, I set aside most of the examples they located through a systematic review as reflecting a simple QUAL + QUAN combination logic. This means they had a qualitative phase and a quantitative phase, but the two were not integrated in a meaningful way. This is the reason there is little overlap between the articles this group located through their systematic search procedures and the articles I use as examples and exemplars in this text.

I ultimately selected nine articles to feature as exemplars of MM-GTM from about 50 articles I studied with considerable intensity. I consulted more than one article about an exemplar when it was possible with the conviction derived from an earlier study that this approach not only yields more data but also provides a more accurate way to gauge integration and the use of a theoretical framework (i.e., Creamer, Guetterman, Govia, & Fetters, 2020). A summary of each of the exemplars is set aside in each chapter in a text box. A list of these appears in Appendix A. All of the exemplars I selected refer to use mixed methods to develop and/or to refine a theoretical or conceptual framework. Each appeared in the form of a peer-reviewed journal article. Each has a rigorous qualitative phase where qualitative data and analytical procedures are not used simply to add color and human interest to reporting, but for purposes of expanding and enriching explanatory insight.

Qualities of the exemplars include the following:

1 Adequate documentation of research methods.
2 A reference list that reflects more than a passing acquaintance with the methodological literature of both traditions. The most methodologically rigorous of these articles reflects knowledge of both mixed and grounded theory methods.
3 Often, an unusual visual.

Table 1.2 provides a list of the exemplars of MM-GTM and identifies the chapter where they are featured. All of these are FIMM-GTM. Table 1.2 lists the articles, their academic field,

TABLE 1.2 List of Chapter Exemplars*, Field, and Distinguishing Features

Exemplar	Field	Lead Author Country	Disciplinary or Methodological Journal	Distinguishing Features
Chapter 1: Kawamura et al. (2009)	Public Health	Japan	Disciplinary	Developed a formal grounded theory with a visualization that distinguished between qualitative and quantitative findings. Built on a conceptual model from the literature.
Chapter 2: Evans, Coon, and Ume (2011)	Public Health	United States	Methodological	Framed by event analysis. Used grounded theory procedures with a visual display.
Chapter 2: Catallo, Ciliska, and MacMillan (2012)	Nursing	United States	Disciplinary	Developed a grounded theory to explain counterintuitive findings. Developed a visual display to trace each participant's decision-making trajectory.
Chapter 2: Westhues et al. (2008)	Nursing	Canada	Methodological	Teamed MM-GT with participatory action research.
Chapter 3: Jones & Kafetsios (2005).	Child Psychology	United Kingdom	Disciplinary	Used grounded theory procedures, including a visualization, to elaborate an existing theory about the relationship between exposure to violence and trauma.
Chapter 5: Carmona (2015)	Urban Planning	United Kingdom	Disciplinary	Integrated visual, quantitative, and qualitative data for a case-based analysis of specific public spaces.
Chapter 5: Kaplan & Duchon (1988)	Management	United States	Disciplinary	Elaborated an existing theory with grounded theory procedures and analyzed group differences to explain dissonant findings.
Chapter 5: Wesely (2010)	Education	United States	Methodological	
Chapter 6: Shim et al. (2017)	Health	United States	Disciplinary	Presented theoretical framework using the paradigm model proposed by Strauss & Corbin (1998).

* Only one article is listed in this table. Some chapter exemplars (e.g., Catallo & Shim) generated more than one publication.

country of affiliation of the lead author, if they appeared in a disciplinary or methodological journal, and identifies distinguishing features.

I distinguish an article as an example, rather than exemplar, because it illustrates a point or shows an unusual approach particularly to integration but otherwise is not distinguished. This is the case, for example, in Chapter 4 that explores some innovative examples of how visuals can contribute theoretical insight but otherwise are not exemplary as MM-GTM. Unlike the exemplars, examples generally underplay meaningful integration. I attribute this to unfamiliarity with the mixed methods literature. The multi-method label is a better descriptor for some of these because they reflect the combination logic I have already referred to. These self-identify as having a qualitative and a quantitative phase but documented few if any steps to integrate them.

Appendix B provides a selected list of examples of articles that voiced an intent to combine mixed methods and grounded theory. This is not an exhaustive list of articles, but one that I have screened for quality. The list by and large is restricted to examples that mention "grounded theory" and "mixed methods" in the title or abstract. It also includes a few that do not refer to "mixed methods" but that make it clear in the abstract that analysis was conducted of both qualitative and quantitative data. Additional examples where mixed methods and grounded theory were combined are identified in chapters by Johnson and Walsh (2019) and Hesse-Biber and Flowers (2019) appearing in the most recent edition of the *SAGE Handbook of Developments in Grounded Theory* (Bryant & Charmaz, 2019). Both of these chapters include examples that I am not comfortable with characterizing as MM-GTM label because it is not one the authors acknowledge.

CONCLUSIONS

There are many different paradigmatic and methodological approaches to grounded theory, just as there are to mixed methods. Both share the methodological resilience to be adaptable to many other research approaches and philosophical paradigms. Fifty years from its initial conceptualization in 1967 and the publication of the book that opened the door to qualitative research, *The Discovery of Grounded Theory*, grounded theory has been around long enough as a methodology that different schools of thought, often led by former students of either Glaser or Strauss, have emerged. First evident as a distinct movement, according to one of its most iconic figures, John Creswell, emerging in the 1990s in the midst of what is referred to as the paradigm wars, there is certainly great diversity of views about it but distinct schools of thought about mixed methods have yet to coalesce. The different perspectives in the prominence they award to the role of design, purpose, paradigm, and the centrality of mixing to understanding its logic. I have not set out in this textbook to erase the differences in perspectives to either logic of inquiry, nor to corral those differences by cataloging them or trying to reduce them to a narrow typology of types. Instead, my goal is to put that diversity center stage with the belief it can provide a springboard for creative and new applications that integrate methods.

As venerable and durable tradition as it has proven to be, grounded theory is not the only qualitative approach that can be used to develop theory (Maxwell, 2012). The next chapter widens the scope of our inquiry by considering the variety of ways that mixed methods have been used in tandem with theory testing and building, including by pairing with a case-based approach and life history analysis. I argue that conceiving a core construct in a multi-dimensional way is the key to thinking in an integrated way. There are a number of quantitative procedures that are highly effective in developing and refining theory, but it is beyond my interest, expertise, and the scope of this text to pursue these.

Cross-cutting themes

A family of cross-cutting themes weaves in and out of each of the chapters, with each chapter gradually adding another layer to our understanding about each one. The themes can be conceptualized in three clusters. Two of the cross-cutting themes are related to an integrated approach to research that involves the collection and analysis of data from multiple sources to build or refine an explanatory, conceptual, or theoretical framework. The second cluster challenges the restrictiveness of a framing of MM-GTM that underscores the purpose of triangulation or confirmation and, instead, highlights its use to expand the breadth, depth, and nuance in an explanation. The third cluster deals with themes related to complexity and dissonance and their contribution to explanatory power. A meta-summary of the contribution of each chapter to the cross-cutting appears in Appendix C.

Table 1.3 helps the reader extract key takeaways from this chapter and to begin to build a wider architecture that provides a link between the key takeaways and the cross-cutting themes. Methodological advances about our understanding of mixed methods approaches have always been driven by the way it has been adapted in real-world examples (Greene, 2008). The extent

TABLE 1.3 Linking Key Points from Chapter 1 with the Cross-Cutting Themes

Cluster	Major Themes that Cross Chapters	Chapter 1 – Key Points
Integrated Approaches to Mixed Methods Research	Integrated mixed methods approaches engage qualitative and quantitative data in many phases of the research process, but particularly during analysis.	Integrated research uses strategies that intentionally leverage interdependence between their sources of data, methods, or approaches.
		The most effective way to become an integrated researcher is to have some competence in multiple methods, including mixed methods.
		Fully integrated mixed methods research (FIMMR) integrates qualitative and quantitative data and analytical procedures in substantive ways throughout the research process. Integration generally serves multiple purposes in this type of study.
Mixed Methods and Grounded Theory	MM-GT is a methodology that embeds the logic of mixed methods in the constant comparative method and grounded theory procedures.	Conventional perspectives maintain the independence of the stands and the view of the purpose of MM-GTM to build theory with qualitative procedures and test it with quantitative ones.
		In MM-GT, the constant comparative method can be applied to quantitative, qualitative, and mixed data.

Cluster	Major Themes that Cross Chapters	Chapter 1 – Key Points
Complexity and Dissonance	The link between mixed methods and complexity.	A dynamic design is needed to adapt to rapidly changing research environments, unexpected results, and to negotiate the different perspectives team members bring to research initiatives.
	The contribution of paradox and dissonance to explanatory power.	A process that is deliberate about engaging the dissonance and paradox often introduced by abduction is the lynchpin that reaches across mixed methods, grounded theory, and complexity.

of inter-method mixing emerging from practice, such as evident in the dozens of examples of MM-GTM I uncovered in peer-reviewed journals, provides evidence that researchers adapt methods in creative and often unexpected ways in the face of the roadblocks and challenges they face as they pursue complex, real-world problems. The type of complexity this introduces pressures us to reconsider our notion of what it means to develop expertise. To call someone a mixed methods researcher is misleading as all but a few people who contribute to the methodological literature also tend to write about their experience with other methods as well. Methodological innovation requires both content expertise and knowledge of multiple different research approaches.

REVIEW QUESTIONS

1. What distinguishes a conceptual framework, an explanatory framework, and a theoretical framework?
2. What is a mixed methods approach to the constant comparative method?
3. What is an integrated mixed methods approach to theory development and how does it vary from the way it was first conceived in the literature?
4. In what ways can complexity influence the design and execution of a study?

SUPPLEMENTAL MATERIALS AND ACTIVITIES

1. To identify some of the challenges of using grounded theory in a doctoral dissertation, read the self-reflective account by Nelson (2017).
2. IIQM/Mixed Methods International Research Association (MMIRA) Archived Webinar: *Mixed Method Approaches to Developing Grounded Theory, March 13, 2018.* Link: www.ualberta.ca/international-institute-for-qualitative-methodology/webinars/mixed-methods-webinar/archived-webinars

CHAPTER 2

Varied approaches to using mixed methods with theoretical frameworks

The chapter provides a glimpse of the range of ways that mixed methods has been paired with grounded theory and how it can serve as an integrative framework at the onset of a study, offer interpretive insight as a study is underway, and/or stand as its principal outcome.

TERMS INTRODUCED IN THIS CHAPTER

- Formal or classic grounded theory
- Design
- Methodological dynamism

INTRODUCTION

Mixed methods research has been widely criticized, including by some of its strongest proponents, for being "method-centric" in its preoccupation with procedures at the expense of both theory and methodology. Uwe Flick, a German author writing about the myths and mantras about mixed methods research, makes this argument when she notes that there is "too much focus on methods instead of theoretical and methodological issues" (2017, p. 46). Sharlene Hesse-Biber, long writing from a feminist standpoint, links the tendency to downplay the integrative functions a theoretical or methodological framework with the pragmatist epistemological framework and the interpretation that it reflects an "anything goes" with research methods. Variously framed as a methodology or a paradigm, the critical or transformative perspective, Hesse-Biber contends "provides the theoretical perspective that links research problems and approach with a particular method or methods of data collection and analysis" (2018, p. 550).

As we will see in this chapter, both a methodology, like grounded theory, and an explanatory framework or model can serve as an integrative structure that links the purpose, conceptualization of the core construct, research questions, literature review, data collection procedures, analysis, interpretation, and reporting. This is what can be characterized as the **design** of study. *A design is a map or a plan about how an empirical study is executed.*

Studies motivated to build theory are more likely to integrate than other types of studies (Boeije, Slagt, & van Wesel, 2013; Evans, Coon, & Ume, 2011) because they provide the framework to identify core constructs, pose links between them, and provide the structure for data collection and analysis (Evans et al., 2011). In a study designed to test, explore, or develop an explanatory framework, both theory and methodology can serve as a map "for combining the what with the why to gain a multi-dimensional understanding of causal mechanisms" (Evans et al., 2011, p. 278). It can shift the thinking about a research problem in terms of a set of variables, or the relationship between a handful of variables to the kind of holistic multi-layered reasoning that generates explanatory power and, in some cases, generalizability.

Purpose, objectives, and contribution

The purpose of this chapter is to demonstrate the creative and varied ways that mixed methods and grounded theory have been partnered, including through their use with two other methodologies – the life course perspective and participatory action research. The discussion continues to center on examples that manage to combine inductive, deductive, and abductive approaches to analysis for purposes of developing theory. By theory I mean an explanatory or conceptual framework, as opposed to a methodological framework. My interest in this discussion is not to provide a recipe for approaching MM-GTM or in any way to attempt to routinize the procedures associated with it. This is evident in my selection of three examples, which by and large do not completely adhere to a foundational or purist views of grounded theory aligned with one of its founders. It is my goal to underscore that a researcher has a wide variety of tools at his or her disposal that can be adapted to his or her own perspectives, values, and those that emerge in the research setting over the life of a single study or multiple inter-related study that constitutes a research program or project. Options about other strategies that can be used to pursue the process of developing a theoretical framework using grounded theory procedures is the topic of Chapter 3.

The principal ideas at the center of this chapter are:

1 MM-GTM has informed research in a wide variety of different ways. It is its adaptability and variety that sustains its continued dynamism and usefulness.
2 Conceptualizing a problem and research questions in a multi-dimensional way can serve as the foundation for thinking theoretically and developing an integrated approach to mixed methods.
3 Launching a project with a conceptual framework sketched or diagrammed during the process of consulting a cross-disciplinary body of literature facilitates integration across research phases.

Organization of the chapter

The chapter begins by considering the word "design" and the implications it carries of conceiving of a research project as an integrated systematic whole where both a methodology, like grounded theory, or a theoretical framework can provide a guide to link the phases of the research process from initial framing of research questions, to sampling plan, data collection, analysis and drawing conclusions in a systematic and coherent way. It shifts next to highlighting the advantages to theoretical insight offered by thinking of a core phenomenon in a multi-dimensional way. The heart of the chapter is in the section that uses three exemplars to underscore the variety of ways that MM-GTM has been used at different phases in the research process, from a driver of design, to serving an interpretive role during analysis, and in a more conventional sense as the outcome of a study.

First, we consider what is meant by the word "design" and how it is linked to quality.

IMPLICATIONS OF THE WORD "DESIGN"

Among researchers using mixed methods it is common to hear the term "design" used to refer to a core set of basic designs advanced by Creswell and Plano (2011). This equates the word "design" with the timing of data collection and analysis. Analysis of qualitative and quantitative data conducted in a parallel manner referred to as a concurrent design and when linked to each other but timed at different points referred to as a sequential design. This approach has been criticized for awarding more attention to procedures than to purpose as the principal driver of research design and for promoting the idea that the procedures set in place during planning phase of a study comes to fruition exactly as planned. A more expansive view is that the word "design" to carry a dual meaning. It implies both thoughtful planning and ongoing adaptability (Hunter & Brewer, 2015). The implications of research design are related to issues of quality because it helps builds consistency across phases of the research process.

Many conceive the word "design" in broader ways, but also see it as a kind of map or plan about how an empirical study is executed. In this way, to design a research study means to conceive of it as a logically coherent whole that begins with a clearly articulated research purpose that is subject to ongoing refinement and revision. When carefully worded, purpose can serve as road map to guide the construction or selection of data collection instruments, the sampling plans, and data analysis. It is the first place to turn in situations where events take an unexpected turn, or findings emerge that are far outside what the literature led one to expect.

Methodologists often mean different things when they use the words "theory" or "design." Reflecting a deep commitment to a feminist perspective, for example, Sharlene Hesse-Biber (2018) refers to the transformative/emancipatory/critical paradigm as a theory because it influences aspects of the research methods, including the type of relationships established with participants, an expectation for reflexivity, and an approach to data analysis that is respectful of diverse points of view. We have already considered how a conceptual framework developed from the literature can play a similar organizational role, just as a grounded theory developed using a qualitative constant comparative approach developed in one phase of a research project can serve as the basis for further analysis and/or testing in a later phase. Although our focus is on theory as an explanatory framework, any coherent framework or methodology that serves to connect content and method could be called a theory.

Kathy Charmaz, a US scholar from California internationally recognized for her role in articulating the foundation for a constructivist approach to grounded theory, maintained that although their approach can be criticized for being positivist (i.e., there's one truth and there is an accurate way to measure it), Glaser and Strauss' original 1967 book was paradigm shifting in that it tamped down the expectation for "grand theories." These are assumed to be like the laws of nature in that they are invariant over time and place. Charmaz wrote that by providing a systematic set of procedures, Glaser and Strauss "democratized theory construction and made it within the realm of the working researcher" (Charmaz, 2014a, p. 1076). The idea of generating theory is less intimidating when it is thought to be a method that uses an inductive approach to generate a set of categories and then to spell out ways they may be linked (Timonen, Foley, & Conlon, 2018).

The first step toward thinking theoretically about a research problem is to expand the way the core phenomenon is conceived. That includes considering the core phenomenon in a multi-dimensional way that frames research questions that extend across levels of analysis (Weisner, 2016). An advantage of this multi-layered approach to data collection is the potential to examine individual attitudes and behaviors as it is embedded in larger social systems (Malagon, Huber, & Velez, 2009). Although this is not the stance taken by practitioners of a classic approach to grounded theory, this type of framing of a core construct requires engaging a cross-disciplinary body of literature.

Conceptualizing a research problem in a multi-dimensional way

Kathy Charmaz continued to build her ideas about grounded theory as both a method and methodology by taking in account of cultures which are increasingly multiple, mobile, and dynamic (2014a, 2017b). Weighing it in light of research involving indigenous groups, Charmaz observed that much Anglo-North American inquiry is driven by a preoccupation with individualism with individual views, perceptions, and actions, and analyzed as if these occur in a vacuum without the influence of friends, social and professional groups, wider communities or neighborhoods, or social, organizational, and economic forces. She described how researchers working with participants from indigenous communities have to consider collective and communal ways of knowing that are embedded in the family, other kinship patterns, and the local community.

> Not only do we gather data from individuals, but also our analysis often remains at the level of individualism.
>
> (Charmaz, 2017b, p. 37)

One of the characteristics of grounded theory is how it situates a social phenomenon in a multi-layered social contexts (Charmaz, 2014, 2017b). Context is multi-faceted and operates at a variety of levels and in ways that are not always consistent or coherent (Pearce, 2015). Conceiving individual attitudes and actions as nested within micro-, meso-, and macro-levels of social structures enhances the capacity for theorizing (Irwin, 2008; Mason, 2006). Micro-level constructs relate to individuals' beliefs, attitudes, interactions, motivations, and aptitudes. Meso-level constructs reflect how individual perceptions or actions might more fully be understood within the broader context of instrumental relationships within groups, communities, or an organization (Irwin, 2008). Macro-level constructs reflect an even wider social context and could include recognition cultural factors, as well as how current socio-political events impact experiences.

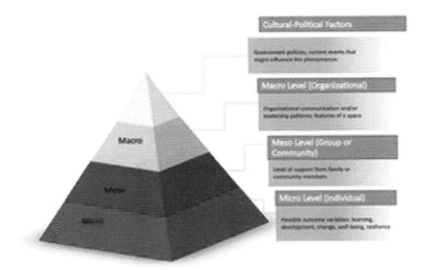

FIGURE 2.1 Framing a Research Problem in a Multi-Dimensional Way

Figure 2.1 supplies a template to expand the conceptualization of a core construct in a multi-dimensional way by weighing individual perceptions and behavior within multiple broader contexts. A multi-dimensional or multi-level way of framing research problems differs from what might be referred to as a bi-dimensional approach that weighs the impact of one variable on another.

Figure 2.1 is not constructed with data that are specific to a single research topic. During the process of defining a research problem, the template might help you to think about a core construct as embedded within a constellation of other constructs that are embedded in a wider social, cultural, and political context. This type of multi-dimensional framework can be informed by Adele Clark's ideas about situational analysis in grounded theory (e.g., Clarke & Friese, 2007; Clarke, 2005).

How we connect or integrate evidence is less a procedural matter than a theoretical one because it reflects wittingly or not assumptions about how change occurs (Irwin, 2008). A theoretical orientation, rather than simply a descriptive one, can be further enhanced by pursuing questions about the interconnections between the constructs. Writing within the context of nursing and research, involving interventions, Marguerite Sandelowski makes the same argument: "Theory is always implicit in the problems that is presented, in the literature reviewed, and most importantly, of the method itself" (1993, p. 215). Theoretical reasoning includes considering not only *what* might be the interconnections, but also about *how* and *why* these might be interconnected.

Embedding multi-dimensionality in research questions

A central reason for the dynamic potential possible when a mixed methods approach is used with theory development and refinement is that multi-dimensional thinking is embedded in the logic. A writer with expertise in complexity theory highlights a role of mixed methods that is central to theoretical thinking, arguing that mixed methods approaches are a "fertile breeding ground" for "research that collects and analyzes data at different levels of granularity (individual, groups, society)" (Koopmans, 2017, p. 17). Framing research questions that link micro- and macro-levels of social experience, including about underlying social processes, necessarily involves different sources and kinds of evidence (Irwin, 2008).

Arguing for the benefits of multi-method and mixed method research, a feminist sociologist writing about inequality, Sarah Irwin, maintains that a single source of data offers only one level or dimension of evidence, and can be not only partial but possibly distorting (Irwin, 2008). This would have been the case, for example, if the exemplar discussed in the next section of the chapter restricted its scope with the individualistic assumption that a single individual, not a wider network of family and community members, contributed to elder care.

An exemplar that models multi-dimensional theorizing

Exploring how the process of caregiving can be embedded and contingent on a cultural context is part of the framework nursing educator, Bronwynne Evans and a set of collaborators in the health sciences bought to a mixed methods study about caregiving pairs among Mexican American immigrants (i.e., Evans, Crogan, Belyea, & Coon, 2009; Evans et al., 2011). They describe how the life-course framework provided a map that facilitated integration and analysis. They write, the framework provides a map "for combining *what* with *why* to gain a multidimensional understanding of causal mechanisms" (p. 278) (italics theirs).

Evans et al. (2011) include two explanatory visualizations in their mixed method article that also were reported earlier in an article about the qualitative phase of the project (2009). The first visualization is a conceptual framework that served as a guide for the design of their study. It frames the literature within key constructs in the life course perspective. A second visualization shows how the initial visualization was refined over the course of the study. Figure 2.2 is reproduced with copyright permission from the Evans et al. (2011) article. It captures a multi-dimensional way of conceptualizing a research problem. It is the first of two figures they include in the article.

Several elements about this visualization are of note. The processes associated with caregiving over a 15-month period are depicted both across the bottom and linked to the timing of life events and adaptive strategies at the top of the figure. Three levels of constructs are depicted at the center of the figure. "Burden and gain" are both individualistic constructs in that they are associated with the caregiver. Cultural influences are associated with family and Mexican American culture. Contextual influences are conceived the most broadly. In the final model, these are narrowly conceived as demographic characteristics (education, social economic status, age, and gender) but could have been conceived more broadly to include, for example, characteristics of the home setting that would accommodate the elderly and/or access to care locally.

Research questions can be worded in ways that reflect that type of multi-dimensionality that is evident in the conceptual model of the caregiving process proposed by Evans et al. (2011). In mixed methods, research questions are often identified in ways that show the link between the questions and either a qualitative or quantitative source of data, with additional questions making clear how the two will be integrated during analysis.

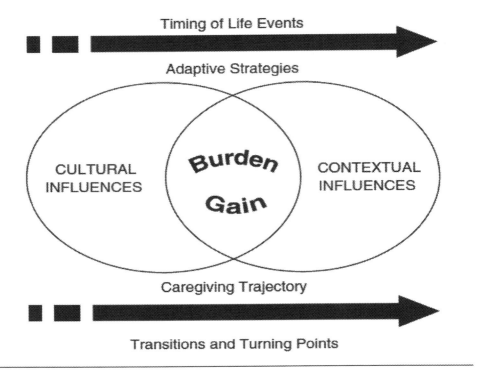

FIGURE 2.2 A Multi-Level Conceptual Model from Evans et al. (2011, p. 280)

Table 2.1 provides an example about how research questions in the Evans et al. (2011) could be worded to make explicit not only how each is linked to a source of data but also how they were or could be integrated.

The first question is purely a descriptive one, written in anticipation of reporting on the results from a quantitative questionnaire. The second and third questions each point to the type of integration that is possible from case-based profiles that were created to synthesize both qualitative and quantitative data about each of the caregiving units. The word "strain" appears in bold to highlight the kind of link across research questions that can facilitate integration of findings from different sources of data.

The research questions posed in Table 2.1 are written in a way that suggests that qualitative data are associated with some constructs and quantitative data associated with others. While this is the most common approach, it is entirely possible that both qualitative and quantitative data could be collected about some of the same constructs. In this study, for example, additional qualitative data could have been collected to more fully contextualize the construct "level of strain." We will be exploring this example in greater detail in the next section, which addresses the variety or "methodological dynamism" (Ralph, Birks, & Chapman, 2015) in the ways

TABLE 2.1 Example Developed from Evans et al. (2011): Framing Multi-Dimensional Research Questions in Ways that Promote Integration

Source of Data	Integration	Research Question
QUANT Measure		What level of **strain** do participants report?
QUAL from Participants' Drawings	Linked through case-based analyses	What cultural, familial, and contextual influences are associated level of **strain**?
QUAL – Interviews	Linked through case-based analyses	What are the physical and emotional consequences of **strain**?

grounded theory has been used when paired with mixed methods, as well as with a feminist theoretical grounding (Kushner & Morrow, 2003; Wuest, 1995).

METHODOLOGICAL ADAPTABILITY OF GROUNDED THEORY

Although there is an ample list of prominent methodologists writing about grounded theory that would very likely breathe fire about this view, others have written in ways that recognize what could be described as **methodological dynamism** in its practice. This is a term that has been used broadly to describe *how methods evolve and remain viable over time* (Ralph et al., 2015). Versed in a variety of perspectives about grounded theory methods, Seidel and Urquhart (2013) and Urquhart, Lehman, and Myers (2010), are committed to its core logic while recognizing its adaptability to a variety of paradigmatic and theoretical positions. "Grounded theory method (GTM) is an evolving method that is subject to idiosyncratic interpretation and flexible deployment," Seidel and Urquhart write (2013, p. 237). Making an observation that applies equally to mixed methods research, Dey (2004) points to the variability in the ways grounded theory methods are used. It is not a single, unified methodology. He writes, "There is no such thing as 'grounded theory' if we mean by that a single, unified methodology, tightly defined and clearly specified" (p. 80).

> Grounded theory method (GTM) is an evolving method that is subject to idiosyncratic interpretation and flexible deployment.
>
> (Seidel & Urquhart, 2013, p. 237)

Evidence of the adaptability of grounded theory includes the gradual shift away from its initial grounding in an objectivist or modernist viewpoint to one that embraces the constructivist orientation (Charmaz, 2006, 2014a). This extends to feminist and indigenous research and other types of critical qualitative inquiry that aims to advance the goal of social justice by studying issues of power and privilege (Charmaz, 2017b). The adaptability grounded theory can also be seen in the ways it has proven amenable to multi-method triangulation that combines qualitative and quantitative methods (Kushner & Morrow, 2003).

CONSULTING THE LITERATURE THROUGHOUT THE RESEARCH PROCESS

The role of the literature and the timing of its use is another topic where there is evidence of methodological dynamism in grounded theory and its adaptability to varied approaches. Founders of the movement, particularly Barney Glaser and proponents of his stance, position engagement with the literature as something that should be postponed until core constructs have emerged. Holton (2008) joins Glaser by insisting that engaging the literature prior to the establishment of the core category can inhibit theoretical sensitivity and block the potential to recognize a new core category that has not been prominent in the literature.

The requirement that no literature be consulted during the process of conceptualizing a grounded theory study is one of the major reasons it is avoided (Urquhart, 2007). Subsequent generations of scholars and who approach grounded theory with a constructivist lens quarrel with the practicality of the purist position that the literature is something to be avoided until the later stages of a project when core constructs have begun to emerge. The idea that it is possible to ignore the literature as pen is put to paper to describe the need and potential contribution of a study is not a practical one (Dunne, 2011). The perception that when using a grounded theory, it is mandatory to abstain from reading the literature, is no doubt one reason why many an advisor might look askance at the idea of using grounded theory in a doctoral dissertation.

> Grounded theory is not an excuse to ignore the literature.
>
> (Suddaby, 2006, p. 635)

A whole chorus of qualitatively minded methodologist has called the notion naïve that a researcher can enter a research project with a blank mind. Charmaz (2014a) is among those who argues that it is often neither practical nor conceptually productive to ignore the literature. She writes "Despite continued injunctions to forgo the literature until after completing the analyses, not all grounded theorists find delaying the literature review to be possible, practical, or conceptually useful" (Charmaz, 2014b, p. 1080). "The idea any research undertakes a study without some level of prior knowledge is simply unrealistic," Dunne observes (2011, p. 117). The idea of a researcher as a blank slate may leave him or her prone to all manner of prejudices and preconceptions (Dey, 1993). It is inherently contradictory to insist that the use of grounded theory is warranted because a topic has not been studied without engagement in the literature to document that claim (McGhee, Marland, & Atkinson, 2007).

My position is that in scholarly research, including in a study using grounded theory methods, a researcher should thoroughly and thoughtfully engage with a wide body of literature throughout all phases of the research process. A researcher from Sweden who writes about grounded theory from a constructivist position, Robert Thornberg (2012), refers to "informed grounded theory" where both the product and the process of grounded theory is informed by an iterative engagement with the literature and theoretical frameworks throughout the research process. He writes that by applying the principle of an ongoing engagement with the literature:

> It is a highly interactive process in which the researcher's coding and questions take him or her to some of the literature, which in turn sends him or her back to the

TABLE 2.2 Contribution of the Literature to Theoretical Reasoning Throughout the Research Process

Phase	Contribution of the Literature
During Planning	Solidify need; develop sensitizing concept: single out key constructs and relationships; locate potential instruments; identify competing explanations.
During Data Collection	Input about sampling strategy and types of additional data, if any required.
During Analysis	Generate explanations for unexpected findings; provide context for the significance of findings, including those that seem counterintuitive; challenge emerging findings, flesh out the properties of emerging constructs; suggest or support emerging themes; contribute to the decision about what to highlight; indicate promising avenues for future research.
During the Process of Pulling Together Results	Clarify contribution; fine tune language that emerged from the coding process to provide links to the way terms are used in the literature; support an argument that findings challenge elements of existing theory; refine audience for work and identify potential publishing venues.

empirical field and to his or her tentative codes and concepts with new lenses and questions.

(p. 252)

Table 2.2 summarizes some of the ways that engagement with the literature and theoretical frameworks can contribute to theoretical reasoning throughout the research process. Although many of the items listed probably cross phases, the list points to contributions during planning, data collection, analysis, and during the process of pulling things together for reporting.

The position suggested by Table 2.2 is more closely aligned with a constructivist view of grounded theory, than with the one advanced by its founders. Wide reading of the literature and other theories, including outside of one's original disciplinary or empirical domain, is instrumental to offsetting a confirmatory mindset.

DEMONSTRATING VARIABILITY IN MM-GTM WITH A GROUP OF EXEMPLARS

The variety of ways that grounded theory procedures can be accomplished through the analysis and integration of qualitative and quantitative data to generate a multi-level grounded theory with a social process at the center is evident in three case examples of MM-GTM highlighted in the next section. Without denying the likelihood that theory plays more than one role and at more than one phase of the research process, the section is organized by the three points of entry of theory in the research process identified by Sandelowski (1993). Theory is used from the onset in the first exemplar by Evans et al. (2011) about caregiving among Mexican American immigrant families. In this case, the life-course perspective served an integrative function throughout the framing, design, and execution of the project. The second exemplar comes for the field of nursing and was one of the publications that emerged from Christina Catallo's dissertation (i.e., Catallo, Jack, Ciliska, & MacMillan, 2013). After a preliminary round of analysis that integrated qualitative and quantitative findings, Catallo generated a formal grounded theory to explain paradoxical findings. The references lists supplied by both the first and second exemplar show a refreshing amount of familiarity with diverse perspectives about mixed methods. The third exemplar illustrates the use of MM-GTM for the classic purpose of generating a theoretical framework as an outcome. The final example by Westhues et al. (2008) produced an integrative grounded theory from a mixed methods community-based participatory action project (CBPR). CBPR is used widely in health sciences, for example, to explore health disparities. The commitment to address inequities in the health care system and to do so by engaging stakeholders as co-constructors of knowledge carried with it from the onset the expectation of diverse points of views.

Each of the exemplars featured in this chapter and their innovative features are summarized in Table 2.3.

The exemplars are described in greater detail in the next sections.

Exemplar 1: using theory to frame and advance the design of a study

Some consider the idea of launching a project by explicitly grounding it in an existing theoretical framework as inimical to the inductive drive that some consider as essential to the logic of grounded theory. Evans et al.'s (2009, 2011) framed a study about caregiving of the elderly among Mexican American families within the life course perspective. These authors demonstrate that new dimensions of theory, including new theoretical constructs, can emerge when a study has a theoretical drive that is inductive (and/or abductive) even when it is framed by a pre-existing theoretical perspective. Another way that this exemplar is unusual is that it shows unusually strong grounding in the methodological literature about mixed methods and qualitative methods.

TABLE 2.3 Innovative Features of the Three Exemplars of MM-GT from Chapter 2

Example	Section in Chapter	Innovative Feature
Evans et al. (2009, 2011)	Demonstrating Variability in the Ways Mixed Methods are Used with GT	Used an existing theory to frame and advance the design of a research method.
Catallo et al. (2013)	Demonstrating Variability in the Ways Mixed Methods are Used with GT	Developed a grounded theory to explain counterintuitive findings.
Westhues et al. (2008)	Demonstrating Variability in the Ways Mixed Methods are Used with GT	Used MM-GTM with a thoroughly interactive, community-based participatory action research project.

The life course perspective derives, like event analysis, from sociology. Major constructs in the life course perspective includes transitions and adaptive strategies. Its focus is on major life transitions. It can be used to study social interactions and events (Happ, Dabbs, Tate, Hricik, & Erlen, 2006). It shares some parallel with core methodological concerns in grounded theory. This includes an interest in a time-ordered social process which in this case involved the caregiving trajectory. In grounded theory, attention to process involves considering how something occurs and under what conditions or circumstances. This is associated with a logic of causality that resides in process theory that deals with events, what influences them, and what connects them (Maxwell & Mittapalli, 2010). Although this is not something Evans et al. consider, the parallel between the life course perspective and grounded theory methodology is also evident in an analytical interest in cultural and contextual circumstances, the physical and emotional consequences to the caregiver, and the strategies they used to adapt to the strain.

Box 2.1 summarizes key aspects of the theory driven mixed methods study by Evans et al. (2009, 2011) that adapted the life course perspective to explore the experiences of how Mexican American immigrants managed the process of caregiving when nursing home options were not realistic. It identifies the design of the study by summarizing the purpose, the way the data were collected, and how integration occurs.

BOX 2.1

Evans et al.'s (2009, 2011) Adaptation of a Life Course Perspective

Purpose: This longitudinal, qualitative dominant mixed methods study adapted the life course perspective from the discipline of sociology to explore caregiving among 110 Mexican American pairs over 15 months. Transitions, turning points, and adaptive strategies are examined in this framework.

Design: Interview data and participant drawn timelines provided the qualitative data, while the quantitative data about key concepts, including caregiver burden/strain, were collected using questionnaires.

Integration: Integration is enhanced in the study by a case-based approach to analysis that combined qualitative and quantitative data in a narrative about each caregiving unit. It was also achieved through quantifying some elements of the participant produced life course drawings.

Unexpected findings: This example illustrates that new dimensions of theory can emerge even when a study is designed to apply a pre-existing theoretical framework. By identifying themes that emerged from the combination of a deductive and inductive approach to coding, these authors identified collective caregiving as a theoretical construct that is new to the literature.

Theory produced: The article includes two multi-dimensional visualizations of the research problem.

The box also summarizes the contribution of unexpected findings to new insight about the caregiving process that normally considers it primarily as one caregiver and one patient, rather than a process embedded in the wider social unit of the family.

In their qualitative article (2009), Evans et al. point to a case-oriented approach as a core component of their study, writing: "The core component of the study is case-oriented approach, which is an intensive, inductively driven study of cases with an eye toward configuration of similarities and differences" (2009, p. 282). In mixed methods, case-based analysis provides an effective way to link qualitative and quantitative data in a narrative or visualization (Bazeley, 2018a). Regardless if the case consists of multiple points of data about an individual, a dyad or family unit, a classroom, an event, or physical location, a case with integration embedded in it can serve as the principal unit of analysis. In the caregiving study (i.e., Evans et al., 2011), data from interviews, a quantitative survey, and data quantified from life course drawings were integrated in a case narrative for each of 110 caregiving units.

The case-based narratives of each caregiving unit were the principal source of data used to answer the research questions. With a mixed methods approach, a case-based approach to analysis differs from a case study in several important ways. These include that (a) they are an intermediary step in the analysis, (b) they integrate multiple sources of data, and (c) they are based on a sample size that exceeds what one would normally find in case study research where an N = 1 is sometimes satisfactory.

In the Evan et al.'s (2011) caregiving study, the case narratives served a formative purpose in that they were used as the basis of further analysis. They were used formatively in a new round of coding to generate working hypotheses for further testing in subsequent phases. The life course perspective also influenced how qualitative data from the life history timelines were quantified. "The quantitizing process also was guided by the theoretical framework as we looked across constructs to identify important comparisons," the authors note (Evans et al., 2011, p. 286). Generalizations drawn from the cross-case comparison were used formatively to generate testable propositions.

Exemplar 2: developing a grounded theory to explore counterintuitive findings

A researcher in nursing, Christina Catallo, carved out a dissertation using MM-GTM within the context of team-based project intended to test the efficacy of a randomized control trial (RCT) designed to increase women's comfort in disclosing partner abuse to emergency room personnel. Catallo et al. produced several articles about this project. A 2012 article concentrates on the qualitative phase when the grounded theory was developed, while the second, 2013 article explicitly frames the study as using both grounded theory and mixed methods (i.e., Catallo et al., 2013).

Box 2.2 summarizes key aspects of the Catallo, Ciliska, and MacMillan (2012, 2013) use of MM-GTM in a randomized controlled trial. It summarizes its purpose, design, and the ways integration occurred, as well as identified the role unexpected findings play, and the type of theory produced.

VARIETY 39

> **BOX 2.2**
>
> ## Catallo et al.'s (2013) Use of MM-GTM to Understand Paradox in a Randomized Control Trial
>
> ***Purpose:*** The complementary rationale is explicit in the purpose Catallo and her colleagues identified for the phase of their research project reported in this feminist, MM-GTM research. They wanted to gain a more comprehensive analysis of abused women's decision-making regarding disclosure of partner violence.
>
> ***Design:*** Following an initial phase of quantitative data collection, the authors turned to a qualitative interview to gain more context about the disclosure process. The authors used an embedded sample in that quantitative data about the type and intensity of violence that was used to select a sample of participants to interview.
>
> ***Integration:*** Integration of qualitative and quantitative data occurred in the second and third phase of the research process where Catallo executed a type of case-based analysis by drawing a change map for each interview participant that contextualized key transition points in her journey toward disclosure.
>
> ***Unexpected findings:*** After executing the first phase of randomized control trial, the authors unexpectedly turned to MM-GTM to pursue the counter intuitive finding that women who reported the most violence on the quantitative measure were the least likely to disclose it to emergency room personnel.
>
> ***Theory produced:*** For her dissertation, Catallo integrated qualitative and quantitative data to produce a formal grounded theory that is visualized in a figure. The model is multi-level in that it identifies constructs associated with the individual (antecedents) and those associated with context, including conditions that promote the disclosure process and its outcomes. Transitions in the disclosure process are depicted at the center of the model.

After executing the first phase of a randomized control trial, Catallo et al. found themselves in the unexpected position of turning to MM-GTM to more fully understand the counter intuitive finding that women who reported the most violence on a quantitative measure administered in the first phase, were the lease likely to disclose in the emergency room setting. To explore these paradoxical findings, Catallo et al. used a type of case-based analysis where the unit of analysis was an individual and their journey through the process of disclosure. They drew what they referred to as "concept maps" or "change maps" that contextualized the qualitative data by pinpointing key transitions or turning points on the journey to disclosure. The change maps revealed patterns of behavior that were evident in the integrated account but probably not to the participant. They drew on both qualitative and quantitative data to test the emerging theory and to determine if they had actually pinpointed the characteristics of women who were and were not likely to disclose intimate partner violence to a health care provider. Catallo et al. (2012) hand drew each change map, incorporating data from the interviews. This kind of visualization can be produced by Computer Assisted Qualitative Data Analysis Software (CAQDAS) (Inaba & Kakai, 2019).

A grounded theory that is visualized in this linear fashion often has a dynamic social process at its core. In this case, Catallo and her colleagues identify three steps in the disclosure process in the 2012 article: (a) establishing readiness, (b) evaluating level of trust, and (c) the decision to seek care.

Catallo et al. (2012) include a figure that reflects the elements of what is referred to as a **formal grounded theory**. *A formal or classic grounded theory is envisioned in a multi-level way. Stages in the progression through a temporal process are at the center of a visualization of formal or grounded theory. Other elements include references to outcomes (anticipated or not), intervening conditions that mediate the outcome, and contextual factors.*

Table 2.4 itemizes the key components of a formal grounded theory, as identified by Seidel and Urquhart (2013). The table provides a definition for each element and extracts examples for each element in the model from the Catallo et al. (2012) study about the process of disclosure to health care professional of intimate partner abuse.

TABLE 2.4 Core Elements of a Formal Grounded Theory, Their Definition, and Key Components of the Catallo et al. Grounded Theory Model to Explain the Intimate Abuse Disclosure

Item	Definition	Example from Catallo et al. (2012)
Casual Condition	Events or incidents that serve as triggers.	"Being Found Out"
Intervening Conditions	Elements in the environment that influence the interactions.	Type of interactions with health care providers
Context	Elements of the location that influence the interaction.	Wait time, lack of privacy, multiple health care providers, concern about losing children to social services
Strategy	Sometimes associated with the participant, but often the activities that influence the outcomes.	Identifying a breaking point
Consequences/Outcome	Outcomes of the actions and interactions.	Self-initiated disclosure; forced disclosure

Exemplar 3: developing a theoretical model as an outcome: an example that combines mixed methods, grounded theory, and community-based participatory action research

It is possible to continue to expand our ideas about the many varied ways that MM-GTM can be approached by consulting an article produced by a multi-disciplinary team (community psychology, sociology, anthropology, and social work) that built an expectation of plurality in the research design (i.e., Westhues et al., 2008). This project involved a five-year initiative designed to "explore, develop, pilot, and evaluate how best to provide community-based mental health services that are reflective for people from culturally diverse backgrounds" (Westhues et al., 2008, p. 702). This team of feminist researchers paired mixed methods, grounded theory, and community-based participatory research (CBPR) to synthesize findings from four sub-projects into a final meta-conceptual model that appeared in a qualitative health research journal. The CBPR framework meant that the team was committed to engaging stakeholders through all phases of the research project, including by engaging community members and data collection and analysis.

Box 2.3 summarizes the purpose and design of Westhues et al.'s (2008) community-based project. It also identifies the ways that integration occurred, and the type of theoretical model produced.

BOX 2.3

Westhues et al.'s (2008) Study About Mental Health Services for Immigrant Populations in Canada

Purpose: The purpose of this collaboratively based mixed methods research project was to build a practice-oriented theoretical framework to enhance mental health services five cultural-linguistic groups in Canada (Punjabi Sikh, Mandarin Chines, Somali, Spanish Latin American, and Polish).

Design: Explicitly labeled as multi-method, mixed methods, and grounded theory, participatory action research (PAR) provided an integrative framework for this complex, multi-site project, which meant, according to the authors, "that we were committed engaging service providers and members of the cultural-linguistic communities in all phases of the study, including data analysis" (p. 702). Data were collected from a comprehensive literature review, focus groups with community members from minority cultural linguistic groups, case studies, and an online service of health care service providers and analyzed concurrently.

Integration: Data from the four methods were first analyzed separately using a combination of an inductive and deductive approach by subcommittees formed for this purpose. The conceptual models produced for each group were then

> triangulated by members of the theory construction committee to produce a final integrative model that included some new synthetic categories.
>
> **Unexpected findings:** It was anticipated from the onset that many stakeholder groups would bring different views to bear on the topic of mental health. They report "the interactive and dialectic use of mixed data helped to discover paradoxes and contradictions in what we had been told, as wells as the similarities and agreements" (p. 714).
>
> **Theory produced:** The meta-model theoretical model produced that integrated separate models constructed from different sources of qualitative and quantitative data uses labels that are comparable to those of a grounded theory model. It includes outcomes, actions that are similar to strategies, and a column that refers to values that promote the transformational process.

The project reflects the complexity involved in a community-based project where the same value-oriented commitment extended to implementing a highly collaborative model of team-based research. The complexity of the project is evident in its methodological grounding and philosophical commitment. It is described as (a) multi-method (data gathered through interviews and surveys), (b) mixed methods (combining qualitative and quantitative approaches), (c) multi-site, and (d) "multi-perspectival." An expectation for diverse points of view was built in the multi-level framing of the project. It was framed by the assumption that service providers, policy makers, and members of the five different cultural linguistic groups would bring very different perspectives.

The account provided by Westhues et al. (2008) is unique in the exemplars I have reviewed in that it describes a research design that is embedded and mutually informed by team dynamics and interaction with stakeholders. In this case, the methodology (CBPR) provided the organizing principle, not a theory like we saw in exemplar using the life-course perspective. The seven-person team appeared to form and reform the task oriented sub-committees initially assigned to analyze the different forms of data, while all the while memoing and communicating actively with each other. The process they describe is dialectical because the same people are moving across tasks and in ongoing communication. In this way, their depiction of the process resonates with the fluid, iterative conceptualization of synergistic fully integrated partnership based mixed methods research generated by Nastasi, Hitchcock, and Brown (2010). They differ in that Nastasi and colleagues imagined ongoing, iterative engagement of qualitative and quantitative data throughout the research process, while the Westhues et al. (2008) account downplays the quantitative data and concentrates on multiple qualitative sources of data.

CONCLUSIONS

The impression that grounded theory methods require the formulaic application of a set of procedures that must be followed step-by-step is one reason researchers avoid it (Timonen,

Foley, & Conlon, 2018). "Descriptions portray theorizing," Weick writes, "as mechanistic, with little appreciation of the often intuitive, blind, wasteful, serendipitous, creative quality of the process" (1989, pp. 518–519). Reservations about the method that emanate from this concern are no doubt further aggravated in the face of the argument that the application of grounded theory methods has been eroded because students have not been taught the differences that evolved between the approaches of its founders (cf. Boychuk Duchscher & Morgan, 2004). Weed (2009) takes a similarly firm admonitory tone in a review of the use of grounded theory in research in sport or exercise psychology, seemingly alarmed to find that authors were not distinguishing differences between approaches.

All methods are hybrid, emergent, and interactive productions.
(Hesse-Biber & Leavy, 2008, pp. 2–3)

Tight adherence to views of the founders who first conceived of grounded theory as a methodology is at odds with the principal argument at the basis of this chapter and why the brief title is "variety." That is that every researcher adapts methods to their skills and circumstances within the inquiry logic of a method, as well as to the requirement for creativity and adaptability demanded changes in the environment, unexpected findings, pluralistic views of collaborators, and diverse perspectives of participants. With foundational grounding that comes from reading the methodological literature, methods can be applied in a systematic and rigorous manner that supports the credibility of the conclusions, without slavish attention to following a narrowly prescribed set of procedures.

Neither methods nor design can be equated with quality (Gorard, 2004). Central to any judgment of the quality of a research report and whether it has an impact is the originality and power of the explanation produced and the extent it resonates with reality (Charmaz, 2014a). Many others emphasize "utility" of theory to both practice and future research as a central measure of quality of research involving theory. The central question to ask about theory is if it is a "model of reality that seems to 'work'" (Hunter & Brewer, 2015, p. 619) and if it assists with making good decisions (Gorard, 2004). Theory is a tentative, partial explanation that is only good as long as it is useful, Gorard (2004) maintains.

Each of the three exemplars featured in this chapter used grounded theory methods with the very practical purpose of helping to inform policy and practice about complex health and well-being questions among members of vulnerable populations. Evans et al. were concerned about family members the care of the home-bound elderly in the Mexican-American community; Catallo et al. with how emergency care personnel interact with women in abusive relationships; and Westhues et al. with developing a health care system that is responsive to the needs of immigrant populations with diverse cultural perspectives.

Adding to the architecture of cross-cutting themes

Table 2.5 adds a second layer of key themes to the architecture of cross-cutting themes introduced in the first chapter. These are designed to help the reader extract important takeaways from the chapter. It is organized around three clusters of concepts: (1) integrated mixed methods designs, (2) MM-GTM, and (3) complexity and dissonance.

TABLE 2.5 Linking Chapter 2 to Cross-Cutting Themes

Cluster	Major Themes that Cross Chapters	Chapter 2 – Key Points
Integrated Approaches to Mixed Methods Research	Integrated mixed methods approaches engage qualitative and quantitative data in many phases of the research process, but particularly during analysis.	Conceptualizing a problem and research questions in a multi-dimensional way can serve as the foundation for thinking theoretically and developing an integrated approach to mixed methods.
		Launching a project with a conceptual framework developed during the process of consulting a cross-disciplinary body of literature facilitates integration across research phases.
Mixed Methods and Grounded Theory	MM-GT is a methodology that embeds the logic of mixed methods in the constant comparative method and grounded theory procedures.	It is possible to sustain an inductive drive in a study that is framed by a theoretical framework from the literature at the onset.
		MM-GT has informed research in a wide variety of different ways. It is its adaptability and variety that sustains its continued usefulness.
		MM-GTM has been paired with a variety of other qualitative research approaches, including participatory action research.
Complexity and Dissonance	The link between mixed methods and complexity.	A theoretical framework can offer interpretive insight about unexpected findings.
	The contribution of paradox and dissonance to explanatory power.	An expectation for plurality and dialectical exchange is built into the design of a MM-GTM participatory action research.

Anticipating the next chapter

The next chapter builds on the idea of the variety that we see in the way MM-GTM has been conducted but narrows the attention to the way that the analytical process can incorporate multiple sources and types of data. My purpose in Chapter 3 is not to revisit a well-worn path by itemizing grounded theory coding procedures or to arduously itemize all the distinctions between the ways the founders view these. This is a task that has been taken on by others. My argument in the third chapter is that mixed methods are adaptable to grounded theory procedures because they can be embedded in an abductive exchange between an exploratory and a confirmatory stance.

REVIEW QUESTIONS

1. How can a conceptual model developed from the literature during the planning stage of a project enhance the design of a study?
2. What is the difference between conceiving a core construct, like identity, in a one-dimensional way from conceiving it in a multi-dimensional way?

3   What distinguishes a grand theory from a substantive grounded theory?
4   What is case-based analysis and how can it promote integration?
5   What are three major points of contention about people who have devoted considerable energy to writing about grounded theory as a methodology?

SUPPLEMENTAL ACTIVITIES

1   Creamer, E. G. (January 2016). YouTube: *Anatomy of a Mixed Method Publication – Highlighting Integration During Reporting (https://youtu.be/5PhV0ocaJ3A)*
2   Using your personal experience and knowledge of the literature, sketch a change map in the form of a grounded theory of your own project. Include activities or strategies, anticipated strategies, and individual and environmental factors that are likely to influence the achievement of targeted outcomes. Create a type of logic diagram that (a) starts with individual pre-disposition, (b) imagines a core sequence with steps suggesting ways change might occur over time, (c) list strategies, activities, interactions thought to influence a positive outcome, and (d) identify possible outcomes, both intended and unintended.

CHAPTER 3
Mixed methods and the process of theorizing

This chapter is about the procedures that advance theorizing, including how qualitative and quantitative data can be integrated through theoretical coding, analytical memo writing, case-based analysis, and theoretical sampling.

TERMS INTRODUCED IN THIS CHAPTER

- Case-based analysis
- Integrated analytical memo
- Integrated case-based analysis
- Saturation
- Theoretical coding
- Theoretical sampling
- Integrated theoretical coding
- Integrated theoretical sampling

INTRODUCTION

In the first two chapters, our attention was directed to the outcomes of empirical research that uses mixed methods and grounded theory procedures in some part of the research process to generate an analytical or conceptual framework to explain a social experience or process. In doing so, our attention was on developing an explanatory framework that is local in the sense that it is grounded in a specific context. This is sometimes referred to as "middle range" theory. These are less ambitious in their scope and claims than so-called "grand" theories where evidence supports the reliability of the constructs across settings. This was the case, for example, in research that people express embarrassment in much the same way across cultures that I reported in my 2018 textbook, *An Introduction to Fully Integrated Mixed Methods Research*.

Chapter 2 highlighted the variety in the ways grounded theory procedures have been used with mixed methods in a wide range of disciplinary contexts. This includes how it can be used as an integrative framework at the onset of a study, to offer interpretive insight as a study is underway, and/or as its principal outcome. Examples presented in that chapter demonstrate that mixed methods and grounded theory can be paired with other research methods, including qualitative approaches like participatory action research and event analysis, to both expand understanding of a complex phenomenon and to provide some measure to confirm its findings.

An emphasis on theory as a product as compared to theory as a process is one of the major differences between the epistemological foundations of thought associated with grounded theory (Apramian, Cristancho, Watling, & Lingard, 2017). Glaser and Strauss characterized these in different ways. In their minds, a theoretical framework is the ultimate endpoint of using grounded theory (Apramian et al., 2017). On the other hand, Charmaz, following a position Clarke took (2005), elevate *theorizing* over theory. Charmaz was explicit in the language she used to frame her preference for theorizing over theory:

> Theories present arguments about the world and relationships within it . . . My preference for theorizing – and it is for theorizing not for theory – is unabashedly interpretive. Theorizing is practice . . . The fundamental contribution of grounded theory methods resides in offering a guide to interpretive theoretical practice, not in providing a blueprint for theoretical products.
>
> (Charmaz, 2006, p. 128)

In an article that identifies "schools of thought" within grounded theory, Apramian et al. (2017) maintain that Charmaz was less enamored with producing a theoretical framework than her predecessors and mentors with a more modernist leaning. Instead, Apramian et al. (2017) assert, her interest in basic social interactions and processes and flexibly deploying analytical procedures that promote the development of the properties of theoretical constructs. Rigor to her was not transferability to other settings or conceptual density. Rather it was to authentically present the voices of participants.

Purpose, contribution, and principal takeaways of the chapter

In this chapter, our lens shifts from what theory or an explanatory framework looks like when it is a product of the systematic application of a set of mixed method procedures to the process of theory generation. This chapter attends to analytical procedures that combine data from qualitative and quantitative methods during the process of theorizing that contribute to analytical understanding. These are not always associated with a final product that is described as a theory. The chapter transgresses traditional approaches to grounded theory by building an argument for the ways a dialectical give-and-take between qualitative and quantitative data can be embedded into the constant comparative method. It offers new ways of applying core grounded theory procedures like theoretical coding, analytical memoing, and theoretical sampling.

The chapter focus on procedures that integrate qualitative and quantitative analytical procedures moves us considerably closer to a model of MM-GTM that reflects a fully equal status in that it contains an equally robust qualitative and mixed methods arm. The approach taken in the chapter widens the options available for MM-GTM to extend well beyond preliminary views that it merely involves applying the constant comparative method to quantitative data as well as qualitative data. Similarly, although it is very likely that a MM-GTM study starts with separate analysis of different sources of data with procedures that maintain the integrity of that method, the emphasis once again is on the types of synergies that can be accomplished by an ongoing interactive exchange, particularly during analysis. The chapter further expands views of ways that data can be collected in grounded theory by offering examples of the creative use of visual methods.

This chapter emphasizes the integration of data collected through qualitative and quantitative methods in core grounded theory procedures. Principal takeaways from the chapter include:

1. There is support for the argument that, rather than being a purely inductive one, the analytical process in grounded theory research is more accurately characterized as an abductive one that moves back and forth between an exploratory and a confirmatory stance. This is an epistemological basis for the compatibility between grounded theory and mixed methods.
2. Promising directions for additional analysis often emerge from an abductive exchange between data generated qualitatively and quantitatively about the same phenomenon.
3. Case-based analyses that integrates qualitative and quantitative data in a narrative or a visualization can resemble a theoretical memo. These can advance theoretical insight about the relationships among constructs, including about the ways they are linked to micro-and macro-level variables that influence the process being studied.
4. Theoretical sampling is a grounded theory procedure that is an extension of the constant comparative method in that additional data gathering is shaped with the purpose of advancing theoretical insight. A promising lead can guide theoretical sampling. Theoretical sampling can be used for both exploratory or confirmatory purposes.

INTEGRATED ANALYSIS USING ABDUCTION

The conception of the analytical process at the center of the constant comparative method as one that combines both an inductive/exploratory stance and a deductive/confirmatory one, is one that has been acknowledged. Charmaz, for example, declared: "grounded theory is not exclusively an inductive method" (2014a, p. 1079). This view of the analytical process in grounded theory as combining different analytical logics is a principal methodological argument for the compatibility between mixed methods and grounded theory. Sociologists Stefan Timmermans and Iddo Tavory (2012) took the position that induction does not produce theory. Instead, they argued that it is the pragmatically grounded analytical strategy of abduction that is the key to generating theory. Pushing back against the characterization of qualitative research as inductive and quantitative research as deductive, Sandelowski (2014) maintained that all research cycles back and forth between the two (p. 6). There is growing recognition that abduction needs further exploration, co-editor with Kathy Charmaz of the *SAGE Handbook of Grounded Theory*, UK academician Anthony Bryant wrote. He maintained that while induction remains central to grounded theory, grounded theory is a "method for enacting abstraction and abduction," Bryant asserts (2017, p. xii).

We encountered abductive reasoning as a type of analytical logic in the first chapter. There, it is defined as an approach to analysis that is both inductive/exploratory and deductive/

confirmatory. It as an extension of the way the constant comparative method is used that often produces unexpected findings. Abduction "refers to the creative inferential process aimed at producing new hypotheses and theories based on surprising research evidence" (Timmermans & Tavory, 2012, p. 170). It often involves finding new concepts to account for puzzling empirical findings (Timmermans & Tavory, 2012). It requires a willingness to abandon old convictions and to generate new ones (Reicherz, 2007).

> In abduction, "the researcher goes beyond data as well as pre-existing theory or theories. It is an innovative process because every new insight is a result of modifying and elaborating prior knowledge and putting old ideas together as the researcher tries to explain the new data."
>
> (Thornberg, 2012, p. 247)

In the context of MM-GTM, an analytical phase involving abduction is very likely to follow an initial phase where preliminary inferences or tentative conclusions are drawn from the separate analysis of different sources of qualitative and quantitative data. For example, in a project about vulnerability among children and homeless adolescents, Jo Moran-Ellis and a set of colleagues from the United Kingdom build an argument for the importance of conceptualizing integration in a way that requires maintaining the methodological integrity or character of each method: "integration involves the generation of a tangible relationship among methods, data, and perspectives, retaining the integrity of each" in a way that gives each method equal weight (Moran-Ellis et al., 2006, p. 51). (Equal weight means that each method is integral to developing the findings [Creamer, 2018d].) They argue this is a strategy to reconcile the epistemological and ontological tensions that arise from using multiple methods, including multiple qualitative methods.

Theory generation is not usually accomplished through a linear process. It is likely to involve an iterative process during analysis as the investigator moved back and forth between induction and deduction and convergence and divergence. Theory generation is not something that can be accomplished in a linear or mechanistic fashion, but requires "simultaneous parallel processing" (Weick, 1989, p. 519).

Visualizing an interactive approach to data analysis in MM-GTM

Although there are other ways it might be executed, iterative exchanges between inductive, deductive, and abductive analytical strategies are often launched, first, with separate analysis of the different sources of data using analytical strategies that are consistent with the method. That is followed in a subsequent phase of analysis by cycling back and forth between the findings beginning to emerge from the analysis of different sources of data. These lead to the generation or what Cronin, Alexander, Fielding, Moran-Ellis, and Thomas (2007) describe as a "promising lead" that offers an explanation for a relationship between data sets. A promising lead is often conceptualized in the context of the literature. Others refer to them as a hypothesis or theoretical proposition. Hiles (2012) refers to them as an explanatory inference. These can take the form of an "if–then" statement about a relationship between constructs (Morgan, 2015).

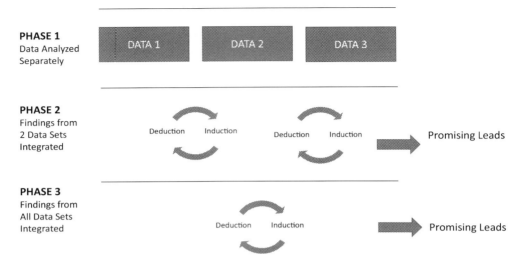

FIGURE 3.1 An Inductive–Deductive–Abductive Analytical Cycle: Integrative MMR-GTM

Figure 3.1 provides what is referred to as a procedural diagram. It visualizes a way analysis might progress in a mixed methods study with a theoretical drive that directly engages qualitative and quantitative data in an interactive and iterative way. It refers to three types of analytical logics: inductive/exploratory, deductive/confirmatory, and abductive.

This generic figure depicts a three-phase process that begins with the separate analysis of each data set. This is followed by investment of time and resources in a second phase where results from the initial round of analysis are engaged dialectically in a give and take that has both inductive and deductive dimensions. Conclusions can be verified or warranted through this back and forth between an exploratory and a confirmatory stance (Morgan, 2020). Dissonance between the results from the different methods or evidence of a gap between what was expected can introduce an unexpected element to the analysis. This integrative step in theorizing can guide additional data collection or analysis or suggest novel directions for the research process.

An example of a promising lead that emerged from an iterative exchange that veered between convergence and divergence is evident in a feminist account of a research project about working mother's involvement in their childrens' school activities (i.e., Weiss, Mayer, & Kreider, 2003; Weiss, Kreider, Mayer, Hencke, & Vaughn, 2005). Their research challenged the prevailing assumption that paid employment is negatively associated with a mother's involvement in their childrens' school activities. Weiss et al. characterized the mixed methods analytical process as a highly interactive one that mirrored the team dynamics. "An intentional and iterative interplay exists between the separate analysis of qualitative and quantitative data sets, such that mixing and integration occurs throughout analysis," they wrote (Weiss et al., 2005, p. 52). The analytical procedures parallel the type of interaction on the team that they characterized as "extensive and respectful dialogue" (Weiss et al., 2003, p. 52).

Abductive reasoning as an extension of a mixed methods approach to the constant comparative method

An argument that prioritizes abduction over induction in the use of grounded theory methods extends the idea of the constant comparative method to one that embraces mixed methods approaches. Conventionally defined as linking data collection and analysis in a qualitative approach by constantly comparing emerging constructs or concepts with new data as it is collected (Urquhart, Lehmann, & Myers, 2010), in mixed methods the idea of using a constant comparative approach to analysis extends to the inductive–deductive–abductive process that brings qualitative and quantitative data and analytical procedures into a conversation.

Abduction extends to pragmatic views about the role of the literature in MM-GTM

Cycling between an inductive/exploratory and a deductive/confirmatory one during analysis assumes familiarity with the literature and existing theory from the very beginning of the research process (Timmermans & Tavory, 2012). The judgment about what is a promising lead that brings dataset together relies on personal experience, familiarity with the data, and knowledge of the literature. It can be sparked by team discussion (Cronin et al., 2007), particularly when interdisciplinary expertise is brought to bear. Familiarity with the literature can amplify the potential implications of inconsistencies, gaps, silences (Creamer & Edwards, 2019). Noting the roots of abduction in a pragmatic philosophical perspective, Robert Thornberg, wrote:

> Thus, by abduction, the researcher goes beyond data as well as pre-existing theory or theories. It is an innovative process because every new insight is a result of modifying and elaborating prior knowledge or putting old ideas together in new ways as the researcher explores and tries to explain the new data.
>
> (Thornberg, 2012, p. 247)

INTRODUCING EXAMPLES IN THIS CHAPTER

A wide reading of studies using MM-GTM yields many examples of the innovative use of a procedure or a visualization that could offer a tool for others with a project with a similar drive underway. Ideas for this chapter go beyond what I had in mind when I first started thinking about its contents. Some of the ideas in this chapter were generated in part from in-depth scrutiny of four studies that I consider in the following sections of the chapter.

I distinguish three as examples and the fourth as an exemplar. All use research methods in original and innovative ways, but I only designate a study as an exemplar when I consider the overall design, particularly the mixed methods component, to be refreshingly robust. I single out a study as an example when a research procedure that integrates data from different sources is used in an original or innovative way that could be adapted in other settings.

Authors of each of the examples situate their work as utilizing mixed methods and at a minimum acknowledge following grounded theory coding procedures. Table 3.1 summarizes the innovative features of each of the four examples discussed at some length in this chapter. Table 3.1 provides information about each set of authors, the section of the chapter where discussion about them appears, and what is innovative about their approach.

The examples reiterate the variety that is evident in research that pairs mixed methods with grounded theory. Each of the examples departs in some substantive way either from conventional practice in grounded theory or mixed methods. For example, in their project about vulnerable populations, Cronin et al. (2007) deviate from definitions of mixed methods that require one method to be qualitative and a second quantitative. What is "mixed" in the Cronin et al. (2007) article is not qualitative and quantitative data, but data that were collected and analyzed with different qualitative approaches.

I showcase the other examples discussed in this chapter for an original feature of their approach to grounded theory. For example, in writing about how undergraduates' definitions of research evolve with experience, Lee et al. (2019) used a unique approach to the process of developing an analytic memo. They were not constructed by a solitary researcher but through multiple exchanges between a group of researchers who were actively engaged in coding the data. In the study about treatment for attention deficit disorder, Bussing and her colleagues (2012) did not collect their own data. This team of researchers was able to leverage a set of data that had already been collected. The expectation that new data be collected in a grounded theory is an assumption that Timonen, Foley, & Conlon (2018) dismiss as not always practical. The last example about the well-being of adolescent in war-torn areas in the former Yugoslavia by Jones and Kafetsios (2005) is at odds with the framing of grounded theory as an exclusively inductive approach that, as Whiteside, Mills, and McCalman (2012) proclaim, begins with no preconceived hypothesis to prove or disprove.

TABLE 3.1 Innovative Features of the Four Examples of MM-GTM from Chapter 3

Example	Section in Chapter	Innovative Feature
Cronin et al. (2007)	Promising leading	Integrating multiple qualitative databases.
Lee et al. (2019)	Integrating through case-based memos	Collaboratively produced integrative analytical memos.
Bussing et al. (2012)	Integration through theoretical coding	Teaming GT with hypothesis testing and data which refuted it.
Jones & Kafetsios (2005)	Integrative theoretical sampling	Composite measure combining qualitative and quantitative data used for theoretical sampling.

Some scholars insist that departures from conventional research practice violate the integrity of the method and contribute to its erosion (i.e., Greckhamer & Koro-Ljungberg, 2006). Others long associated with grounded theory, like Anthony Bryant, take a different position. Bryant (2002) sees it as a negative that grounded theory is still so strongly associated with its founders, arguing it inhibits innovation. For a research method to remain viable and dynamic over time, particularly when it is used across disciplines, it must be adaptable to diverse circumstances (Ralph, Birks,& Chapman, 2015).

Advancing integration through a promising lead

Those with an epistemological bent that predisposes them to qualitative approaches will take comfort in a methodologically reflexive account produced by a team of researchers that set out to more fully understand experiences of vulnerability by integrating findings from data generated from four "mini" qualitative studies (i.e., Cronin et al., 2007) that used grounded theory procedures during coding. In an account of these small-scale studies that seem more like a pilot study than a full-fledged research project, these researchers accentuate the role of a "promising lead" in integrating data from different sources. A promising lead is "a lead for further analysis involving an iterative interrogation of all data sets" (Cronin et al., 2007, p. 576).

The most creative part of this project is its shift from an interview to less conventional and more naturalistic means of data collection. An impression that interview participants were concerned "to present their life accounts as stories" led the researchers to make a course adjustment and to add life history as a data collection method. The promising lead they trace emerged from the data gathered through visual methods. Physical safety emerged as a strong thread in the visual component of the study that included photo-elicitation interviews and video-recorded neighborhood tours with participants who were homeless. The team subsequently chose to explore this thread in their interview and life history data by creating what they referred to as a "data repertoire" that aligned information from all the data sources in a single matrix. The article concludes with a statement resonant with theoretical implications but falls short of presenting a fully developed explanatory framework.

A promising lead can make an appearance in the form of a hunch or burst of creative insight. These often rise to surface when each method produces a different, but likely overlapping, understanding of the over-riding research question. In the Cronin et al. (2007) study this was about the ways that economic, social, and physical vulnerability are manifested. Singling out the role of a promising lead as a way to link findings from different sources of data points to a research design that requires adaptability of methods to emerging findings. The choice to pursue an unexpected finding revealed by the juxtaposition of findings from different methods rests on the researcher. Regardless of method, the act of analysis is always an interpretive one (Fielding & Fielding, 1986). The choice of new ideas to pursue and those to let fall by the wayside is an interpretive one made within the context of the research questions and a firm grounding in the literature.

The team working with data about vulnerable populations (i.e., Cronin et al., 2007) constructed what in the realm of mixed methods is referred to as a data display for each promising thread. The juxtaposition of data from different methods about a promising lead or a theme is used formatively in that it generates further analysis that engages the iterative, inductive–deductive–abductive exchange

TABLE 3.2 Illustrative Example of a Data Display from Multiple Sources of Data

	Sources of Data Related to Physical Safety Theme, by Participant Fabricated from Cronin et al. (2007)		
Fictitious Participant	Narrative Interviews	Photo-Elicitation Interview	Video-Recorded Neighborhood Tour
Lou Ellen	History of physical assault as a child	Photo of drug paraphernalia near a school playground	Time of day influenced perceptions of safety, as did an unfamiliar location

described earlier. At reporting, this kind of display can support an argument for validity by providing documentation of the source of conclusions drawn. It could well generate further rounds of data collection and in grounded theory what is referred to as theoretical sampling to further embellish gaps and silences disclosed by the juxtaposition of data collected with different methods.

It is a shortcoming in reporting that while the text fully pursues the lead about physical safety as an aspect of vulnerability, there are no visualizations related to the analysis in the Cronin et al. (2007) article. As we talk about in the next chapter, whether in the form of table or figures, these types of visualizations can play an important role in supporting the conclusions of a study. Table 3.2 is designed to help a researcher visualize what a data display might look like. I have extended the Cronin et al. article by extracting ideas articulated in the article to create the first few lines of what a data display might have looked like in this study.

When coded in the same way, these types of visual displays can be generated by software that aids in the analysis of qualitative and visual data. If not in the final report, data displays like the ones described by Cronin et al. (2007) would be helpful as supplemental materials.

The richest data from the Cronin et al. study (2007) came from naturalistic sources. These include field notes and a less conventional, participatory approach to data collection referred to as neighborhood mapping. Charmaz (2017b) joined other feminist and critical theorists in the commentary she offers of the limitations of conventional data collection strategies and, most notably, the semi-structured interview with marginalized populations, arguing, as have others, that it reflects very Western cultural assumptions. More creative strategies like using visual methods as described in the next chapter will generate more authentic and robust data with groups of participants where the spoken word is not the best vehicle for communication. This might include, for example, children, non-English speakers, and those with special needs. The appearance of terse, two to three words quotes appearing in the findings section of an article speak to the limitations of the over-reliance on interviewing as a method of data collection in much qualitative research.

SINGLING OUT CORE GROUNDED THEORY PROCEDURES

Despite the diversity of perspectives voiced about grounded theory, there is a surprising level of consensus about its terminology and generally about what constitutes its core characteristics (Rieger, 2018). Table 3.3 narrows our attention to eight core characteristics of grounded

TABLE 3.3 Core Grounded Theory Procedures and Definitions

Core Feature	Definition
Coding (open, focused, and theoretical)	An increasingly abstract system of coding that begins with descriptive (open codes) and moves to a more narrowly defined set of codes that can include deductive codes.
Constant comparative method	New data is constantly compared to data previously collected and tentatively coded.
Core category	Central concept that could begin as a sensitizing concept that becomes the focal point of the theoretical explanation.
Logic model, conditional matrix, or formal grounded theory model	A conceptual model that includes contextual factors, inputs, outcomes, a process of strategies, and factors that mediate them.
Memo writing	An ongoing process of recording reflections about the research process and emerging theoretical ideas.
Saturation	A judgment made by investigators about when sufficient data has been collected when new rounds of data collection yields little new insight.
Social process	A temporal, time-ordered sequence that is at the center of a logic model.
Theoretical coding	Theoretical coding generates constructs to conceptualize the relationships between categories.
Theoretical sampling	A type of purposeful sampling where participants are selected for purposes of advancing theoretical ideas.

theory. Table 3.3 synthesizes information about eight grounded theory procedures and provides a definition of each. Authors reporting on a grounded theory study rarely acknowledge more than a couple of these (Guetterman, Babchuck, Howell Smith, & Stevens, 2017).

Table 3.4 reflects a subjective judgment of the different weighting that is given to the core procedures by leaders of different schools of thought defined within methodologists writing about grounded theory. While the work of each of these authors is linked to different ontological and epistemological assumptions, with the exception of Charmaz's affiliation with constructivism, there is little agreement among experts what philosophical grounding is attached to each school.

Table 3.4 adds to the table that precedes it by recognizing that leading voices writing textbooks about grounded theory methods differ in the amount of space they dedicate to each procedure. The location of the Xs in the table is subjective, but it is informed by a number of articles devoted to discriminating between the methodological, ontological (nature of reality), and epistemological (how knowledge is constructed) priorities of each (e.g., Apramian et al., 2017; Rieger, 2018; McCall & Edwards, 2021; Sebastian, 2019; Timonen et al., 2018). Some authors single out Adele Clarke's situational analysis (2005) as an additional school of thought (e.g., Apramian et al., 2017; Timonen et al., 2018; Morse et al., 2009). The placement of the Xs in this table is eminently debatable.

There is a modest level of consistency across the three schools of thought identified in Table 3.4 about the centrality of three core procedures as being essential to a grounded theory study. That is not to say they may not make a passing reference to the others. All three schools

TABLE 3.4 Priority Awarded to Core Grounded Theory Procedures by Schools of Thought

Procedure	Classic/Formal Glaserian GT	Straussian GT with Corbin	Constructivist GT Charmaz
	Positivist	Realist	Constructivist*
Coding (open, focused)	X	X	X
Constant comparative method	X	X	X
Core category	X		
Logic model, conditional matrix, or formal grounded theory model		X	
Memo writing	X	X	X
Saturation	X	X	
Theoretical coding	X		
Theoretical sampling	X	X	

Source: Apramian et al., 2017; Rieger, 2018; Sebastian, 2019

TABLE 3.5 Frequency of the Use of Core Grounded Theory Procedures in an Analysis from a Systematic Review of 64 MM-GT Articles by Guetterman et al. (2017)

Procedure	Number/Frequency (N = 61 Articles)
Constant comparative method	26 (42%)
Coding	36 (59%)
Generated a theory/framework	20 (33%)
Analytic Memos	8 (15%)
Saturation	18 (30%)
Theoretical sampling	5 (8%)

of thought are in agreement about the centrality of a structured, increasingly abstract approach to coding, the constant comparative method, and memo-writing. Differences among these authors is most evident on three items. The constructivist emphasis in Charmaz's (2014a) work is in that she awards less attention than the other two authors on theory as the product of grounded theory procedures, theoretical sampling, and saturation.

Authors of the articles comparing the approaches differ in the language they use to situate the paradigmatic grounded of each. Leading methodologists differ in their views about the paradigmatic grounding of the different schools of thought approach (e.g., Apramian et al., 2017; Rieger, 2018; Sebastian, 2019). One group of authors position Glaser's and Strauss' initial framing of the methodology as post-positivism and modernism and Strauss and Corbin as symbolic interactionists (Ralph, Birks, & Chapman, 2015) (see Table 3.5).

Estimating the frequency of the use of core grounded theory procedures

A systematic review and analysis of peer-reviewed MM-GTM articles executed by Tim Guetterman and his colleagues (2017) offers some insight about how rarely most core grounded theory procedures are acknowledged in empirical MM-GTM articles. Researchers on this team dissected each article to catalog many features, including by the type of mixed methods design and the types of grounded theory procedures documented. Although conventional, the search terms they used have a lot to do with weaknesses in the sample of 61 articles yielded in their search. They write, "search terms were 'grounded theory,' and one of the following: 'mixed method*, 'multi-method,' or 'quantitative' and 'qualitative'" (p. 184). A telltale sign of the weakness in the articles Guetterman et al. uncovered is that they found no example where the two methodologies were given equal priority. The search terms were not effective in locating a sample of articles with the type of meaningful integration during the analysis of the type that is considered in this book.

The team of researchers concluded that there was not much recognition of core grounded theory procedures in most MM-GTM articles they located during their search process. The majority of articles (62%) recognized four or fewer core characteristics. Their cataloging revealed that none of the 61 articles recognized all of the core grounded theory procedures. They write: "Researchers employing grounded theory in mixed methods research rarely drew upon all or even most of the majors features of grounded theory" (Guetterman et al., 2017, p. 188).

Guetterman et al. (2017) equate research quality with methodological transparency. They rely on the identification of six core procedures as an indicator of quality and transparency in a MM-GTM article. Reinforcing the idea that most of the time a reference to grounded theory as a method refers to the coding procedures and not its theoretical purpose, authors of 59% of article referred to developing a coding scheme. Only about one-third produced a theoretical framework. Memo writing and theoretical sampling were acknowledged only in a small number of studies.

There are many reasons why researchers involved in complex, cross-disciplinary, team research executed in several sites may not use many of the core grounded theory procedures other than coding over the course of executing a project. Lack of in-depth knowledge of grounded theory is only one of several possible explanations. A second is associated space limitations in journals and conventions about how much space is devoted to methods in content-oriented articles. The majority of insight of creative uses of MM-GTM procedures comes from methodological articles or content-oriented articles that devote an unusual amount of space to documenting research methods.

Embedding the engagement of qualitative and quantitative data in core grounded theory procedures

While leading methodologists devoted to grounded theory have long championed the potential to use many kinds of data to generate theory, the recognition has been at the level of data and not the procedures. The emphasis placed on data is evident in the wording of the argument put forward about MM-GTM. For example, by Holton and Walsh (2017) maintained: "For grounded theorists, using both qualitative and quantitative data opens a vast realm of additional empirical possibilities for generating theory" (p. 11). They maintain the separation between the two approaches, aligning themselves with the view that the principal way to imagine MM-GTM is in a two-phase study with a qualitative phase devoted to theory generation and a second, quantitative phase attending to demonstrating its generalizability. Possibly because this requires multiple studies to execute and the likelihood that these are reported in separate articles, Walsh (2015) is one of the few examples I was able to locate that used this approach.

An alternative to the emphasis on data as the source of an alliance between mixed methods and grounded theory is one that situates it in the analytical approach (constant comparative method, abductive reasons) and procedures (coding, memo writing, theoretical sampling, etc.). This is a topic I first entertained in a 2018 article, "Enlarging the Conceptualization of Mixed Methods Approaches to Grounded Theory with Intervention Research" (Creamer, 2018b). In that article, I introduced an argument for the potential for a fully integrated MM-GTM (FIMM-GTM) where qualitative and quantitative data are integrated at multiple phases of the research process, including during analysis. I closed that article noting that potential to use a mixed methods approach to advance theory development had not been actualized and proposing that future research set out to identify the ways the two methods have been teamed: "There has been little acknowledgment in the literature about MM-GTM that the use of some procedures that are central to the process of developing grounded theory, including theoretical sampling and theoretical coding" (p. 13). This is the idea that launched this book.

In the second chapter, I reviewed ways that qualitative and quantitative approaches can be integrated to produce a final explanatory model. In the next section of the chapter, I keep the focus on the act of theorizing and use three different examples of MM-GTM to follow up on the idea that mixed methods can be embedded in grounded theory procedures like theoretical coding, analytic memo writing, and theoretical sampling. Each of the examples point to the ways that mixed methods and grounded theory can be employed together in synergistic ways.

THEORETICAL CODING

Considerably more attention has been paid in the methodological literature to descriptive types of qualitative coding (i.e., open, axial, and selective or focused coding) than to an advanced type of coding referred to as **theoretical coding**. *Theoretical coding generates constructs that conceptualize the relationships between categories.* "Redefining beauty" might be an example of a theoretical code generated as a core construct in a study about how women adjust their body image following a mastectomy. Theoretical coding can be a way to generate hypotheses or themes that subsequently can be tested quantitatively (Walsh, 2015), qualitatively, or with mixed data.

Theoretical coding typically occurs later in the process of developing a coding scheme. It is framed in the literature as following an initial phase of open or emergent coding. This is the most descriptive phase of coding. It can be developed using a subset of the data. The next round of coding is referred to as focused coding. Normally, this refers to the phase of the coding process where clusters of codes referring to similar constructs are grouped together. Johnny Saldaña (2009), the author of a coding manual for qualitative researchers that greatly expanded ideas about ways to approach coding, defines theoretical coding as a strategy that leads to the discovery of a core category. Theoretical coding generally follows earlier more descriptive phases of coding. It is the leverage point that moves coding from descriptive to analytical or abstract. In the real world of practice, theoretical coding can be introduced at many points in the analytical process.

Charmaz (2014a) ranks with her other methodologists writing about grounded theory in the way she presented theoretical coding. "The extent theoretical coding is an application of an emergent process is somewhat ambiguous," Charmaz wrote (2014a, p. 150). She suggested that a coding scheme can include both inductive (or emergent codes) and deductively derived codes from the literature and other theoretical frameworks. To illustrate that point, she suggested that Glaser's (1978a) coding families could prove useful. These include constructs such as context, conditions, consequences, and causal mechanisms that are central to developing a formal theoretical model. This type of model is illustrated in Chapter 6.

In the process of moving from the realm of the descriptive to one that is more analytical and potentially theoretical, an investigator's frame of mind shifts to one that is more overtly interpretive. One reason this level of coding is considered abstract is that it requires identifying patterns and regularities detected in the text but rarely apparent to the participant (Morgan, 2015). It is unlikely to find a participant, for example, that uses language about causality or about how one event or set of circumstances contributed to an outcome. The depth and nuance of theoretical coding depends on investigators' personal experience, breadth of knowledge of the literature, and willingness to simultaneously juggle more than one possible explanation.

An example of integration through theoretical coding

We turn to an example from a project about attitudes about treatment options adolescents with attention deficit disorder (ADHD) to spark ideas about what **integrated theoretical coding** might look like. *Integrated theoretical coding is a mixed methods analytical strategy that engages findings from more than one type of data to generate theoretical propositions or hypotheses about the relationship among categories.* I use two articles produced from this long-term project that are explicitly labeled as mixed methods to explore the ways that integrated theoretical coding can be used in tandem with conventional grounded theory procedures (i.e., Bussing et al., 2005, 2012).

The 2005 Bussing et al. article is unconventional in that the authors describe their project as using grounded theory inductively with a theoretical framework that had already been developed. This is a pragmatic approach to developing a coding scheme that is not uncommon in practice. Both the 2005 and 2012 articles characterize the approach to coding of qualitative data as one that combines both inductively and deductively derived codes. "The mixed-method approach used in this study utilizes both inductive and deductive research methods," that authors write (Bussing et al., 2005, p. 87). The movement back and forth between deductive and inductive coding meant a near seamless connection between the quantitative and qualitative data.

In the earlier article (Bussing et al., 2005) described a process of developing analytical insight that reflected that the team of researchers used a highly interactive approach. Linking team dynamics to the construction of analytical memos, Bussing et al. (2005, p. 89) wrote: "Throughout the analysis process the research team took notes and shared memorandum, both analytical and reflexive." The conceptual model was produced through this process. We see a similar process and outcome in an example from Lee et al. (2019) about engineers' views about research that I discuss later in the chapter.

In researching views about treatment options for ADHD, Bussing et al. (2012) had an opportunity to apply grounded theory methods to analyze an unusually robust body of data generated in response to an open-ended question on a survey about concerns about the undesirable effects of treatment options. While it is quite common, if not always applauded, for someone to refer to a survey with open- and close-ended questions as mixed methods, this team of researchers had access to an unusual number of responses (1356) that ranged in length from one word to lengthy paragraphs.

Bussing et al. (2012) coded the data supplied in response to an open-ended question on a survey in ways the combined conventional grounded theory coding procedures with theoretical constructs from the literature and that had emerged in prior phases of the research project. They describe a process of inductive coding that followed the usual sequence of open coding, axial coding, and selective coding but also included already established codes. Theoretical codes "were used to create an integrated model" (p. 97). Through this process, the team generated three theoretical codes that reflected reasons participants held negative views about a treatment option: negative attitude/dislike, perceived ineffectiveness, and burden. The "burden" theoretical code contained axial codes like cost and disruption of daily activities.

Theoretical coding is directly linked to the construction of theoretical models that, according to Charmaz, have an internal logic "that more or less coalesces into coherent forms" (2006, p. 128). Figure 3.2 reproduces the model Bussing and her colleagues (2012, p. 97) generated as a result of an analytical procedure that integrated deductively and inductively derived theoretical constructs. The journal where it appears is open access. I reproduce the model in full for a

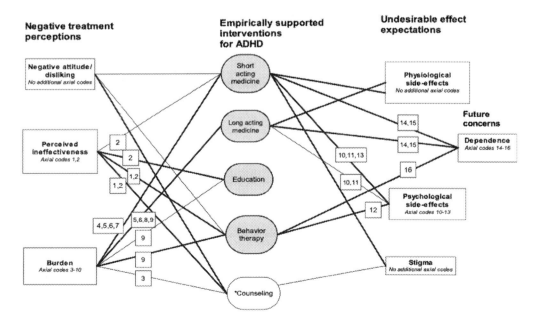

FIGURE 3.2 Conceptual Model from Bussing et al. (2012)

number of reasons, including that: (a) it reflects theoretical coding; (b) it is concise but highly nuanced, leading to more than one interpretive conclusion; and (b) the practical implications about reasons patients may resist treatment are clearly evident. Paths connecting constructs in the model are based on the frequency of responses, with the darker shading indicating more than 20 responses. Small boxes with numbers make it possible to understand each path in terms of codes derived from an open coding phase.

The figure contains key elements of a grounded theory, including causal conditions, the treatment or strategy, and the outcomes. The shaded lines in this figure connect the theoretical codes in the left column (negative attitudes, perceived ineffectiveness, burden) with the treatment options in the center of the future (short-acting and long-acting medicine, education, behavior therapy, and counseling) with outcomes that are the undesirable effects anticipated (physiological side effects, dependence, psychological side effects, stigma.

The insights in this model could be visualized in other ways. In the section of *Coding Manual for Qualitative Researchers* (2009) devoted to coding for causality, Johnny Saldaña demonstrates a way that the types of interconnections shown in the Bussing et al. (2012) figure can be displayed to highlight the potential causal links between the theoretical in causal matrix or flowchart (p. 192). This type of table helps to disaggregate a complex figure by sorting out the results in terms of each treatment option.

In Table 3.6, I apply the Saldaña (2009) strategy to tracing the paths in the grounded theory model produced by Bussing et al. (2012) by extracting information about three of the treatment options: long-term medication, education, and behavior therapy. The "more than" sign implies a linear orientation often embedded in a grounded theory model.

Causality is implied in by the theoretical codes that offer an explanation for the "why" between the outcomes anticipated and the treatment option. The search for evidence about the "why" behind relationships between constructs builds internal validity (Eisenhardt, 1989). So, for example, education as a treatment option is not perceived to have undesirable effects but it is not the treatment option most strongly endorsed by participants because of the concern is that it might not be effective.

Bussing et al. (2012) feature the model in the section of the article devoted to reporting on the qualitative analysis but an argument can clearly be made for what they represent as mixed

TABLE 3.6 Illustrating Causal Pathways in the Grounded Theory Model Produced by Bussing et al. (2012)

Theoretical Code: "Negative Treatment Perceptions" >	Strategy (Treatment Option) >	Outcome – "Undesirable Effects" >
Burden (e.g., cost, adhering to a dosing regime)	Long-acting medications	Physiological side effects
Burden (interference with daily routine) Perceived ineffectiveness	Education	None
Burden Perceived ineffectiveness	Behavior therapy	Dependence Psychological side effects

data and mixed data analysis as one way to acknowledge that the lines between a qualitative and quantitative approach can be blurry. Rather than one that can be pigeon-holed as quantitative or qualitative, a "mixed position" is when some aspect of the quantitative analysis is pursued inductively or some aspect of the qualitative analysis is pursued deductively (Pearce, 2015). The constructs depicted in the model can be considered as "mixed" because the lines between those quantitatively derived and those qualitatively derived are blurry. Some were inductively derived through grounded theory methods and others were deductively derived. The figure can be considered "mixed analysis" because the paths between the constructs were not derived inductively, but by quantifying the frequencies of the responses. Bussing et al. (2012) could have afforded more methodological transparency to readers by devoting a section of the manuscript to explaining how mixing occurred and what was achieved by it.

MIXED ANALYSIS THROUGH INTEGRATED CASE-BASED MEMOS

Memo writing in its various forms is widely recognized as one of the core characteristics of grounded theory analytical procedures. Writing memos is an on-going process in grounded theory. they are a record of reflections about the research process and emerging theoretical ideas. The priority awarded to memoing as a procedure that enhances theorizing spans different schools of thought about grounded theory, including those associated with formal theory (Glaserian) (Timonen, Foley, & Conlon, 2018). Memos can be in a written as a narrative or constructed through a visualization like an informal sketch that captures preliminary ideas about the links between codes and sub-codes, between constructs embodied in categorical or selective codes, or that traces an idea about a temporal sequence. A field note from an observation could serve as a memo that could be coded later in the analytical process. Initially, memos are brief and constructed in a tentative way. Excerpts from a memo might appear in a manuscript, but their main purpose is to advance analytical reasoning.

I refer to a memo that keeps a record of key decisions points in the analytical process as procedural memo and distinguish it from a more abstract and potentially theoretically significant analytical memo. Memos are another type of data that serve as the fundamental bridge between data and emergent theory (Lempert, 2007). "If data are the building blocks of the development of theory, memos are the mortar," Lempert wrote (2007, p. 119). A memo that toggles between description and abstraction can be the basis of an argument for patterns and relationships unlikely to be evident to a participant. More abstract than raw data in the form of interview transcripts or field notes, memos become data that can be the basis for further rounds of coding and theme development. Some memos grow in complexity and become an enduring part of the emerging theory, while others quickly fall by the wayside and can seem embarrassingly naïve in retrospect. An eye to the literature during the iterative process of developing a memo can alert the researcher "to gaps in theorizing, as well as the ways that . . . the data tells a different, or more nuanced story" (Lempert, 2007, p. 254).

An integrated analytical memo *integrates data collected from qualitative and quantitative methods to advance theoretical insight*. These are readily adaptable to communicating a coherent narrative or to encapsulating the type of temporal sequence associated with change over time. An analytical memo can integrate qualitative and quantitative data and serve as a stepping-stone for further analysis, particularly when this involves case-based analysis by recontextualizing what otherwise may seem the fracturing that occurs during open coding. The cycling back and forth between insights drawn from different sources of data that is involved in the construction of an integrated analytical memo is another example of the way the logic of mixed methods can be embedded in a grounded theory procedure.

Analysis that is based on a case that integrates qualitative and quantitative data can be characterized as mixed analysis. **Integrated case-based analysis** *is a mixed methods analytical strategy that leverages data generated from qualitative and quantitative methods into a narrative or visualizations in ways that advance the analysis*. A case might revolve around a core construct. It can be about an individual or an incident or event, like a public protest. Other units of analysis for a case-based analysis could be a caregiving dyad, a classroom, a community organization or hospital ward, a school, a neighborhood, a community, monument, or a piece of land. The development of cases allows a researcher to reconnect segments to the context (Cronin et al., 2007).

Prioritizing case-based analysis as the "lynchpin for integration" in a mixed methods study, Pat Bazeley wrote: "Each case holds data from different sources and different types together, thus cases provide the lynchpin for integration of data" (2018a, p. 26). In MM-GTM, an integrative case-based memo might take the form of a narrative that weaves together information from different sources to construct an account of steps or transitions in the process of change. This is similar to the "change maps" used by emergency room nurse, Christine Catallo, Ciliska, and MacMallan (2012) featured in Chapter 2. She sketched one for every participant and used them to pinpoint key transition points in the process leading to disclosure about partner abuse. The purposeful integration of qualitative and quantitative data for purposes of further analysis is one feature that distinguishes case-based analysis from qualitative approaches to case study.

In her description of it as mixed analytical strategy, Dutch scholar, Judith Schoonenboom, refers to the process of developing a case in ways that suggest the abductive process of moving back and forth between an exploratory and a confirmatory stance. She refers to this as "spiraling cycles of ideas and evidence" (2019, p. 1). The priority she places on discordances and discontinuities in the construction of cases suggests that Schoonenboom's perspective inclines to the postmodern. She traces different steps in the construction of a case, concluding that they often begin what she refers to as the "controversial case." This is evidence that supports more than one conclusion about the role of a theoretical construct in a larger process. She also singles out what she refers to as "moderating cases." These further address complexities emerging from the analysis of different data sources by developing an understanding of the conditions or circumstances under which core ideas do not apply.

An integrative case-based memo or visualization is not simply a descriptive compilation like a data matrix, but a construction that involves interpretation, a winnowing down of the data, and organization in a way that communicates a coherent logic without concealing nuances in the ways it is experienced. In that way, it is similar to the reliance in fields like geology on producing field notes from observations. The lines between qualitative and quantitative data can be kept distinct in an integrated case-based memo, as we will see in the example described in the following section where making meaning of the dissonance between the two was part of the task. In other circumstances, an integrative memo can be constructed so seamlessly that it is difficult to discern the lines between the data generated by different methods.

An example of an integrative case-based memo

During a phase of intense coding and analysis of interview data, an innovative group of researchers at Clemson University led by Lisa Benson (Faber et al., 2019; Kajfez et al., 2021; Lee et al., 2019) unexpectedly found themselves adding a step in their grounded theory project that involved developing an integrative analytical memo about each participant. Their interest in the role of real-world research experiences in the process of the development of an identity as a researcher is a good match with the emphasis placed on process in constructivist grounded theory. Team members central to the analytical process needed a wider context to understand undergraduate students' evolving and sometimes contradictory understanding of the nature of research and what it means to be a researcher. The process of constructing the memos helped members of the team further explore what appeared to be the contradictory statements participants made during the interviews when they were asked to explain what they were thinking when they completed an item on the survey asking them to rate their view of themselves as a researcher.

Dennis Lee took (Lee et al., 2019) took the lead in an article that documented the procedures team members used to develop and refine memos for each participant that integrated interview data with responses collected on a survey a few months earlier. The original authors of each of the 20 memos had conducted the interview and were well versed in the theories related to epistemology and identity that informed the research project. Each memo was formatted in a similar way, with a final section called "cross case analysis" devoted to the constant comparative act of weighing the in light of other memos. Each memo went through multiple revisions during the process of interaction among the two people who co-constructed the memo and the reviewers who subsequently provided feedback about them. This resonates with Eisenhardt's (1989) observation that the process of building theory from case study research is a "strikingly iterative one" (1989, p. 546).

The interactive process of constructing a detailed integrative memo about each participant led to downplaying the significance of the quantitative number respondents assigned to their response to survey items related to identity as researcher. Part of the researchers' reluctance to base their analysis on the quantitative response was the realization that it froze a response about researcher identity to a single point of time. A quote that appeared in the memo about a participant, Taylor, captures the fluidity of the meaning of the number assigned and how it was impacted just a few months later by experiences that had occurred since completing the survey.

> I feel like, from the time I answered your survey to now, I feel a lot more like a researcher, just in the sense that I've had a lot more exposure in the last few weeks to doing engineering-related research, so I've been exposed to another field in that sense. If I answered "7" for whatever reason on that, I would probably put myself at a an "8" now.
>
> (Taylor, quoted by Lee et al., 2019, p. 4)

The evolving nature of Taylor's experience fits with Lempert's (2007) warning to be cautious about imposing linearity on a participant's experience. Not all social processes unfold in a linear or for that matter, systematic, way, Lempert observed (2007).

Integrative memos (cases) can be constructed to serve many different functions that advance theoretical insight. They can be organized to explore causal processes, to identify moderating variables that influence the outcomes, to pinpoint outcomes, or to describe the process of change (Johnson & Schoonenboom, 2015). They can be analyzed to reveal under what circumstances the social process (Rule & John, 2015). Lee et al. (2019) listed five main benefits that accrued from the use of these case-based analytic memos in generating a theoretical framework. These are: (a) support the description of relationships between theoretical constructs, (b) integrate what was often seemingly contradictory quantitative and qualitative data, (c) facilitate the use of the constant comparative method, (d) enhance data analysis and model building, and (e) verify a grounded theory model. They also served several practical purposes of consolidating data management and facilitating communication among team members about the data. As the final model began to coalesce, members of the research team returned to the integrative memos as a way to test model fit and to consider the new insight afforded by those who do not seem to fit the model. Their search for cases that appeared *not* to fit the emerging model is a strategy more strongly associated with Strauss and Corbin (1998), than it is the constructivist position put forward by Charmaz (2014a).

THEORETICAL SAMPLING

Theoretical sampling is a third core grounded theory procedure designed to advance theorizing that can be readily adapted to include multiple sources of data. It follows a very different sampling logic than one that is based on trying to achieve representativeness. In a conventional sense, it is defined *as an emergent and purposeful approach to sampling that follows and initial purposeful sampling that is designed to advance theoretical insight by adding to the understanding of concepts, categories, relationships and themes*. In the foundational literature about grounded theory, the purpose of theoretical sampling is to gain better understanding of categories and concepts and possible variations in them (Timonen, Foley, & Conlon, 2018). Emergent themes can be explored by adding questions to an interview protocol (Levina & Vaast, 2008) or expanding an observation protocol.

Others writing about the use of theoretical sampling take a more expansive view of the purposes theoretical sampling can serve. It can include sampling to verify constructs or themes, to achieve saturation, or to pursue negative cases (Morse & Clark, 2019). It can be used to find an explanation for group differences, as well as to find an explanation for inconsistencies between data sources. Theoretical sampling based on the identification of disconfirming cases is often used during the cyclical process of theory building and testing (Booth, Carroll, Ilott, Low, & Cooper, 2013). It is possible to imagine theoretical sampling undertaken to understand gaps and silences in the data about elements of the phenomenon that were not raised by participants but expected from the literature.

In MM-GTM, the analytical logic of abduction can be the engine that drives theoretical sampling. An abductive logic can enter the scene when a coding scheme has begun to solidify. "Theoretical sampling involves abduction as the researcher accounts for puzzling findings," Charmaz noted (2019, p. 172). Maintaining her qualitative perspective, she framed the back and forth as occurring between the data and the emerging theory. Findings emerging from quantitative data or from quantitative analytical procedures would be a third partner in this arrangement in MM-GTM. For example, in intervention research in a health context where preliminary results ran counter to the assumption that a treatment would be effective, an abductive approach to theoretical sampling would pursue additional qualitative and quantitative data to support or refute multiple possible explanations for that finding.

Saturation

The argument for **saturation** as an indication of rigor now extends across many qualitative approaches but the originators of grounded theory originally conceived of it as the end point, if not the point, of theoretical sampling. In their first publication, Glaser and Strauss (1967) described saturation in terms of fleshing out the characteristics of categories, rather than a theoretical model. "Saturation means that no additional data are being found whereby the sociologist can develop properties of the category. As he [sic] sees similar instances over and over again, the researcher becomes empirically confident that a category is saturated" (1967, p. 61). The pursuit of saturation can contribute to careful attention to the development of the properties of a category and produce "the sharply defined, measurable constructs that are necessary for strong theory," Eisenhardt (1989, p. 542) maintain.

Others define saturation in more practical terms. Eisenhardt (1989) defined saturation as a point in the analytical process "when marginal improvements become small" (1989, p. 533). Nursing educator and editor of a qualitative journal, Janice Morse, sees this differently. She that data collection ends when there is "enough data to build a comprehensive and convincing theory. That is, saturation occurs" (1995, p. 148). It is not the quantity of data, she out, but "valuing variation over quantity" (p. 147). An indicator of saturation is when the theoretical categories and model resonate with the literature (Nelson, 2017).

There are wide variations in the way that theoretical sampling can be used in MM-GTM. It can depart from views of it framed in conventional grounded theory textbooks by serving a confirmatory purpose. Its use for confirmatory purposes is evident, for example, in a mixed methods study that used some grounded theory procedures to study depression among Japanese immigrants (i.e., Saint Arnault, 2009). She identified theoretical sampling as the strategy she used to test hypotheses generated in a previous phase of a study.

Theoretical sampling does not always require additional data collection. A certain portion of the data can be reserved to verify findings (Bruce, 2007). The study by Bussing et al. (2005) about attitudes about treatments for attention deficit disorder explored earlier in the chapter, for example, used theoretical sampling with data that already had been collected. A similar strategy could be used with themes generated from an integrated case-based analysis. In a study of Indigenous empowerment, for example, Whiteside et al. (2012) demonstrate a way that theoretical sampling can be used with secondary data.

Integrated theoretical sampling *engages multiple types of data to advance theoretical insight about categories, concepts, relationships, and themes.* In the exemplar described next, these are used with a carefully matched sub-sample from the larger population.

Box 3.1 summarizes key features of the design of the MM-GTM study of the effects of childhood trauma during war by Jones and Kafetsios (2005). I distinguish this study as an exemplar, rather than an example, because of the way that the intent to integrate different sources of data and engage the dialectically is embedded at many points in the research process.

> **BOX 3.1**
>
> ## Jone's and Kafetsios's (2005) Study About War-Related Childhood Trauma
>
> ***Purpose:*** This mixed methods publication is part of a larger body of work related to an ethnographic study by a team of researchers in the United Kingdom investigating adolescents living in two neighboring cities on the opposite sides of a war in Bosnia (1992–1995) that involved ethnic genocide. Its declared aim was to better understand the relationship between overall exposure to political violence and well-being and the contextual factors that influence it.
>
> ***Design:*** This study is explicitly situated as mixed methods with a "primarily qualitative methodological stance" (p. 159). Study authors characterize their research as following the basic principles of grounded theory. The priority awarded to mixed methods is evident in the numerous sources of data and the multiple ways they were engaged interactively. Data were collected through interviews with adolescents and a parent, the administration of multiple questionnaires, including those related to trauma and well-being, and stories and life history timelines.
>
> ***Integration:*** Findings from multiple sources of data were integrated at many points in the research process and in many innovative ways. The most innovative of these included the quantification of the life history timelines and the creation of mixed data through the construction of a composite measure of well-being that was informed by subjective judgment and quantitative indicators. Both qualitative and quantitative were collected simultaneously through a survey that was administered orally where participants described their response to a variety of different types of trauma associated with war (bombing, pet killed, family member injured, friend killed, etc.) and then ranked their frequency (how often) and intensity (duration)
>
> ***Unexpected findings:*** The "promising lead" that emerged fairly early in this project is that findings were not consistent with the initial assumption that the well-being of adolescents in the two villages would differ because one had been the target of more sustained and intensive bombing. Because habituation leads to less feelings of threat, findings were described as "paradoxical" about quantity of shelling.

> **Theory produced:** The research extended the original theoretical framework. Although not explicitly stated in a theoretical way, well-being (outcome) was influenced by contextual factors, most notably, the "degree to which an event disrupts the adolescent's personal network, and their personal sense of security" (p. 172).

Although there are many fascinating elements of the methods used in this study, the discussion that follows draws attention to the creative ways that data from different sources were intermingled in the sampling strategy.

An exemplar that launched theoretical sampling with a promising lead

The Jones and Kafetsios (2005) study about the effects of ethnic violence was shaped by the theoretical assumption that the more intense and sustained it is, the more traumatic the experience and the more likely it is to damage a sense of well-being or security. This logic guided initial sampling procedures and the selection of adolescent youths from two villages that had experienced different levels of bombing during the Bosnian War between the Serbs, Croats, and Muslims that occurred between 1992 and 1995. The authors situate the study as mixed methods with a "primarily qualitative methodological stance" (Jones & Kafetsios, 2005, p. 159). The second round of sampling procedures was influenced by an unexpected finding that operated like a "promising lead" discussed earlier in the chapter. The authors point to this theoretical anomaly when they write: "Initial readings of the [interview] transcripts showed the importance of exposure in one town but not the other, yet there seemed to be an equal number of less well adolescents in each city" (Jones & Kafetsios, 2005, p. 163). This puzzling finding influenced subsequent integrative sampling procedures to further understand the theoretical implications of the relationship between exposure to violence and symptoms of trauma.

Jones and Kafetsios (2005) used a unique approach to integrative theoretical sampling that was grounded in both qualitative and quantitative assessments. They built a mixed data composite measure of psychological well-being based that contained both a quantified change score, school grades, and the subjective judgments of parents, teachers, and the researcher who had been engaged in the field. Particular weight was given to the change score. That was the difference between the initial and final score participants assigned to their well-being as they drew their timeline.

Jones and Kafetsios (2005) quantified findings from participant drawn timelines but did not include any examples of them in the paper. As this is a strange omission for a study that used visual methods, I constructed the visualization in Figure 3.3 from the narrative provided in the article in the study about adolescents during the Bosnian conflict to illustrate how data provided in the life history timeline was quantified. Participants drew a dot on the timeline reflecting an assessment of their well-being for each year of their life after age five. A line was drawn to connect

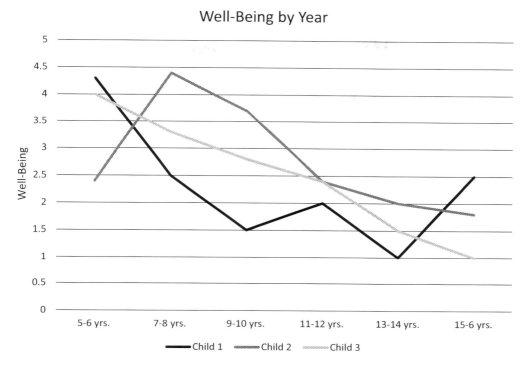

FIGURE 3.3 A Facsimile of the Timeline Completed by Participants in the Study About War-Related Trauma

the dot to produce a trajectory. Differences between the highest and lowest point of well-being were then calculated.

A timeline can be "qualitized" (Onwuegbuzie & Leech, 2019) by asking a participant to provide context for points on the timeline.

CONCLUSIONS

The attention in this chapter has been on procedures that promote theoretical reasoning by engaging more than one source of data and more than one analytical approach (inductive, deductive, and abductive). I have used several examples and one exemplar to illustrate the potential of embedding an abductive and dialectical exchange between qualitative and quantitative data in three core grounded theory procedures: theoretical coding, analytical memoing, and theoretical sampling. The same logic readily extends to other grounded theory procedures such as axial coding and saturation.

It would be disingenuous to suggest that the process of generating a theoretical framework with grounded theory and mixed methods can be reduced to a few formulaic steps that are useful in all settings. One set of authors writing about grounded theory research undertaken with a feminist perspective compare doing grounded theory to preparing a gourmet meal. They write: "Doing grounded theory, rather than a tidy process, is as messy as preparing a gourmet meal where all the parts need to come together at the end" (Keddy Sims, & Stern, 1996, p. 450). This relates to the multi-dimensionality of the constructs and the complexity of the phenomenon being studied. An approach characterized by a high level of interaction among collaborators and that integrates findings from different types of data inevitably introduces new ideas and unexpected findings.

Adding to the cross-cutting themes

The final table in the chapter, Table 3.7, adds a third layer to the cross-cutting themes identified in the first and second chapter by singling out key points from this chapter. The table is organized around three clusters of concepts: (1) integrated mixed methods designs, (2) MM-GTM, and (3) complexity and dissonance.

TABLE 3.7 Linking Key Themes from Chapter 3 to Cross-Cutting Themes

Cluster	Major Themes that Cross Chapters	Chapter 3 – Key Points
Integrated Approaches to Mixed Methods Research	Integrated mixed methods approaches	A narrative or visualization that integrates qualitative and quantitative data is a case-based mixed method analytical strategy that can serve a formative purpose by promoting other kinds of analysis.
	Fully integrated mixed methods research (FIMMR)	Fully integrated mixed method grounded theory (FIMM-GTM) embeds both qualitative and quantitative data in basic grounded theory procedures like theoretical coding, analytical memoing, theoretical sampling, and saturation.
Mixed methods and grounded theory	MMR contribution to explanatory power	The inductive and exploratory component in MM-GT means that new insight with theoretical implications can emerge even in a study with a purpose to test an existing theory or hypothesis.
	MM-GTM	The constant comparative method is not simply an inductive analytical approach, but one that also engages deduction and abduction.
		In MM-GTM, the analytical logic of abduction can drive theoretical sampling.
Complexity and dissonance	The link between mixed methods and complexity	
	The contribution of paradox and dissonance to explanatory power	A strategy for theoretical sampling can emerge from unexpected findings that emerge from comparing preliminary findings from different databases.

With an eye toward visual displays

An integrative approach to grounded theory analytical procedures extends the widespread acknowledgment that both qualitative and quantitative data can play a role in a grounded theory study but moves well beyond any conventional approach to grounded theory. I continue this more expansive and creative logic in Chapter 4 where we continue to explore ideas related to case-based analysis by offering new ideas about the role visualizations that integrate qualitative and quantitative data can play in promoting more nuanced reasoning and in reporting.

REVIEW QUESTIONS

1. How can case-based analysis promote integration of diverse sources of data?
2. How can a dialectical logic be built into the way core grounded theory procedures are used during analysis?
3. What is an example of how multiple sources of data can be engaged for purposes of theoretical sampling?
4. Under what circumstances can the inductive drive of grounded theory be maintained when a study is framed with an explanatory framework from the literature?

SUPPLEMENTAL ACTIVITY

1. Creamer, E. G. (March 13, 2018). Webinar: *Mixed Methods and Grounded Theory* sponsored by the Mixed Methods International Research Association (MMIRA) and hosted by the International Institute of Qualitative Inquiry (IIQM): www.youtube.com/watch?v=n_-oTXK8s1U&feature=youtu.be

CHAPTER 4
Advancing theoretical reasoning with visualizations

This chapter considers the ways that in empirical research, visual displays represent ideas at the same time they generate them. The chapter introduces creative approaches to integrating different sources of data in visual displays to advance theoretical reasoning. These include mapping, timelining, and variations of cluster mapping.

TERMS INTRODUCED IN THE CHAPTER

- Graphic elicitation
- Integrative display
- Joint display
- Matrix mapping
- Participatory photo mapping
- Quantitizing
- Timelining

INTRODUCTION

Diagrams, tables, and figures constructed by participants and/or researchers not only serve as a tool to succinctly communicate what was discovered through analysis but also as an analytical tool that generates insight (Buckley & Waring, 2013). In mixed methods, a joint display is the most commonly used tool for integration (Creswell & Plano, 2011). A display that integrates data from different sources can help a researcher visualize links between constructs, envision a core construct that is at the root of an interactive social process, or recognize conditions that mediate an expected outcome. Participatory procedures using **graphic elicitation** during data collection, such as through mapping and timeline activities, readily flow over to create a platform for an initial round of an analysis. *Graphic elicitation is a data collection procedure where participants physically create and/or verbally edit a diagram or other visual display.*

In the last chapter, I re-imagined many core grounded theory procedures, like the writing of analytical memos and theoretical sampling, from their roots in a qualitative tradition to one that readily embraces a mixed methods approach. These go beyond the simplistic idea that mixed methods approaches to grounded theory are simply a matter of adding quantitative data to what is otherwise a profoundly qualitative set of procedures. In this chapter, I take on the same task with visual methods. These, too, have almost exclusively been presented as qualitative procedures. I re-purpose them as accommodating many different types of data and methods even when maintaining a drive that moves back and forth between an inductive/exploratory and a deductive/confirmatory stance. I provide examples of the use of mixed methods during data collection and analysis with participatory mapping, timelining, and what I refer to as matrix mapping. The examples are provided to inspire creative thinking about ways that they can be adapted and modified to fit other topics and context. The examples are meant to encourage researchers to think beyond procedures like interviewing and surveys that are not the best fit with marginalized or invisible populations, youth, or to those where formal verbal exchange is unlikely to produce rich and meaningful data.

Purpose, contribution, and principal takeaways of the chapter

The use of visualizations is positioned as a critical step in the analytical process in both qualitative (Miles & Huberman, 1994) and mixed method (Onwuegbuzie & Teddlie, 2003) research but their use in the development or refinement of theory has not been explored (Buckley & Waring, 2013). At the same time, that there is little guidance about how to use them in mixed methods research (Plano Clark & Sanders, 2015), much less how they can be used to promote explanatory and theoretical insight in MM-GTM.

The aim of this chapter is to invite readers to consider a range of examples of mixed methods studies that use visual displays in creative ways to integrate qualitative and quantitative data and/or approaches during data collection and analysis. My focus is on visual displays that have an iterative component. I take an unconventional stance by distinguishing these as an integrative visual display rather than using the more generic term of joint display. The discussion about each of the examples underscores the key point of the chapter. That is that integration of findings from different sources of data in a visual display can be instrumental to advancing analytical and theoretical insight. While there are important links to qualitative software and to quantitative procedures, like multi-dimensional scaling, I must leave that topic to others to pursue.

The chapter highlights the use of visual displays in mixed method research used in tandem with grounded theory procedures. It singles out strategies, including mapping, timelining, and other variations of diagramming that have been demonstrated to be compatible to integrating multiple sources of data in ways that generate new analytical insight. I return to one of the cross-cutting themes by considering ways that visual displays can reveal diverse perspectives and expose dissonance between findings from different analytical methods. My ambition is to provide examples that others could leverage in their own research. I postpone to the final chapter discussion of two types of visual displays that are a central feature of the expectations for reporting of a MM-GTM study. These include procedural diagrams (Creamer, 2020) and visual representations of substantive theoretical models.

Principal take-aways from the chapter include:

1 A visual display can be used as a protocol to structure participatory data collection.
2 While integrative and joint displays play a critical role during reporting, they can also play an instrumental role in advancing analytical and theoretical insight.

3   Joint and integrative displays can reveal diverse perspectives and expose dissonance between findings from different analytical methods.
4   Data from integrated visual displays can be used as the basis of case-based analysis and facilitate cross-case comparisons.
5   Visual displays have the potential to generate theoretical insight by helping an investigator envision patterns, time ordered social processes, and relationships among constructs.

Organization of the chapter

The chapter begins by considering the types and purposes of visual displays that integrate qualitative and quantitative data and/or approaches. The next section of the chapter is devoted to describing several different ways that participatory approaches have been used during data collection, including through mapping and timelining. The fourth section of the chapter shifts the focus away from the use of visual displays during data collection to that serve as a platform to integrate data during analysis. In the last part of the chapter, we consider a hypothetical example involving the effect of nature on well-being that illustrates the interactive interplay that can occur when data collection and data analysis overlap.

JOINT AND INTEGRATIVE VISUAL DISPLAYS

The use of visual displays, like diagrams, tables and figures, is widely endorsed in books about grounded theory, including those written by Corbin and Strauss (2008), Charmaz (2006), and Birks and Mills (2015). A display "is a visual format that presents information systematically, so the user can draw valid conclusions and take needed action" (Miles & Huberman, 1994, p. 91). In mixed methods, a **joint display** encourages the integrative engagement of data (Bustamante, 2017). *It is a table or figure that arrays and sometimes links qualitative and quantitative data about the same constructs, research question, or themes* (Guetterman, Fetters, & Creswell, 2015; McCrudden, Schraw, & Buckendahl, 2015; Plano Clark & Sanders, 2015).

While it is customary to highlight the communicative role of a visualization in reporting findings, they can also play an important role during data collection and analysis. Buckley and Waring (2013) expand the discussion about visual displays by noting their multiple functions: "Diagrams, pictures, images, photographs, conceptual maps, matrices, tables and charts not only serve as visual representation of what is being discovered through analysis but also as generative/analytical techniques and communicative tools" (p. 149). Visualizations can contribute to ***developing*** as well as ***supporting*** the conclusions of a study (Maxwell, Chmiel, & Rogers, 2015). That means visual display is not just a representation of what has been discovered but also provides a strategy to help the analyst generate new analytical and theoretical insight (Buckley & Waring, 2013; Shannon-Baker & Edwards, 2018). They may reveal elements that are keys to theory development or refinement, including by providing information about the sequencing of events, relationships among constructions, and connections between a social process and outcomes (Weick, 1995). The role of joint and integrative displays in developing the conclusions of a study is consistent with Charmaz's emphasis on grounded theory as a methodology for theorizing. Analytical joint displays can be creative. They integrate data and discipline-based expertise for purposes of knowledge discovery (Dickinson, 2010) and theory construction and refinement (Creamer, 2018b).

> Diagrams, pictures, images, photographs, conceptual maps, matrices, tables, and charts not only serve as a visual representation of what is being discovered through analysis but also as generative/analytical techniques and communication tools.
>
> (Buckley & Waring, 2013, pp. 148–149)

Joint displays can serve both summative and formative purposes (Creamer & Edwards, 2019). A summative joint display summarizes or visually portrays data during reporting. Qualitative and quantitative data are often juxtaposed in a summative joint display in ways that implicitly confirm parallels between them, leaving task of drawing inferences or conclusions largely to the reader. Joint displays can be used formatively. This is when visualizations serve as a form of data for analysis and/or as a mode of analysis (Shannon-Baker & Edwards, 2018). A formative visual display can be like a theoretical memo that plays an intermediary role during analysis. These are well suited to explore inconsistencies and contradictions because they encourage further analysis by presenting qualitative and quantitative data in the same analytical framework (Maxwell et al., 2015). When used formatively, a joint display or visualization could be used as a new source of data that offers additional insight about patterns and relationships.

I depart from the conventional practice among members of the mixed method community by making a distinction between a joint display and an **integrative display**. The word "joint" in joint display narrows that function of this type of figure or table to two types of data. An integrative visual display can include visual data or symbols, as well as quantitative and qualitative data. I reserve the term "integrative display" to *a figure or table that integrates more than one type of data during analysis in a formative way that advances analytical or theoretical insight*. As is the case with a figure that depicts a theoretical model, an integrative display can provide more holistic understanding by including qualitative and quantitative data on different constructs. This differs from Guetterman, Creswell, and Kuckartz's (2015) assumption that a joint display link qualitative and quantitative data on the same constructs.

Overlap between visual methods, grounded theory, and mixed methods

Knigge and Cope (2006) coined the expression "grounded visualization" in a way that explicitly links it to theorizing. They defined it as an analytical strategy to "more fully integrate diverse forms of data toward building theories and drawing strong conclusions" (p. 2021). They identified four areas of overlap between grounded theory and visualization that extends to mixed methods as well. These are that they: (a) can be used for exploratory purposes to build themes inductively, (b) are often executed in ways that involve multiple rounds of data collection and analysis, (c) simultaneously consider *particular instances* and *general patterns* (italics theirs), and (d) encourage *multiple views* and perspectives for building knowledge (Knigge & Cope, 2006, p. 2022). The multiple interpretations emerging from a visualization reflect complementary perspectives, with each source of data filling in information not available in another source of data. It can reflect interpretations that are on the one hand, consistent, and on the other, contradictory (Knigge & Cope, 2006).

Purposes served by integrative visual displays

Integrative displays can serve multiple purposes at different points in the research process in MM-GTM. Table 4.1 is organized by phase of the research process, beginning with data collection and ending with reporting. It identifies a wide range of different purposes that visual displays can serve in MM-GTM. The table highlights synergistic ways that visual displays, including both as data and as a mode of analysis.

Purposes identified in Table 4.1 extend beyond procedures strictly associated with analysis and include offering a way to communicate with stakeholders or to pursue member checking. Examples used later in the chapter illustrate the ways that a visual, like a matrix or mapping activity, can be used to enhance the potential to collect rich data as well as to provide an instrument to promote theoretical reasoning.

TABLE 4.1 Purposes of Integrative Visual Displays in MM-GTM, by Phase

Phase	Purpose
Data collection	• Enhance potential for authentic data collection (Umoquit et al., 2013), including about sensitive topics (Kesby, 2000). • Engage stakeholders in ways that will inform later stages of the project. • Create a context for participants to tap into ideas and thoughts they have not yet articulated. • Expand the diversity of participants that can be involved in a research project.
Data analysis	• Serve as a catalyst for discussion among team members. • Serve as an "instrument of thought" and "evoke deeper elements of human consciousness" (Buckley & Waring, 2013, p. 149). • Facilitate cross-case comparison (Onwuegbuzie & Dickinson, 2008). • Provide the basis for a case-based analysis. • Enhance the ability to understand theoretical complexity and to detect patterns, relationships between theoretical constructs, and a sequence of events. • Reveal inconsistencies or contradictions between qualitative and quantitative data. • Facilitate member checking.
Drawing conclusions	• Explore the best possible explanation through visual and spatial reasoning (Buckley & Waring, 2013).
Reporting	• Provide transparency by documenting the link between data and conclusions. • Communicate linkages, a hierarchy, a temporal sequence through the spatial arrangement. • Highlight key findings and help the reader understand how the theoretical framework was developed. • Access a wider audience than by text alone (Buckley & Waring, 2013).

DIFFERENT TYPES OF INTEGRATIVE DISPLAYS

Visual methods are approaches in which visualizations are developed, analyzed, and/or disseminated to examine specific phenomenon (Prosser, 2007). In writing about the use of visual methods with mixed methods, Shannon-Baker and Edwards (2018) conceptualized visuals in four different categories: (a) when pre-existing visuals are used as data, (b) when visuals are created as a form of data to be used in analysis, (c) when visuals are created in the process of doing analysis, and (d) when visuals are created to report research findings. Research that uses visual methods with existing graphics might base analysis on photographs, artifacts in the home (e.g., Sheridan, Chamberlain, & Dupuis, 2011), wine labels (e.g., Tiefenbacher, 2013), or use data available from online archival websites like those devoted to restaurant menus or newspaper advertisements. The alignment of data in a visual can prove pivotal to seeing patterns in data that are not otherwise evident. Visuals that are created to report findings are often in the form of a conceptual model or theoretical framework in MM-GTM.

There are a wide variety of visuals displays that can be used in MM-GTM in ways where they serve both as a form of data and as a medium to promote theoretical thinking. Table 4.2 lists and provides a definition for the different types of integrative displays that will be explored in this chapter. These include concept maps, diagrams, mapping, joint displays, and what I refer to as matrix mapping.

There are other types of visual displays used with mixed methods, like social network analysis, that I do not cover here. Sometimes referred to as ecomaps (Bravington & King, 2018), the spatial arrangements in this type of diagram communicate relationships among constructs.

TABLE 4.2 Definitions of Different Types of Visual Displays in MM-GTM

Term	Definition
Concept map	A diagram or drawing constructed by participants that is used as data.
Diagram	Operates like a theoretical memo by tentatively sketching links between categories developed through inductive, deductive, or, abductive reasoning.
Mapping	A grounded visualization procedure that involves the visual representation and analysis that includes geographic data (Knigge & Cope, 2006).
Matrix mapping	Shares qualities with a concept or cluster map, but what appears within the map is based on qualitative and quantitative data participants enter in a matrix with four or more cells.
Integrative display	A visualization that integrates qualitative and quantitative approaches in ways that advance analytical and theoretical insight.
Joint display	A type of visual display that combines, aligns, or links qualitative or quantitative data in a table or figure.
Timelining	Timelining is a participatory graphic elicitation method that encourages the construction of rich, time-ordered narratives of peoples' life and experiences, often through diagramming or sketching combined with open-ended interview (Sheridan et al., 2011).

EXPLORING EXAMPLES OF MIXED METHODS USED WITH A VISUAL DISPLAY TO GENERATE ANALYTICAL INSIGHT

This chapter diverges from all the other chapters in this book in that it incorporates no exemplar but singles out three examples for discussion instead. The distinction, as noted in Chapter 1, is that for purposes of this chapter the authors used a visual display in an innovative way that might be useful to other researchers. They are not exemplary in other ways relevant to this context.

The chapter introduces three examples of mixed methods studies that used visual displays to integrate qualitative and quantitative data in ways that promoted analytical insight. Each used participatory methods in that they were constructed or co-constructed with participants in a dynamic and interactive way. Table 4.3 provides information about each of the three publications. It identifies the source, the disciplinary affiliation, the purpose of the display, and which stages of the research process that the visual display was used. Visualizations are used in these examples in ways that recognize that interpretation plays a role throughout research process. Bazeley (2018a) argues this is true for all research methods.

Visual displays are used in each example in a different way. Each extends reasoning into additional dimensions of time or space. Timelining works well with narrative approaches, research about the lifespan, or event analysis that center on processes that unfold over time. The research using mapping introduces a spatial dimension. It works well with research involving interactions, such as occurring in public spaces or built environments, where the research is about human–environment interaction. All are intended to create a setting that helps the analyst to explore meanings and patterns that underlie diverse experiences and points of view.

Each of the examples illustrates the use of a fully integrated approach to mixed methods (FIMMR) because there is attention to the integration of qualitative and quantitative methods across data collection and analysis. The examples differ in their approach to mixed methods. The example using grounded visualization through mapping (i.e., Teixeira, 2016) and the

TABLE 4.3 Examples of Visual Displays, by Field, Type, Purpose, and Stage of the Research Process

Example	Field	Type	Purpose of the Visual Display	Stage(s) of the Research Process
Youth views of housing abandonment (Teixeira, 2016)	Built environments	Mapping	To annotate photographs during a youth-led neighborhood walking tour.	Data collection and analysis
Changes in poverty status over time in rural Bangladesh (Davis & Baulch, 2011)	Economics	Timelining	To co-construct a time-ordered narrative.	Data collection and analysis
Fabricated example of the impact of nature on well-being	Environmental sciences	Matrix mapping	To generate a set of themes for additional analysis and cross-case comparison.	Data collection and analysis

hypothetical one that used matrix mapping were executed in an iterative way that continuously moved seamlessly back and forth between data collected through different methods. This can be referred to as braided approach to mixed methods (Watson, 2019). The qualitative and quantitative phases are more distinguishable in the timelining exercise completed by two economists using data collected in Bangladesh (i.e., Davis & Baulch, 2011). The data collection and data analysis phases are distinct in this study. In their typology of mixed methods design, Leech and Onwuegbuzie (2009) would categorize this as a sequential fully integrated design.

We move to consider three examples that used integrative displays during data collection and/or analysis in the next section of the chapter. First, we study an example that used photographs with geospatial data to explore participants' views of an urban neighborhood. The link to theorizing is clearest in this one. The second example shifts attention from space to time and a research strategy called timelining. This example was produced by a pair of economists who studied changes in poverty status over time among farmers in Bangladesh. The third example pivots around the use of data matrix to collect both qualitative and quantitative data about the relationship between an experience in nature and well-being. The cells in the 2 × 2 matrix afford a dimensionality that facilitates cross-case comparisons. Grounded theory methods are not well developed in any of these examples.

Participatory photo mapping, grounded theory, and mixed methods

Participatory photo mapping (PPM) is generally categorized as a qualitative approach but it is readily adaptable to mixed methods. **Participatory photo mapping** (PPM) *is a graphic elicitation method that integrates photography, community mapping, and walk-along interviews to learn about people's experiences in a spatial context. It can also utilize diagramming* (Teixeira, 2014). "Maps provide a visual representation of the spatial dynamics of a social phenomenon or process" (Rucks-Ahidiana & Bierbaum, 2015, p. 99). These can be hand drawn by participants, by an investigator, or they can be co-constructed together. Photo mapping borrows procedures from photovoice (cf. Wang & Burris, 1997) but prioritizes the insight that is afforded about a public space like a community garden, museum, tourist spot, or neighborhood that could influence well-being or identity. A quantitative component can be added by using a software mapping platform to identify the coordinates of the geolocation for a photograph. This type of data collection strategy joins other participatory approaches in setting out to promote authentic communication with youth, marginalized populations like the homeless or disabled, and/or with groups with limited language skills. A participatory approach challenges conventional (positivist and post-positivist) approaches that position the researcher as an independent, neutral observer.

Studies with a geospatial component have been used in a wide range of mixed methods studies. These include in a study designed to promote campus safety (e.g., Hites et al., 2013). Other mixed methods studies have used hand-drawn figures to explore environmental factors that promote physical activity (Hume, Salmon, & Ball, 2005), how community gardens foster an attachment to place (Knigge & Cope, 2006), and others by feminist geographers exploring land-use patterns in rural settings (e.g., Nightingale, 2003; Rocheleau, 1995). A drive to explore underlying structures, like gender, race, and poverty, that perpetuate inequality is associated with a feminist and transformative paradigm.

An example of participatory photo mapping

In the next section, we consider two articles by the same author (Teixeira, 2014, 2016) about youths' attitudes about urban neighborhoods. Teixeira modeled her work using participatory photo mapping as a grounded visualization from Knigge and Cope (2006). In this case, the grounded visualization was the bridge that linked grounded theory and mixed methods. It integrated the analysis of qualitative and quantitative data through grounded theory with visual representation and the analysis of geographic data (Knigge & Cope, 2006). Data in the Teixeira study included photos taken by youths, field notes recorded by the researcher during a walkabout, interview data, and geospatial coordinates that marked the location of each photograph taken by the youths in the study.

> Grounded visualization is "a research strategy at the analysis level, which will more fully integrate diverse forms of data toward building theory and strong conclusions."
>
> (Knigge & Cope, 2006, p. 2021)

As with the study by Knigge and Cope (2006) that it is modeled after, that most unusual element of Teixeira's research is its documentation of the creation of an interactive database that merged multiple different types of data in Computer Assisted Qualitative Analysis Software (CAQDAS). Constructing a database that merges data on qualitative and quantitative constructs is the key to meaningful integration (Bazeley, 2018a; Creswell & Plano, 2011). In the study with the mapping exercise, integration occurred during analysis through the innovative linking of the multiple sources of data through a multi-media interactive map with hyperlinks using mapping software. Each location point was associated with one of the youth photos, a GIS coordinate, street map, and coding schemes created by both the youthful participants and the researcher.

Teixeira (2016) included a screenshot from the mapping software (ArcGis) she used in her article (see Figure 2, p. 591, in Teixeira). The software made it possible for her to toggle back and forth between multiple different types of data about a specific location in a neighborhood that appeared in a participant's photograph. It is not difficult to imagine how a researcher with this type of interactive database could use the kind of abductive process described in earlier chapters that moves back and forth between generating new ideas and supporting or refuting them.

Teixeira's two articles (2014, 2016) reveal different aspects of the project. The first article (2014) details the participatory side of the project and its transformative aim to promote community change. The focus shifts away from participants in the subsequent 2016 article where the author elected to situate her work within an existing theory, broken windows theory, as presented by Knigge and Cope (2006). From my perspective, the pairing with the broken windows theory is not consistent with the participatory action model. The translation is less than optimal because the broken windows theory is framed in language about "urban decay," "blight," "vacancy," and "abandonment" that has negative connotations. The author acknowledged that participants did not resonate with the negativity embedded in the language she adopted from Knigge and Cope (2006). The language was far harsher than the language participants used to describe their neighborhood. This is a case where my strategy to consult more than one article exposed a clash between the pre-existing theory that was utilized and how the author reported her interactions with participants in the field.

This research is plagued by significant methodological weaknesses that ruled out my identification of it as an exemplar, including in the very small sample size based on convenience sampling. Despite these limitations, several qualities distinguish this study of participatory photo mapping, both in terms of grounded theory and mixed methods. These include:

1. Its purpose is consistent with grounded theory because it reflects a localized theory of a social process developed using an inductive approach that was grounded in the experience of the participants.
2. The quantitative, geospatial data helped to point to patterns and commonalities across the sites identified by participants in the photo mapping activity.
3. Qualitative and quantitative data were integrated during data collection through a group mapping activity.
4. Data were merged during analysis to create an interactive, integrated database.
5. In a second phase, the locally developed theory was compared to a well-known existing theory in ways that challenged it and invited further exploration.

We turn from a use of visual methods that prioritizes spatial arrangements to one that attends to time, critical events, and the sequence of events.

TIMELINING AS A VISUALIZATION STRATEGY THAT ENABLES INTEGRATION OF DIFFERENT TYPES OF DATA

Timelines or lifelines are generally cast as a qualitative data collection method but are readily adaptable to approaches that integrate qualitative and quantitative data along a chronological dimension. **Timelining** *is a participatory graphic elicitation method that encourages the construction of rich, time-ordered narratives of peoples' life and experiences that is accomplished through diagramming or sketching combined with an open-ended interview* (Sheridan et al., 2011). A timeline used in data collection can have both a vertical and a horizontal axis (Bravington & King, 2018). These are not necessarily restricted to collection at a single point in time but can be constructed over the course of several interactions to capture key transition points or change. The act of creating the diagram and annotating it can shrink the emotional and physical distance between the researcher and participant (Sheridan et al., 2011) in ways that enhance the quality of the data. Timelining activities are used more widely with adults than other types of drawing and diagramming procedures.

Timelining is a visual method that can be effective to study topics where the interest, as is typical with grounded theory, is with a social process that changes over time. In his dissertation, Michael Kutnak (2017), formerly a doctoral student in higher education, used a mapping activity to gain understanding of key points in the collaborative decision-making process that academics, planners, architects, and engineers working together used to reach agreement about design of new academic buildings. He collected written and spoken language and symbols by handing each participant a set of magic markers and a sheet of paper from a flip chart and asking them to talk out loud as they diagrammed important steps in the process. Field notes were an important part of his data, along with images constructed by his participants.

Like other visual methods, timelining is readily adaptable to a mixed methods approach. This procedure can be utilized either through data collection, during analysis, or through an approach that integrates that two. As we saw in one of the exemplars featured in the previous chapter about the experiences of adolescents in a refugee camps by Jones and Kafetsios (2005), both qualitative and quantitative data can be collected on a timeline. In this case, participants first tracked the frequency of their exposure to war-related violence over time on the horizontal axis. Subsequently, researchers asked them to elaborate their responses by annotating the timeline. Data in timelines are often quantified for purposes of analysis. A straightforward way to do this is by creating a dichotomous variable to code a timeline for the presence or absence of a specific event.

A MM-GTM study used a timelining activity in the qualitative phase of a study about parents' help-seeking behavior for a child with an attention deficit disorder that was reviewed in an earlier chapter. During semi-structured interviews, Regina Bussing et al. (2005, 2012) asked parents to describe their help-seeking behaviors. Further analysis was conducted to quantify different elements of the help-seeking behavior appearing on the timeline, including about the types of treatment sought. When combined with quantitative indictors, these researchers reported significant differences by both race and gender, particularly for African American girls, in help-seeking behaviors by parents with children with attention deficit disorder.

An example of using timelining and case-based analysis to understand changes in poverty status

An international team of researchers involved in a large-scale, longitudinal study about changes in the poverty status in communities in rural Bangladesh (i.e., Davis & Baulch, 2011) created an innovative approach to timelining to reconcile dissonance between their qualitative data and a quantitative measure that had become a gold standard for the field. This conventional index is based on a single measure of expenditures. It documented an improvement in economic status, while the investigators had confidence in their qualitative data that presented a more pessimistic conclusion.

Davis and Baulch (2011) developed case-based timelines to track the changing poverty status of their participants. Figure 4.1 reproduces a figure the researchers created to represent the experiences of a 57-year-old woman. The figure includes quantitative data (a quantitative score that denotes one of five different poverty states at different points of time) and qualitative data that summarizes comments by the participant to explain the ups and downs in the graph line. The trajectory depicted in the timeline reproduced in the article shows a few up-ticks, but by and large it shows deteriorating circumstances between 1950 and 2007.

VISUALIZATION   83

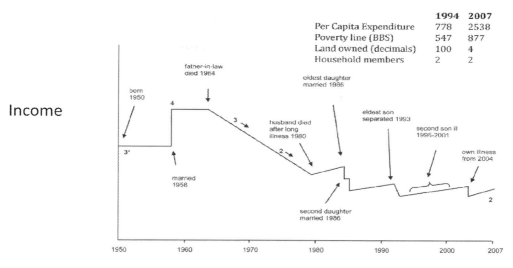

FIGURE 4.1 Example of a Case-Based Timeline

The timeline depicted in this figure is an example of the type of data that motivated Davis and Baulch (2011) to shift from a one-dimensional measure of poverty to a multi-dimensional one that factored in more than simply expenditures. This is a case where the inconsistencies between the insights gained from the qualitative and quantitative data revealed different dimensions. Because expenditures increased over time, but land ownership declined, the figure captures a personal narrative where a single measure concealed shifts in personal and family economic well-being. The downward trajectory of the timeline shows how fragile these lives were and how a single, unexpected event could propel a person back into poverty. Analytical procedures that combined qualitative and quantitative indicators provided evidence to warrant the effectiveness of a more nuanced and multi-dimensional way to measure economic well-being.

Davis and Baulch (2011) further integrated their qualitative and quantitative data through an unusual joint display. They generated a creative set of symbols to depict different trajectories graphed on the timelines. Symbols in the joint display reflect both the direction (declining, stable, improving) of the graph line, as well as if the progression was an even or uneven one. The number of cases in each category and the weight that was given to those cases in the quantitative analysis also appear in the joint display. A similar approach could be used to distinguish the trajectory of change over time about many constructs, including activity level, weight gain or loss, or recovery from illness or addiction, to name just a few possibilities.

Table 4.4 reproduces the joint display from Davis and Baulch (Table 7, 2011, p. 126) that uses a set of images to embody what they refer to as common life trajectory patterns in their data. These were quantified for subsequent analysis.

TABLE 4.4 Davis and Baulch's (2011) Visual Depiction of Common Life Trajectories

Direction	Pattern	Depiction	Number of Cases	Weighted Per cent of Cases
Stable	Smooth		8	1.47
Improving	Smooth		3	1.43
Declining	Smooth		2	0.36
Stable	Saw-tooth		135	44.98
Improving	Saw-tooth		76	26.15
Declining	Saw-tooth		30	6.90
Declining	Single-step		2	0.48
Declining	Multi-step		37	18.22
Total			293	100

Integrating data through a matrix-mapping exercise

Researchers using mixed methods have integrated qualitative and quantitative approaches through visual displays they sometimes refer to as a concept map and sometimes as a cluster map. When used as data, concept maps are generally hand drawn or diagrammed by participants in ways that depict a network of related concepts. Qualitative software like NVIVO, Dedoose, MAXQDA, or ATLASTI can be used to quantify qualitative data in ways that reveal similarities in coding or text. Qualitative software has the capability to produce or map or figure of a complex construct, like sustainability, in ways that make it possible to discern relationships among constructs.

There are multiple creative examples of the use of cluster or concept mapping in mixed methods. Following a structured approach used in evaluation and assessment, Windsor (2013), for example, used qualitative software and a concept map to cluster qualitative data about the dimensions and consequences of abuse in a distressed community. Another team (Walker, Block, & Kawachi, 2012) used similar procedures to map factors that influence the food-buying preferences of people living in locations where the options for buying groceries are more or less abundant. In the field of agriculture, Santiago-Brown, Jerram, Metcalfe, and Collins (2014) created a concept map to group statements reflecting different dimensions of wine growers' definitions of sustainability based on their frequency. In a longitudinal grounded theory study with patients with advanced Parkinson disease, Williams and Keady (2012) used a series of concept maps they co-constructed with their participants to document how an illness narrative became more and more central to their definition of self over time.

The research that distinguishes itself from a mixed method concept analysis or cluster analysis uses a type of mixing that relies on data transformation. Most often this is when qualitative data are quantified for purposes of statistical analysis. This is a mainstay of research using a mixed methods approach that is referred to as **quantitizing** (Sandelowski, Voils, & Knafl, 2009). *This is a type of data transformation where qualitative data are quantified for purposes of statistical analysis.* In a structured approach to content analysis, this is often done by asking participants to assign a score so that the relevance or importance of statements generated during a brainstorming session can be ranked. In mixed methods studies, visual preference surveys quantitize visual data by asking participants to rate or score a photograph or image (e.g., Sweeney & Von Hagen, 2015). In their use of mixed method concept mapping, both Walker et al. (2012) and Windsor (2013) used qualitative software to cluster the line numbers of text that appeared in close proximity. The closer the line numbers on this type of cluster map, the more the statements were assumed to share an underlying meaning.

In the next section of this chapter, I accept the challenge that I have presented to the reader to be creative in experimenting with integrative displays that advance the analytical insight in ways that move beyond simply quantifying qualitative data. I describe a hypothetical example about the benefits of a walk in a forest that I have used as an interactive activity in workshops about MM-GTM. I refer to the procedure as a participatory matrix-mapping activity. **Matrix mapping** is an interactive graphic elicitation method that asks participants to, first, enter the intersection of a quantitative score on a scale on the vertical axis and a second score on a scale on the horizontal axis and then to annotate the point of intersection with a few words to describe it.

A matrix-mapping activity produces a type of cluster map that is plotted by participants rather than by qualitative software that quantifies qualitative codes or language. It is an integrative display that collects both qualitative and quantitative data concurrently. Participants plot the intersection of their scores on two behavioral scales to generate a quantitative score. A qualitative component is added when a participant adds explanatory comments in a matrix with four cells.

An example of a matrix-mapping activity conducive to MM-GTM

I illustrate the way that a matrix-mapping activity might be used as a grounded visualization from an idea that was sparked by a review of the popular media book, *Nature Fix*, that appeared in the *New York Times*. Jason Mark (2017), a writer specializing in the environment, expressed some skepticism about claims made about the benefits to physical and psychological well-being of experiences of nature that promise to help us be happier, healthier, and more creative. Nature neuroscientists purport that a walk in the woods as short as 15 minutes can reduce the stress hormone, cortisol, and when as long as 45 minutes, can significantly enhance cognitive performance and possibly generate feelings of generosity. One explanation is that the experience has its most profound impacts when it is an immersive one that engages all the senses from sounds (bird song, wind, rain) through the aerosols present in evergreen trees that act as a mild sedative.

Not entirely convinced that these findings extend to the real world, Mark (2017) expressed skepticism that these claims might be "aspiration dressed up as a hypothesis." In other words, that the unpredictability of the real-world experience, along with the potential introduction of unexpected weather, pests, wildlife, and equipment malfunctions might yield for less positive benefits.

Figure 4.2 represents the type of 2 × 2 matrix that could be used to collect data to explore the link between well-being and an appreciation of nature, as evident through recollection of a single incident of a walk in the forest. In this hypothetical example, during the first phase of data collection, participants would plot the intersection of two scores, each using a one- to four-point scale with the vertical Y axis collecting an assessment of overall well-being and the X axis a measurement of appreciation of nature during a specific experience. In Figure 4.2, each circle represents a single participant. The label applied to each circle could be generated by the participant and/or the researcher and then used as the basis for a group interview or discussion. The data in Figure 4.2 are hypothetical. It is completed as if there are only six participants when considerably more would be needed to either confirm or develop a theory about the impacts of an immersive experience in nature.

There are a lot of different ways this type of activity could involve participants both in data collection and analysis. Figure 4.3 is a flowchart that captures the way the research process might unfold in this matrix-mapping activity.

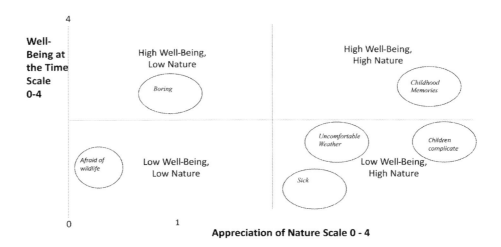

FIGURE 4.2 Generating Analytical Insight from a Matrix-Mapping Activity

VISUALIZATION

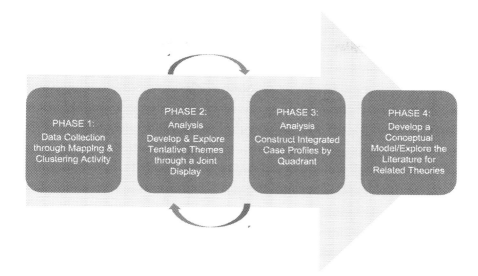

FIGURE 4.3 Procedural Diagram of the Design of Matrix-Mapping Activity

Participants involved in the first phase of the research might plot and annotate their scores on a data matrix and then explain their logic in a group setting. In the second phase of the process, preliminary themes could be developed that explore differences within and between the quadrants in the matrix. A comparison of the experiences of participants positioned in the different quadrants very likely would uncover a diverse set of personal and environmental conditions that effect the experience. A case-based approach to analysis could be used in a third phase where the research analyst might draft analytical memos or a summary case profile for each of the four quadrants or for the extremes (high well-being, high nature; high well-being, low nature; low well-being, high nature; low well-being, low nature). Bazeley (2018a) suggests that a similar exploratory strategy could be used with a quantitatively generated cluster analysis.

The use of a matrix or cluster map that integrates qualitative and quantitative data for analysis can extend to the use of a joint display. Qualitative and quantitative data are often aligned side by side with questions, themes, and/or statistics in a joint display (Guetterman et al., 2015). By and large, this type of visual display devotes more attention to words than does an integrative display. Meaning can also be communicated in an integrative display through such visual devices as shading, dotted and solid lines, curved or straight lines, and arrows.

Illustrating the use of a joint display to advance analysis

Joint displays array or align qualitative and quantitative data on the same constructs. Some conceptualize joint displays primarily as a table with a two-column format that juxtaposes or links qualitative and quantitative data. These typically represent less fluidity in the interaction between data from different sources than the type of integrative display I have been reviewing. Early conceptualizations of the formatting of a joint display were extended in a recent publication by Johnson, Grove, and Clarke (2019). They inserted a column at the center of a conventional joint display in a process they referred to as "pillar integration." They used the center column to document the themes that emerged when data from two sources were integrated. In an article I singled out as an exemplar in my first textbook (Creamer, 2018a); Castro, Kellison, Boyd, and Kopak (2010) accomplished the same thing by adding a column to the right of a two-column display. Key themes were proposed in the right column that emerged from the alignment of the qualitative and quantitative data in a rank order.

Table 4.5 uses a small amount of fabricated data extracted from the 2 × 2 data matrix constructed from the matrix-mapping activity shown in Figure 4.2. The first two columns are characteristic of most joint displays in mixed methods. The first column lists quantitative scale scores. The second column lists fictional data extracted from interview data matched to the score. The table is ordered by the score in the first column.

The third column is what positions this joint display as an intermediary step in the analysis, rather than exclusively as a tool for reporting that represents the data. The third column lists examples of the types of themes that might emerge from considering the qualitative and quantitative data together. The influence of past experiences is noted by two participants, for example, and produced the theme: past experiences, positive and negative, influence the present experience. The themes are posed as tentative statements that can be explored through additional rounds of data collection and analysis. Quantitative analysis might, for example, yield distinctions between the scores of individuals that describe interactions with and without other people or those with and without past memories.

TABLE 4.5 Illustrative Joint Display Linking Qualitative and Quantitative Data from the Data Matrix from the Forest Example

Scores on Well-Being and Nature Scales	Qualitative Data	Generated Themes
3.8, 3.8	Whenever I walk in the woods, I remember how my family used to camp when I was a kid.	Theme 1: *Pat experiences, positive and negative, influence the present experience.*
2.5, 1.0	I really like the first half an hour or so of a walk in the woods, but after that I find I stop paying attention and start to think of other things I need to be doing.	Theme 2: *Unpredictable elements of the experience and the environment interfere with the ability to become immersed in nature.*
1.75, 3.0	I really enjoy hiking, but I have run into some pretty scary weather.	
1.5, 3.5	I was enjoying the walk with my family until my daughter was stung by a bee.	
1.0, 0.5	I am very anxious about running into a bear.	
0.75, 2.2	Someone in the group got sick and we had to get him medical help.	

The scores on the two scales in this hypothetical example yield a moderately strong, positive statistical correlation. The limitation of basing conclusions on this quantitative index is that it obscures the distribution of the scores across the space depicted in the matrix. It supports the idea that there is a relationship but does not tell us anything that is theoretically intriguing about what influences that relationship. It conceals substantial variability in the immersion experience that could be explored through further analysis. Further analysis could well lead our imaginary researcher to conclude that it is difficult to replicate the idealized immersion experience of the laboratory in the real world where bugs, bears, insects, and weather can interfere with the ability to savor the experience of a walk in the woods.

CONCLUSIONS

The use of visual displays that integrate qualitative and quantitative data in ways that advance theory development has not previously been explored (Buckley & Waring, 2013). In this chapter, I took on the task of reconceptualizing some procedures like timelining, concept mapping, and geospatial mapping, which have previously been viewed exclusively as qualitative methods as mixed methods procedures that can be used with grounded theory. There are many creative ways that qualitative and quantitative can be integrated in a visual display that extend well beyond the over-used practice of quantifying qualitative data.

There are a number of ways that a visualization can contribute to developing theoretical insight. When a researcher is looking to develop, test or refine a theory, a visual display can help the researcher to specify patterns and to detect relationships between constructs (Bazeley & Jackson, 2013). The juxtaposition of qualitative and quantitative data can help a researcher envision a core construct that might capture an instrumental feature of a social process or to identify and recognize conditions that mediate an expected outcome. It can also provide evidence of change over time.

One of the challenges in reporting mixed methods, including in the final formatting of a visual display, is to find effective ways to communicate with what is often a cross-disciplinary audience (Hay, 2016). Members of this audience may share some content expertise, but it is often the case that their interest is as much about how the methodology is used as about what is learned from it. Figures and tables can be off-putting to readers when they are too complex, span more than a single page, use abbreviations that are not self-explanatory, or are packed with small print and a lot of detail.

Guidelines for constructing effective joint and integrative displays

Despite the variability that can be found in the way integrative and joint displays are constructed, there are some common guidelines that can boost their effectiveness during the reporting process. These include the following:

1 Provide a title for the display that acknowledges it demonstrates integration when it's appropriate.
2 Even if they have been defined in the text, avoid abbreviations that are likely to be unfamiliar to many readers. This includes using abbreviations for variable names from computer output.

3. All abbreviations and symbols should be explained in a footnote to the table or figure.
4. Clearly label what is qualitative data and what is qualitative data.
5. Avoid duplicating data across tables and figures.
6. Take advantage of using color and shading in journals in situations where an article will be displayed online.
7. Avoid inserting page shots of output from statistical software, especially those that use variable names that are not self-explanatory. To consider the limitations of this, see an example of MM-GTM by Yang, Richardson, French, and Lehman (2011).
8. Acknowledge inconsistencies between findings from the different data sources by creating a symbol system. For example, a dotted line around a box can be used to signal weak or contradictory support for a variable.

Adding to the architecture of the cross-cutting themes

Table 4.6 adds yet another layer to the cross-cutting themes identified in the first chapter, by filling in information about key points from this chapter. The table is organized around three clusters of concepts: (a) integrated mixed methods designs, (b) MM-GTM, and (c) complexity and dissonance.

TABLE 4.6 Linking Key Themes from Chapter 4 to Cross-Cutting Themes

Cluster	Major Themes that Cross Chapters	Chapter 4 – Key Points
Integrated approaches to mixed methods research	Integrated mixed methods approaches	Joint and integrative visual displays are a strategic way to integrate findings from different methods during analysis. They can also be used to involve participants during data collection.
		Joint and integrative visual displays can provide a way to visualize patterns and connections that have theoretical implications.
		Constructing a database that merges data on qualitative and quantitative constructs is the key to meaningful integration.
	Fully integrated mixed methods research (FIMMR)	Quantifying qualitative data for analysis is an over-used strategy in mixed methods research.
		In some fully integrated mixed method (FIMMR) designs, the qualitative and quantitative phases may be difficult to disentangle, while in other cases, the phases are quite distinct. FIMMR designs can be executed in a concurrent or sequential manner.
Mixed methods and grounded theory	MMR contribution to explanatory power	Timelines, matrices, concept maps, and other types of integrative visual displays can be used both to collect and analyze data.

Cluster	Major Themes that Cross Chapters	Chapter 4 – Key Points
Complexity and dissonance	The link between mixed methods and complexity	Visual displays can reveal diverse perspectives and expose dissonance between findings from different analytical methods.
	The contribution of paradox and dissonance to explanatory power	

Appendix A consists of a multi-page table that summarizes the key points by the cross-cutting themes for all the chapters.

Bridging to the next chapter

We saw the potential of dissonance to make a contribution to analytical insight in all three of the case examples considered in this chapter. For example, there was a sizable gap between the views of participants in the mapping activity reported by Teixeira (2014, 2016) and the theory the researcher adopted. The economists exploring changes in economic well-being in the timelining example found that a widely adapted measure could not capture the multi-dimensional nature of the phenomenon. The design of the instrument used to collect data in the example weighing the relationship between an immersive experience in a walk in the forest and physical and psychological well-being yielded a diverse array of conditions that were very likely to mitigate a positive outcome.

While many might find these kinds of gaps disconcerting and possibly an indication of poor research, I am in agreement with those that argue that the opportunity to explore differences that emerge when findings from different data sets are considered together as a characteristic that distinguishes mixed methods as a methodology. Erzberger and Kelle (2003) maintain, for example, that divergent findings should not necessarily be taken as an indication of poor-quality data or research methods but should be considered "as a pointer to new theoretical insight" (p. 475). Authors of an early textbook about mixed methods, Abbas Tashakkori and Charles Teddlie, value theoretical consistency and interpretive agreement, but acknowledge inconsistency between the inferences that emerge from different methods "might be considered a unique benefit from conducting mixed methods research" (2008, p. 116).

In the next chapter, we link to one of the cross-cutting themes by exploring the possibility that inconsistencies in the findings generated by different methods is indeed a principal value-added of pairing mixed methods with grounded theory. In that chapter, first we pick up the task of demonstrating how dissonance between findings can contribute to theoretical insight in MM-GTM. Second, we explore the conditions when this is most likely. We also look at the flip side of the issue by excavating situations where exceptions to a pattern may carry little significance. We revisit the argument for the importance of visual displays by exploring the role they can play in documenting the credibility of conclusions.

REVIEW QUESTIONS

1. How might a joint display or an integrative display be used for a case-based analysis?
2. What kinds of variables could be quantified in a research project collecting data through a timelining activity?
3. In what ways can a visual display contribute to theoretical insight?

SUPPLEMENTAL ACTIVITY

1. Guetterman, T. (2019, August). *Using joint displays to integrate qualitative and quantitative data.* You-Tube Video from International Institute of Qualitative Inquiry/Mixed Methods International Research Association Webinar Series. www.youtube.com/watch?v=U5Jv9qY7OQA

CHAPTER 5

Leveraging dissonance to advance theoretical reasoning

The opportunity to engage dissonance and incongruities in the results emerging from different methods is a unique benefit of a mixed methods approach. When pursued systematically, these often generate original insight.

TERMS INTRODUCED IN THE CHAPTER

- Initiation rationale
- Rupture theorizing
- Theoretical sensitivity
- Theoretical triangulation
- Verification
- Warranting

INTRODUCTION

Many find it unsettling when their qualitative and quantitative analytical procedures yield results that run counter to their initial drive to build credibility by seeking another method to confirm findings. There certainly are occasions when unexpected or counter intuitive findings are not worth the investment of time and resources to pursue, including when there is only a small amount of data to support them or there are clear indications that the data or instruments were used in ways that were methodologically flawed. There are other circumstances when there are distinct benefits, including to the rigor of the research, when unexpected findings are pursued through additional analysis and/or data collection. "Divergent findings should not always be considered as an indicator of a poor research design; instead they may be considered a pointer to new theoretical insight," Erzberger and Kelle wrote (2003, p. 475).

The commitment to engage difference and to pursue paradox and contradiction is central enough to the methodology that undergirds mixed methods to warrant a separate designation in a widely used framework that identifies the principal rationales for its use. The originators of a classification system for the rationales for using mixed methods that continues to be widely applied, Greene, Caracelli, and Graham (1989) followed Rossman and Wilson (1985) in singling out what they referred to as the **initiation rationale**. *This is one of the five principal rationales for integrating data that involves additional rounds of data collection and analysis to further explore unexpected, contradictory, or paradoxical findings.* Rossman and Wilson (1985, p. 637) described the initiation purpose in this way: "Initiation is an analytical function that turns ideas around. It initiates new interpretations, suggests areas for further exploration, or recasts the entire research questions." The word "initiation" signals the expectation that the discovery of contradiction initiates additional analysis. Greene et al. defined this rationale with these words: "Seeks the discovery of paradox and contradiction, new perspectives and frameworks, the recasting of questions or results from one method with questions or results from another method" (1989, p. 259). Greene et al. observed that qualitative and quantitative data tend to be given equal weight in this type of study.

> Initiation is an analytical function that turns ideas around. It initiates new interpretations, suggests areas for further exploration, or recasts the entire research question.
> (Rossman & Wilson, 1985, p. 637)

The initiation rationale extends to research seeking to make meaning from gaps and silences and to consider what is missing or not there. In some situations, this can involve exposing assumptions in conventional measures used in research about a phenomenon and what they conceal. The pursuit of gaps and silences is evident, for example, in a study by Weiss, Mayer, and Kreider (2003) that probably set out to contest what now seems an outdated hypotheses that working mothers are less engaged in their children's schoolwork than mothers not employed outside of the home. These authors described their turn to mixed methods as an "act of desperation" as they discovered that the conventional way mothers' engagement was measured erased any of the mothers' activities that occurred in locations outside of the school complex.

Fielding (2012) argues that the "radical potential" of mixed methods lies not in terms of confirmation but its contribution to "sophisticated analytical conceptualization" (p. 125). As is exemplified in a study by Jang, McDougall, Herbert, and Russell (2008) about school success in challenging circumstances, this often occurs when results of statistical analysis gloss over differences between sites or participants that are evident in the more nuanced qualitative data. It is the central thesis of this chapter that the discovery of empirically supported incongruities or gaps between the findings drawn from an initial analysis of data from different sources, when framed within an understanding of the literature and solid data, can spark original insight.

Purpose, contribution, and key points

The chapter expands ideas about how robust MM-GTM research can be designed and executed by addressing two main purposes. The first is to build an argument for the potential for unexpected and sometimes paradoxical findings that emerge from the integration of different sources of data, analytical procedures, methods, and/or theoretical perspectives to contribute to original theoretical and methodological insight. The second purpose is to illustrate a range of procedures, including those associated with grounded theory, to explore or interrogate provocative and theoretically meaningful inferences in a systematic way.

For purposes of the discussion here, the terms dissonant, paradoxical, incongruent, and discordant are used interchangeably to refer to situations where the integration of data, methods, theoretical frameworks, and/or perspectives produces unexpected findings. With the intent to explore their contribution to theoretical insight, I bring forward examples of articles that use mixed methods with grounded theory procedures that provide more than common reflexivity about the strategies they used to investigate dissonant findings. This approach necessarily prioritizes research that gives comparable weight to both qualitative and quantitative procedures. It excludes examples where researchers reconciled inconsistencies between findings from different sources of data by setting aside one set of findings because of methodological limitations or philosophical priorities.

Goals for the chapter are:

1. Explore different sources of dissonance.
2. Consider how views about discordant findings are influenced by philosophical paradigm.
3. Identify ways that the intent to engage multiple perspectives can be incorporated into the way a study is designed.
4. Summarize a range of analytical procedures that can be used to explore dissonance in a MM-GTM study.
5. Investigate the ways that dissonance was leveraged to generate original insight in the case exemplars.
6. Introduce ways that findings can be warranted.

Principal takeaways from the chapter

As with each of the four chapters that have preceded this one, the principal takeaways from the chapter align and expand four cross-cutting themes that are summarized in Appendix C. The principal points made in this chapter are:

1. When it is not due to methodological weaknesses, dissonance between results from different methods often signals complexity in the phenomenon being studied.
2. Dissonance is more likely to materialize in mixed method designs where there is ongoing interaction between the qualitative and quantitative strands than in a component mixed method design where the interaction between qualitative and quantitative phases of the research is limited to the point of drawing conclusion.
3. Different schools of thought about grounded theory are associated with different paradigms. These differ in the priority they award to diverse viewpoints, exceptions, and/or disconfirming evidence.
4. The theoretical implications of dissonant findings cannot be fully appreciated without familiarity with the literature associated with the phenomenon.

5   Case-based analysis can be used to investigate disconfirming cases and unexpected findings.
6   Rupture theorizing occurs when results from the empirical analysis challenge an extant measure, instrument, or theoretical framework.
7   The link between major findings and empirical data can be documented with a figure or table.

Organization of the chapter

The chapter begins broadly with a discussion of different sources of dissonances in mixed methods research, including when findings from different sources of data or analytical procedures are not in agreement, when findings dispute extant theory, or when the analysis reveals limitations of a widely used measure or instrument. It shifts next to an acknowledgment that attitudes toward dissonance and how it should be resolved vary by philosophical paradigm. The remaining sections of the chapter are designed to arm the reader with a wide array of procedures they could deploy to engage unexpected findings. It provides an extended discussion of two exemplars and a number of examples that used mixed methods with grounded theory to systematically investigate discordant findings. A third example utilized mixed methods and case study to build theory. The chapter closes by considering the implications of prioritizing dissonance, and consequently complexity, in the design of MM-GTM.

DIFFERENT PERSPECTIVES ABOUT THE CENTRALITY OF DISSONANCE TO THE RESEARCH PROCESS

Attitudes about what is the appropriate way to address exceptions to research findings and dissonance is influenced by philosophical assumptions or paradigm (Creamer, 2018c). Proponents of different schools of thought about grounded theory take different positions on the necessity and even relevance of exceptions to the categories, themes, and overall framework that emerge. This is true about a commitment to **verification** as well (Dey, 1999). Verification refers to *procedures to verify findings that contribute to the rigor of a research study, construct validity, and in some contexts the reliability of findings*. Recognizing that grounded theory has been approached from diverse perspectives, including in ways that have an effect on viewpoints about the role of verification, is an important element of developing the methodological expertise needed to report findings in a credible way.

There is a good bit of variability in the position that is taken about the importance of verifying findings in grounded theory approaches (Morgan, 2020). The originators and some of their proponents resist the idea that there is a need to verify findings (Dey, 1999). On the other hand, Strauss recognized the role of exceptions. He linked the role of exceptions to theoretical sampling and saw them as playing a role in developing the properties of a category (Apramian, Cristancho, Watling, & Lingard, 2017). With its relativist assumptions, those writing from a constructivist perspective do not devote much attention to exceptions or to verifying findings. It is not in the philosophical tenants of constructivism to differentiate between contradictory perspectives (Fielding, 2009). Morgan (2020) describes Charmaz as "explicitly unwilling to accept the idea of verification" (p. 71). Dey expressed reservations about a methodology that "so resolutely refuses any refutations" (1999, p. 213).

The role of dissonance and the intrigue of paradox move to center stage for those whose views put them outside a strictly relativist stance. The description of difference and exception is central to purpose of theory development from a postmodern perspective (Apramian et al., 2017). From this perspective, differences between findings from different sources of data are not a methodological weakness that must be overcome or reconciled. Those operating by and large from a postmodern frame "accept difference as inevitable and ever-present" (Freshwater, 2007, p. 135). In mixed methods, this extends to philosophical grounding in dialectical pluralism and an approach that centers the intent to consider multiple viewpoints, perspective, and standpoints in its definition (Johnson, Onwuegbuzie, & Turner, 2007).

The decision to pursue contradictions that emerge both within and across methods with further analysis and/or data collection shares with a constructivist approach the view that there may well be more than one "right" answer. This may be the reason Charmaz and a Swedish academic Robert Thornberg (2020) positioned themselves as among those who ascribe to a more recent, non-positivist methodology that embraces dissonance. They describe this type of methodology as "acknowledging multiple realities, seeking diverse perspectives, and engaging in critical analysis throughout the research process" (Charmaz & Thornberg, 2020, p. 7). It is an entirely different matter to acknowledge diverse perspectives than it is to promote procedures that explore and ultimately find a reasonable explanation for dissonance.

Table 5.1 singles out some of the major distinctions in perspectives about exceptions and dissonance among proponents of the four "schools of thought" associated with grounded theory, as broadly sketched by Apramian et al. (2017), Rieger (2018), and Sebastian (2019). None of these authors recognize pragmatism as an analytical logic used with grounded theory (cf. Morgan, 2020). The table lists associated spokespersons, perspectives about exceptions and dissonance, implications for mixed methods designs, and limitations of this methodological perspective.

Hadley (2019a) points out that the different approaches should not be viewed as contradictory but as part of a loosely interconnected network. An advantage of sketching out different viewpoints about the role of exceptions and dissonance in grounded theory is that it allows the up-and-coming researcher the opportunity to clarify his or her own views about it. Postpositivist and modernists lean toward a strategy that allows for the systematic elimination of alternative explanations. Those whose mindset moves between constructivism into post modernism are likely to be most enthusiastic about experimenting with many of the strategies I describe in the next sections of the chapter.

> The variety of approaches to GTM need not be constructed as contradictory, but as part of interactive, interdependent network.
>
> (Hadley, 2019a, p. 568)

TABLE 5.1 Varying Points of View about Exceptions, Dissonance, and the Need for Verification in Grounded Theory and the Implications for Mixed Method Designs, by School of Thought

School of Thought/ Spokesperson	Perspective about Dissonance	Implications for Mixed Methods Designs	Limitations of the Approach to MM-GT
Classic Glaserian grounded theory Straussian grounded theory Charmaz's constructivist grounded theory	Resists the idea of the need for verification or for explaining deviant cases as antithetical to an inductive approach (Dey, 1999). View different perspectives as endemic to the method and not something that requires reconciliation.	Well adapted to a design where the qualitative and quantitative strands are separated with the qualitative methods used first to generate theory inductively, followed by a quantitative phase where its generalizability is tested. Dissonance between findings from different methods less likely to occur with this approach.	Underplay the potential to use grounded theory procedures to add to or refine an existing theory.
Postmodern Clarkeian grounded theory	Exceptions are part of complexity. Difference is a fundamental part of the theory-building process (Apramian et al., 2017).	Adaptable to more iterative approaches to mixed methods where findings from one method may drive further data collection and analysis in another.	Blurs the distinction between qualitative and quantitative methods.

POTENTIAL SOURCES OF DISSONANCE THAT EMERGE OVER THE LIFE OF A RESEARCH PROJECT

In grounded theory, being open to new or unexpected interpretations and their theoretical implications is part of **theoretical sensitivity**. *This is defined as having sufficient familiarity with relevant bodies of literature to recognize the theoretical implications of findings.* Theoretical sensitivity allows the investigator to recognize nuances in the data and subtle differences in the way participants are using language. It paves the way for agility in combining the literature, data, experience, and prior knowledge (Suddaby, 2006).

The discipline of generating multiple explanations

The potential to leverage dissonance can be built into framing the need for a study and through its analytical procedures. It can also be like an uninvited guest who arrives with little advance warning asking to spend a few nights sleeping on your couch. Unexpected or incongruent findings can encourage the discipline of the alternative hypotheses or multiple explanations (Eisenhardt, 1989; Edwards, 2008). It does not introduce conflict when there is the epistemological conviction that there is one best answer that will prevail (Creamer, 2004). This is the "disciplined consideration" of a range of possible explanations before conclusions are drawn

(Thorne, Kirkham, & O'Flynn-Magee, 2004). It is also the process of deliberately seeking evidence that would disprove one hypothesis or explanation over another that is so central to science (Edwards, 2008). This type of strategy for building strong conclusions can "unfreeze thinking" by driving an investigator to go beyond initial impressions and avoid foreclosing prematurely on the obvious explanation (Eisenhardt, 1989). Teams that are constituted with members with expertise in diverse areas can offset bias and contribute to the disciplined approach to alternative explanations (Eisenhardt, 1989). A quizzical mindset can register gaps in the theory about the aspects of the phenomenon that are rendered invisible when applied to existing theory (Rule & John, 2015).

A strategy to generate multiple explanations for a finding is well adapted to a grounded theory approach designed to generate a theoretical framework. This could occur, for example, with a theme or theoretical proposition that suggests a link between a contextual factor and an outcome. It can contribute to strong analytical conclusions in resisting what Johnson and Schoonenboom (2015) refer to as a binary "either/or logic." Associating this with a dialectical perspective that is compatible with grounded theory, these authors recommend: "Instead of using an 'either/or' logic, we need a 'both/and' logic in which different forms of evidence are bought into dialogue, constantly compared, and combined into a whole that is more than the sum of the parts" (p. 591). We will see how an investigator might document support for a range of alternative hypotheses in the final section of this chapter devoted to using visual displays to warrant findings.

Unexpected sources of dissonance

Research projects have habit of unfolding in ways that are not entirely predictable. This is part of the real-world messiness of research that demands adaptability in research designs (Plano Clark & Ivankova, 2016; Sanscartier, 2018). Due to the inclusion of multiple perspectives and approaches mixed methods research is inherently complex, dynamic, and undetermined in practice because "insights and tensions cannot be fully anticipated or predicted" (Plano Clark & Ivankova, 2016, p. 277). As we see in the example by Teixeira (2014, 2016) in the preceding chapter, the "mess" and the tensions introduced by unexpected findings are often air-brushed out of reporting. This can be understated as in Teixeira's case (2014, 2016) where a single sentence acknowledges that participants in her study resisted the negative language she used to characterize the urban spaces she studied.

The ambiguity and uncertainty associated with this type complexity can emerge at any point in the research process. It can be introduced during the design phase when an investigator must tackle differences in the epistemological assumptions of different methods. This might occur, for example, when a grounded theorist using mixed methods finds it philosophically unacceptable to ignore what was learned in an earlier, quantitative phase of the project. "Mess" also makes an appearance once research is underway and the empirical findings diverge from what is expected (Sanscartier, 2018). Dynamics among team members and contextual factors, like differences between research sites, is yet a third source of complexity that can emerge while research is underway. In participatory action research or evaluation research, engagement with stakeholders often introduces unexpected views or needs. The type of complexity often encountered in

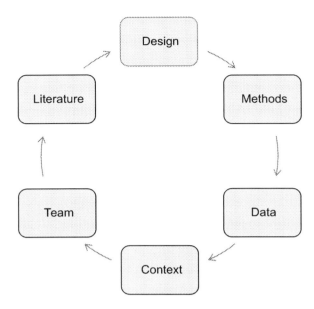

FIGURE 5.1 Potential Sources of Dissonance in a MM-GTM Study

mixed method research requires that investigators have the skills to spontaneously and creatively adapt the research design to their environment (Poth, 2020; Sanscartier, 2018).

Figure 5.1 identifies some of the potential sources of unexpected dissonance that might arise in a MM-GTM study. These can occur at any point in the research process, including during the design phase, during implementation, and in the follow-up phase of reporting.

Dissonance introduced through team dynamics and the engagement with diverse bodies of literature or expertise are elements that weave throughout the research process.

Factors that mitigate the significance of unexpected findings

As intriguing and intuitively appealing as some unexpected findings can prove to be, there are situations where competing demands make them impractical to pursue. Practical reservations present themselves when the finding would lead researchers away from the declared purpose of the research, require an investment of time and resources that is not feasible at the moment, or be too detrimental to the established timeline. A lack of sufficient empirical foundation is an additional reason why a researcher might be forced to set aside tantalizing findings for another day. The most important of these is when empirical grounding is not robust enough to warrant their pursuit (Bazeley, 2018a). Methodological limitations include miscalculation in the research design, quantitative measures with low reliability or statistical power, and small sample sizes in either the qualitative or quantitative data (Edwards, 2008). In cases where methodologists on a team believe that qualitative and quantitative data cannot be combined because they are different paradigms, "uncovering points of disagreements may be the best that researchers can achieve" (Loo & Lowe, 2011, p. 33). This is one explanation for why some authors allow multiple interpretations to stand alongside each other during reporting and defer their resolution to the reader (Moran-Ellis et al., 2006).

DESIGNING FOR DISSONANCE

There are a wide range of ways that the assumption that engaging dissonance and multiple explanations is associated with stronger inferences and original insight can be woven into the design of a research a project (Johnson & Schoonenboom, 2015). Designing for divergence in anticipation of better understanding reflects a methodological commitment to dialectical pluralism (Johnson & Schoonenboom, 2015). Some of these procedures can be built into the design of a research study from the outset, while others emerge as a response to the unexpected ways a research project often unfolds.

Table 5.2 provides a list of some of the procedures that recognize the benefit of a dialectical orientation to inference quality. Although many can weave throughout different phases of a research project, the table organizes the strategies most closely associated with the design phase, analysis, and reporting.

The strategies listed in this table are not limited to MM-GTM. They have wide applicability to other types of mixed methods studies. The centrality of an ongoing dialectical dance between existing literature and theories about the phenomenon is underscored with its appearance in multiple places in the table. Embedded these types of strategies in the initial planning of a study has the potential to invite the kind of creative tensions that lead to new insight.

TABLE 5.2 Procedures that Leverage Dissonance in Ways that Advance Theoretical Reasoning

Phase	Procedure
Design	Frame the need for a study with competing theoretical frameworks and/or in results reported in the literature.
Analysis	Generate theoretical propositions form a case-based analysis or through an integrated joint display.
	Generate and test alternative explanations for key results.
	Explore group differences.
	Explore cases that seem to be exceptions through theoretical sampling.
	Explore unexpected outcomes and the conditions associated with them.
	Create a coding system that incorporates multiple competing explanations.
	Test results through theoretical sampling with new data.
	Consult literature in other domains to explain unexpected findings.
	Get stakeholder input on discordant findings.
Reporting	Warrant conclusions by documenting the link between data and findings through a visual display.
	Communicate information about findings that are not consistent in a visual display through dotted lines, shading, or other graphic tools.
	Seek explanations for unexpected findings in the literature in other disciplines.

Although it is certainly a way to generate interest in a publication, I have encountered few examples of articles that are framed in ways that suggest the drive to understand dissonant findings or dissonance between findings reported in the literature was the driver for an initial plan for how the research would be executed. In the next section of the chapter, I explore three exemplars that tackled dissonance as part of the theory-building process during at least one phase of the analytical process. All differ from a classic approach to grounded theory and the view that engagement with the literature should be postponed until an analytical framework begins to solidify. Each of the exemplars was launched with familiarity with the literature, including theoretical frameworks. In all cases, authors described a process where there was back and forth with the literature during analysis that is recognized as part of an abductive approach (Timmermans & Tavory, 2012).

THE CHAPTER EXEMPLARS

The exemplars underscore how commonplace it is for researchers to find that unexpected incongruities emerge when qualitative and quantitative data or analytical procedures are actively engaged during analysis for purposes of developing a grounded theory or elaborating an explanatory framework already available in the literature. In each of the exemplars, wrestling with unanticipated findings through additional analysis sparked original insight.

The chapter exemplars each used different procedures to interrogate incongruities. The first exemplar by Kaplan and Duchon (1988) comes from the field of management. It is the only exemplar to explicitly frame the study as MM-GTM. These authors found that examining group differences helped to explain unexpected findings. The second exemplar, Carmona (2015), comes from the field of urban planning. Carmona engaged diverse perspectives from the literature by building case profiles that integrated qualitative, quantitative and visual data about a carefully selected sample of public spaces in a city. The third and final exemplar from Wesely (2010) reflects on the process used to find an explanation for findings that challenged the theoretical assumption that in the context of a voluntary language immersion program, that motivation and persistence are linked in a significant positive way.

Table 5.3 singles out innovative features of each of the three chapter exemplars.

Innovative features of the first chapter exemplar are explored next, as are the tensions introduced by team dynamics where members clearly distinguished their expertise as either quantitative or qualitative.

TABLE 5.3 Innovative Features of the Chapter Exemplars

Example	Innovative Feature
Kaplan & Duchon (1988)	Explored group differences to explain dissonance.
Carmona (2015)	Integrated visual, quantitative, and qualitative data for a case-based analysis of public spaces in a city; generated theoretical propositions from the cases grouped by type.
Wesely (2010)	Engaged competing theoretical perspective after unexpected findings emerged.

Exemplar 1: developing an explanation for contradictory findings by investigating differences between groups or sites

Despite its publication in 1988 when mixed methods had barely begun to be formalized as a distinct methodology, a methodologically oriented article by Bonnie Kaplan and Dennis Duchon has qualities that make it still innovative today. There is an explicit acknowledgment in this article that the authors combined qualitative and quantitative methods with grounded theory. The reference list includes quantitative, qualitative, and mixed methods references that suggest an uncommon breadth of methodological expertise. The methods are still relevant, if perhaps the findings now seem out-of-date.

There are reasons related to reflexivity and research methods that undergird the choice to single out the Kaplan and Duchon (1988) as an exemplar. I consider it worthy of replication; first, because of the reflexivity about the research process that is reported, and second, because of the refusal to disregard discrepant findings, and third, the methodological transparency afforded by amount of text that is devoted to highlighting the value-added of combining methods. Mixed methods made two contributions in this study. The first relates to triangulation. Findings confirmed an original conceptual model. The second relates to what is referred to in mixed methods as an expansion purpose. Findings also elaborated the existing theoretical framework by introducing a new construct in the form of a condition. Kaplan and Duchon summarized the contribution of mixed methods this way: "Mixing methods can also lead to new insights and modes of analysis of that are unlikely to occur if one method if one method is used alone" (Kaplan & Duchon, 1988, p. 582).

Box 5.1 summarizes key features of the Kaplan and Duchon article (1988). This includes the purpose of the research, information related to the design of the study, including the timing of data collection and analysis, how integration occurred, unexpected findings, and the nature of the theory produced.

Several elements of the research design of the study reported by Kaplan and Duchon (1988) are also unusual. The first is the utility shown for developing a grounded theory model at the mid-point of the analysis as a way to propose an explanation for the discrepancies observed. This followed an initial round of analysis where the qualitative and quantitative data were analyzed separately by different investigators. Most original is the choice to re-analyze the quantitative questionnaire data based on new variables introduced by the grounded theory model that emerged from the initial phase of qualitative analysis. The additional round of data analysis contributed to the conceptual framework by providing statistical support to document the intermediary role of work orientation in explaining attitudes about the implementation of new management software.

Part of the reflexivity evident in this article is its documentation of the dissonance introduced by team dynamics. The article also points to the tensions on the original four-member team because it involved members who are not methodological boundary spanners but unilateral in their ideas about how to approach research. The article authors who were what remained of the original team, refer to the "tenacity" that was required of the lead author not to abandon the insight she drew from the initial independent analysis of the qualitative data. The co-authors acknowledged that it took intense and ongoing negotiations to find

> **BOX 5.1**
>
> **Exploring Group Differences in a Study About the Implementation of Management Software by Kaplan and Duchon (1988)**
>
> *Purpose:* This methodological article reports on the first phase of a multi-method longitudinal project. The purpose of the study was to explore what happens when a new management information system was installed in commercial laboratory settings. The authors developed and tested a grounded theory model.
>
> *Design:* In some ways, this study fits a core component design and can be referred to as using an exploratory, two-phase sequential mixed methods design. Multiple forms of a qualitative data were collected first, followed by the construction of a questionnaire. Analysis occurred in more than two phases, however. The contradictions between the inferences drawn from the independent analysis of the qualitative and quantitative data and the construction of a grounded theory model at the mid-point meant that researchers returned to reanalyze the questionnaire data during a third phase of analysis.
>
> *Integration:* Data from the first phase of analysis were linked to the second because they were used for purposes of instrument development. Later in the analytical process, the approaches were merged in the construction of a grounded theory model.
>
> *Unexpected findings:* Results from an independent analysis of the qualitative and quantitative data were contradictory. The initial analysis of survey data did not support the findings from the qualitative data analysis that indicated strong differences in the work orientation of laboratory team members in different settings.
>
> *Theory produced:* The theoretical model developed distinguished between laboratory workers by the priority they placed on the product or on the processes associated with producing them through benchwork. Those who prioritize their job as producing reports saw the new management system as helpful, while those who prioritized the process viewed it as increasing the workload.

a way to integrate the findings from the qualitative and quantitative analysis. They wrote it required: "a strong determination to accommodate each approach and to reconcile apparently conflicting data resulted in an interpretation that synthesized the evidence" (Kaplan & Duchon, 1988, p. 582). Transparency about the challenges faced by members of the team with non-overlapping areas of expertise introduced a polyvocality to the text that is rare (Creamer, 2011).

In Chapters 2 and 3, we considered the ways that a case-based approach can be leveraged in MM-GTM to yield new insight in much the same way a theoretical memo can. Investigators can use a case-based approach to integrate qualitative and quantitative data in a narrative or a visualization in ways that resemble a theoretical memo. In the section that follows, we expand the discussion of a mixed methods approach to case-based analysis by looking at the roles it can play to advance understanding of discordant data.

EXPLORING DISSONANCE WITH A CASE-BASED APPROACH IN MM-GTM

Eisenhardt (1989) centers the exploration of paradoxical evidence through the analysis of multiple case studies. In another article that pre-dates the formalization of mixed methods as a distinct methodology, Eisenhardt (1989) wrote about the ways that multiple investigators and multiple sources of data can "foster diverse perspectives" and strengthen the grounding of a study (p. 533). She maintains the emphasis on diverse points of view as the purpose of cross-case comparisons that can force investigators to look beyond initial impressions and "see evidence through multiple lenses" (p. 533).

> Building theory from case studies centers directly on the juxtaposition of contradictory or paradoxical evidence. "That is, attempts to reconcile evidence across cases, types of data, and different investigators, and between cases and the literature increase the likelihood of creative reframing into new theoretical vision."
>
> (Eisenhardt, 1989, p. 546)

Other examples of the ways that a case-based analysis could be used to understand dissonance include:

1 Constructing a detailed case to explain what appear to be exceptions to the theoretical framework that has been developed.
2 Shifting away from a qualitative approach by extracting variables, such as about conditions that impact an outcome, and quantifying them in ways that would allow for statistical analysis.
3 Constructing cases to compare how individuals or groups experience a social process and to find clues about causal factors that explain why it happens.
4 Generating a set of theoretical propositions or themes from cross-case comparisons.

Including visual data in a case-based analysis

Case-based analysis does not necessarily have to rest on a narrative form. It is possible to envision that a case could include not only words and numbers, but also visuals like photographs or diagrams. We see that, for example, in a study about weight that integrated multiple different types of data, including a timeline, record of weight change over time, and visuals like photographs and images drawn by a participant (i.e., Chamberlain, Cain, Sheridan, & Dupuis, 2011). These do not necessarily have to be presented in a narrative form to prove useful during analysis.

It is possible to envision the use of visual data as part of the data in a case-based analysis of the type we see with the next exemplar with a hypothetical example involving a public space. In this case, imagine the types of spaces that have been included in office buildings, residence halls, and libraries that have been designed with the intent to facilitate collaboration. Table 5.4 is not from a real-world study. It integrates three kinds of data about a single location in the library at my own university to illustrate a creative approach to presenting a case study that incorporates visual data. This is the type of grounded visualization described by Knigge and Cope (2006).

A real-world study would import many examples of this type of data into qualitative software for analysis. This hypothetical example of case-based analysis that includes qualitative, quantitative, and visual data about a physical location will resurface later in the chapter in the section about documenting sources of data that support alternative hypotheses.

The case study captured in Table 5.4 has two visual components. One column contains a photograph of the space. A second column pinpoints its location on a blueprint. This type of data could prove useful in a later stage of analysis in this imagined study by providing a way to measure aspects of the space, such as access to an exit or bathroom, which might influence how often the space is used by student groups. The third column integrates qualitative and quantitative data, as well as the results from qualitative and quantitative analytical procedures. The succinctness of the data presented about the case and the way it is displayed in table form could serve as vehicle to facilitate cross-case comparisons.

My intent in synthesizing information about a mixed methods exemplar from urban planning that follows in the next section is not to endorse the idea that it should be replicated in its entirety. Instead, it is my goal to provide enough information about it that a reader might come out with some creative ideas about how some elements of its approach to data collection and/or analysis could be adapted to other contexts. Although the study as a whole has its weaknesses, the use of integrated mixed methods case studies described in the article might inspire others to think creatively about ways to incorporate visual data in a case-based analysis.

TABLE 5.4 Example of Data for a Case-Based Analysis with Visual Components

Data: Square footage
Data: Distance from exit
Data: Noise and traffic level
Data: Index of frequency of usage
Results of QUANT analytical procedure: Measure of overall student satisfaction.
Results of QUAL analysis: Favored aspect: mobility of walls

DISSONANCE

Exemplar 2: using mixed method case studies for purposes of theory development and elaboration

The second exemplar from urban planning by Matthew Carmona (2015) featured in this chapter was framed from the onset by a bold intent to disrupt existing ways of theorizing public spaces in urban settings. Carmona (2015) reveals his impossibly ambitious intent when he declares that the goal of the project was "re-theorization of the nature of contemporary public space" (p. 374) in a way that counters a dominant narrative that characterize urban spaces, like squares and parks, negatively in terms of decline, crime, loss, and decay. This is the very language that we witnessed in the previous chapter in the article by Teixeira (2016) about grounded visualization. Teixeira adapted that language of "urban decay" and the theoretical assumptions of its link to crime from the literature even as she acknowledged that it was language that her adolescent participants resisted.

Box 5.2 singles out key design feature of the Carmona (2015) article.

BOX 5.2

Using Mixed Method Case Studies to Theorize Public Space in London by Carmona (2015)

Purpose: The purpose of the project is explicitly theoretical. Its purpose was to use mixed methods case studies to develop and generalize a theory about "the multiple processes of designing, developing, using, and managing public space" in an urban setting (p. 377).

Design: The mixed method project unfolded in two sequential phases. The first phase began with field observation of 130 public spaces distributed throughout London. Features of these spaces, like accessibility and comfort, were cataloged using a pre-determined typology and these data were subsequently used to identify a stratified, purposeful sample of cases that represented a broader class of cases. The second phase of the research was devoted to the case-based analysis.

Integration: Integration of findings from different analytical procedures and sources of data was embedded throughout this research project in a fully integrated way. There were multiple levels of increasingly abstract analysis. During the first phase of the analysis, theoretical propositions resembling themes were drawn from individual cases (a public location) that were constructed using multiple sources of data, including photographs and maps showing the location and size of the space. During the second phase of the analysis, cases were grouped by type (e.g., domestic spaces, consumer spaces, service spaces, etc.) and an

> additional set of theoretical propositions/themes were generated from comparing cases in the group.
>
> **Unexpected findings:** The "counter narrative" presented by the author presents a theoretical perspective that is in "rupture" with the idea that all public spaces should share the same design features. The strength of a city is that there are many public spaces and that these meet the needs of a diverse population by serving diverse needs.
>
> **Theory produced:** The article concludes with what could be considered a series of ten, inter-related theoretical propositions. The product of the research is described as theory, but it falls short of presenting a coherent conceptual framework or structure.

Carmona characterized both the intent and outcome of his mixed method project in ways that resonate with what Walsh (2015) referred to as "**rupture theorizing.**" As compared to "incremental theorizing" which is far more common, *rupture theorizing occurs when results from the empirical analysis challenge an accepted measure, instrument, or a theoretical framework*. Researchers that produce rupture theories reframe conventional constructs in radically new ways (Walsh, 2015). During reporting, they refer to their contribution as diverging from conventional practices for measuring the construct or for understanding it.

Language used throughout Carmona's article (2015) signals his intent to disrupt conventional views. Examples of wording appearing in this article that communicate an aim that is consistent with rupture theorizing include the following:

- Produce a "counter narrative" that "subverts" the dominant narrative.

    (p. 397, 398)

- Challenge "formula-driven approaches."

    (p. 395)

- Espouse a "questioning approach."

    (p. 396)

- "Turn critiques on their head."

    (p. 397)

The theory produced subverts the normative convention that assumes that there "is a single, idealized blueprint for public spaces" in an urban setting in favor of a more complex narrative that accepts that "users are diverse and will seek different things from their spaces" (Carmona, 2015, p. 398). Dissonance framed the final, meta-analytical framework because the case-study work "ultimately challenged many of the global space critiques" (p. 381).

Using case-based analysis to develop theory

Carmona's (2015) research displays originality involving mixed methods and theory development, but it cannot be said to use grounded theory procedures. The author's purpose for using mixed methods is explicitly linked to developing a theory. Carmona, and no doubt an invisible team of other researchers, declared that he used mixed methods to develop in-depth, mixed method case studies of 14 public spaces in the city of London "as a basis from which to generate (and generalize) theory" (2015, p. 397). The analyses had a strong emergent quality, but in setting up the study to weigh findings against the critique in the literature, it has a deductive drive that is an uneasy fit with the grounded theory methods.

The author observed that the benefits of going back and forth between findings from different analytical procedures were both to triangulate results from different analytical procedures and to build theory. An iterative approach to data analysis means that there was back and forth between an exploratory and a confirmatory stance and different types of data. According to Carmona (2015), the back and forth between results from different analytical procedures made it possible to see connections between different sources of data "that might otherwise not be so obvious" (p. 381).

Providing evidence of originality

One way that originality is demonstrated in this ambitious piece of research is in the breadth and creativity of the sources of data and the range of analytical procedures utilized. Data were collected through participant observation, documentary evidence, user assessment, informal interviews, geospatial data, content analysis of reviews in popular media, and time-lapse photography. Data for each case included a photograph; a map pinpointing its shape, size, and location in the city; and additional details about when it was constructed, its function, and whether it was a public or private space. Data for each of the 14 public spaces were summarized as one row in an integrative table, rather than in the more conventional narrative form.

The case-based analysis in this exemplar became increasingly abstract as it moved from a micro-level, to a meso-level, to a macro-level perspective and in ways that ultimately led to the development of an overarching theoretical framework. The first level of analysis was at the micro-level. It cataloged the characteristics of a large number of public spaces in the city of London. The second level of analysis was at the meso-level or group level. It focused on developing a list of themes about a class or group of spaces that shared similar physical attributes. The third iteration of the analysis is at the macro-level. Themes or theoretical propositions were developed during this iteration of the case-based analysis that singled out the similarities and differences between the groups of case studies clustered by type.

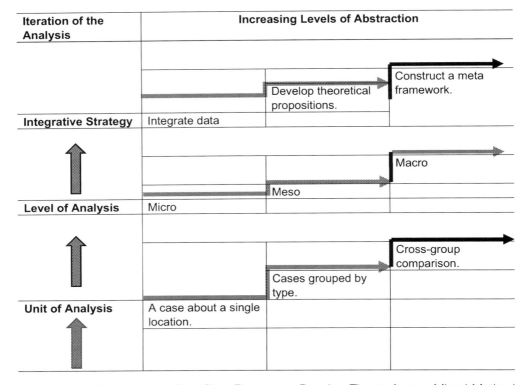

FIGURE 5.2 Embodying a Stair-Step Process to Develop Theory from a Mixed Method Case-Based Analysis

Figure 5.2 is my attempt to visualize the steps used in the exemplar to develop a theoretical framework from a mixed method case-based approach to analysis. The figure incorporates the visual metaphor of a stairstep to characterize the analytical process and how the level of abstraction increased across each of three iterations of the analysis. A micro-level of analysis refers in this case to an analysis based on individual cases; meso-level refers to analysis built from insight gained by comparing cases within a group; and macro-level analysis emerges from insight gained by a cross-case comparison across groups.

The unit of analysis, level of analysis, and integrative strategy changed over the course of the process of building theory in the Carmona (2015) study.

Methodological tensions introduced by the exemplar

Carmona's 2015 article is explicitly labeled as empirical mixed methods research with the purpose of theory development. It lacks details about the procedures that normally would be developed in greater detail in a methodological article. It is clear that results from the different research methods like the analysis of historical documents were incorporated in the cases, but no details are provided about how these analyses were conducted. A further critique is about the lack of transparency in the article about other members of the team and how they worked together during data collection and analysis. Unlike the first exemplar by Kaplan and Duchon (1988), which is characterized by polyvocality, Carmon's article is written with a single authorial voice. It erases what was no doubt the very significant contribution of members of the team that must have been involved in such a long-term and large-scale project.

Even though it is unlikely that a doctoral student or early career investigator could tackle such an ambitious project in its entirety, the use of mixed method case studies to develop a theoretical process through an iterative process could be emulated in other contexts. The procedure used to generate theoretical propositions from a group of cases that shared a similar function, could be adapted to research about other physical locations that serve educational purposes, promote well-being, or foster community. This could include, for example, research considering the layout of classrooms, playgrounds, parks and green spaces, homeless shelters, or food distribution centers.

The final exemplar in this chapter did not use visual data or a case-based analysis. It's unusual in its recognition of the role extant theoretical frameworks played in explaining dissonant findings.

Exemplar 3: drawing on multiple theoretical frameworks during analysis

A methodologically oriented article published by Pam Wesely (2010) illustrates the discipline of generating alternative explanation. The approach used by Weseley could be referred to a **theoretical triangulation**. Theoretical triangulation *contributes to internal validity by drawing on multiple theoretical frameworks as a means to explain findings and weigh competing explanations*. The research reported by Wesely (2010) is original in that it was not only purposeful about pursuing counterintuitive results during analyses but that the investigator drew on multiple theoretical frameworks from the literature to guide later stages of the analysis. Theoretical triangulation can serve as a test for internal validity by virtue of its ability to incorporate competing hypotheses (Jick, 1979).

The puzzle Wesely (2010) was left to explain at the mid-point of the mixed analysis she conducted for her dissertation research was related to the inadequacy of her original theoretical framing in motivation theory to explain the quantitative findings about student attrition and persistence in a language immersion program. The students who were most interested in language and most motivated to learn it, were not necessarily the ones who remained enrolled in the program. Defending her decision to use multiple theoretical frameworks, Wesely observed: "Accessing multiple theoretical frameworks is important in a mixed methods study when the primary theoretical framework corresponds strictly with either quantitative or qualitative approaches" (2010, p. 297).

Box 5.3 summarizes key design features of this fully integrated MM-GTM study about a language immersion program by Wesely (2010). It reflects mixed priority because the conclusions derived from mixed method analytical techniques.

> **BOX 5.3**
>
> ## An Exploration of the Link Between Motivation and Persistence in a Language Immersion Program by Wesely (2010)
>
> ***Purpose:*** The purpose of the study and the purpose of the article are different. The purpose of the study is framed in a quantitative way. It was to explore students' motivation to learn another language and its relationship to attrition from an intensive language immersion program. The purpose of the article is explicitly framed to explore the complexities of the relationship between language learning and motivation.
>
> ***Design:*** The article is organized by six distinct phases of analysis that followed data collection. The first, second, and fourth phases were qualitative. The third analyzed survey data. Mixed methods were used in the fifth and six phases.
>
> ***Integration:*** The secondary theoretical frameworks influenced how integration occurred during the later phases of analysis. Coders refined the initial, inductive coding scheme and grouped statements to reflect additional theoretical frameworks identified from the literature. Two additional theoretical frameworks were added to the constructs to the socio-educational model: attribution theory and investment theory.
>
> ***Unexpected findings:*** Students' attitudes toward learning a language did NOT necessarily have a strong impact on their decision to persist in an immersion language program. They did, however, seem to have a profound misunderstanding of what language learning entailed.
>
> ***Theory produced:*** Attitudes toward language learning were related to motivation, but not the intention to persist in language study. In other word, highly motivated students who appreciated languages might well leave a program for reasons unrelated to the program or language.

The exemplar featured in Box 5.3 is unusual in that the author explicitly positioned the paradigmatic grounding of her research. She described her approach as consistent with the dialectical perspective, writing: "My philosophy of mixed methods research corresponds with the dialectic thesis where opposing viewpoints of different methods and their interaction can create tension and be revealing in their own way" (Wesely, 2010, p. 300). She used a type of dialogical mixing (Creamer & Edwards, 2019) in the fourth phase of the analysis where she refined and added codes to her qualitative analysis to reflect the theoretical constructs and vying theoretical explanations that emerged from engagement in a more expansive body of literature. While she did not produce an over-arching explanatory framework, her findings were complementary in that she found it necessary to add a new set of constructs to explain the contradictory findings.

WARRANTING INFERENCES THROUGH VISUAL DISPLAYS

Transparency about methods and procedures is prized by all research approaches but is no guarantee of the credibility or validity of findings (Maxwell, 2013). **Warranting** *is a type of methodological transparency in reporting that supports the credibility of conclusion, generally through a visual display that documents the empirical support for them.* Bazeley described a warranted statement as "An assertion that is warranted is one that is convincingly argued and supported by research evidence" (Bazeley, 2018a, p. 278). Other methodologists well known to the mixed methods community suggest that a conclusion is warranted or defensible "in terms of documenting results, substantiating results, and validating conclusions" (Collins, Onwuegbuzie, & Johnson, 2012). The task of documenting a conclusion is particularly critical when a conclusion is paradoxical or runs counter to long-held views.

Warranting is most commonly provided through a visual display like a table or figure. "It is critical to invest in developing well-crafted tables, appendixes, and visual aids to demonstrate the underlying empirical support and the anticipated richness of the case data, and to tie those tables clearly to the text," Eisenhardt and Graebner advise (2007, p. 29). In mixed methods, warranting can be accomplished through different types of visual displays, including a joint display that integrates qualitative and quantitative data or findings. A concordance table is one type of joint display to documents the strength of support for themes or theoretical propositions.

Triangulating through a concordance table

A concordance table is a type of a joint display that combines findings from qualitative and quantitative data. Its purpose is related to warranting because it shows the extent that key conclusions, inferences, themes, and/or hypotheses are corroborated by analysis from more than one source of data. These can contribute to theoretical insight when they are organized by theoretical propositions (Eisenhardt & Graebner, 2007). This type of table generally reveals areas where findings are consistent, as well as areas where they are not in accord. Acknowledging themes or constructs where findings are inconsistent is an item that is often incorporated in standards for reporting in mixed methods (e.g., Wisdom, Cavaleri, Onwuegbuzie, & Green, 2012).

Table 5.5 is a shell of a simple concordance table. It is organized by themes that might emerge from a qualitative analysis, from an abductive one that spread across both qualitative and quantitative data, or from quantitative analytical procedures. This hypothetical concordance table is comparing the extent that different hypotheses from a theoretical model were judged to be supported by the case data. It is only showing a few cases. More would be required in a real-world example.

TABLE 5.5 Shell of a Concordance Table Illustrating a Way to Document Strength of Support Across Cases

Theoretical Proposition	Case 1	Case 2	Case 3
Proposition # 1	Low	Moderate	Moderate
Proposition # 2	Strong	Strong	Low

This type of table could also be organized by participant or by source of data. A type of extreme case sampling could be used if the number of cases or participants was large enough. Contrasting patterns in the data can more readily be observed by sampling very high and very low performing cases (Eisenhardt & Graebner, 2007). In some circumstances, it could prove useful to develop a scheme to quantify values in the table by assigning a number to "absent," "low," "moderate," and "strong" and using this transformed data in further quantitative analysis.

Walsh (2015) included a more elaborate type of concordance table in an appendix to a paper reporting on her MM-GTM study about factors the influence the adoption of a new information system (p. 25, table not included). Walsh's table is like an integrated database. It lists six theoretical codes or propositions, identifies that extent the generalizability had been demonstrated, and reports findings from the secondary data, primary qualitative data, and primary quantitative data. Walsh describes the theoretical codes or propositions as emerging "through constant iterations between quantitative and qualitative data as they were collected and through the analysis of all of our data as one set" (2015, p. 14).

A concordance table can play multiple roles for both the investigator and members of the audience of the article. For the investigator, the table and others like it could play a formative role by helping the researcher weigh the strength of the support and what it might add to the theory that is being developed. The role of the literature in understanding and elaborating the theoretical propositions was so strong that Walsh (2015) included it in her merged data set and referred to it as secondary data. For a reader or audience member, the table is summative. It provides a large enough slice of the data to offer a keyhole into an investigator's line of reasoning. When there is enough data in the table, it allows a reader or audience member to form his or her own conclusions and to reach a judgment about whether the line of reasoning is convincing. Tables with raw data, as we see in the appendix supplied by Walsh (2015), make it possible for another investigator to build on the work and to see if it is possible to reproduce the findings.

Using a joint display to warrant conclusions from a study

A joint display that integrates qualitative and quantitative data can serve to warrant conclusions when it is arrayed in such a way as to communicate a pattern of association between variables that becomes central to an explanatory framework. This table is different from a concordance table in that it does not document record levels of agreement between different sources of data or cases but is used to highlight patterns or to summarize key qualitative and quantitative findings.

An article by Eisenhardt (1989) that partnered grounded theory and case study methods included a joint display that integrated findings from the analysis of qualitative and quantitative

TABLE 5.6 Excerpt from a Joint Display from Castro et al. (2010) that Reveals a Clear Pattern

Case Number	Life Satisfaction Score	Quoted Statement About Machismo Self-Identification	Story Lines
Highest on Life Satisfaction			
ID 133	2.17	"I care about my family"; "For me it's acting like a gentleman"	*Story Line 1:* Men who value and engage in family caretaking exhibit high levels of caballerismo (positive machismo) in their male gender role identity, are giving and responsible, and they also experience *high* levels of life satisfaction.
ID 147	1.57	"I'm respectful of women"; "I never bring shame to the family"	
ID 164	1.50	"I do my best to take care of my family"	
ID343	1.48	"I treat women with respect and don't beat them"	

data about the leadership style of chief executive officers in nine for profit firms (see Table 3, p. 543; table not included). The organization of the table underscores key results from the study. A link is shown between qualitative quotes and a "CEO Power Score." The alignment of the two sources of data revealed a strong pattern of association between an authoritarian leadership style and more consensus-oriented approaches. The table is not reproduced here because the cost of reproduction is prohibitive.

The insight that can be gained by aligning a score on a quantitative indicator with excerpts from qualitative data in a way that reveals a pattern is also evident in an example of a mixed methods study by Castro, Kellison, Boyd, and Kopak (2010). One of the last tables in that article demonstrates a link between qualitative data reflecting views of masculinity and a quantitative index of well-being. One reason this table is effective is that it sorted not by participant or case, but by a well-being score. An excerpt from interview data is aligned with the well-being score. It provides credibility for a single conclusion. That is that there is a relationship between views about masculinity (machismo) and well-being.

Table 5.6 reproduces a small portion of the joint display from Castro et al. 2010, Table 3 (p. 355) that is available through fair use policies. The column on the far right refers to a "storyline" that was generated by exploring the alignment of the qualitative and quantitative data. In the terminology of MM-GTM, this might be referred to as a theoretical proposition that integrates qualitative and quantitative data.

The format of this table could be helpful to communicate the empirical support for key theoretical propositions emerging from a MM-GTM study.

Documenting support for alternative explanations through a visual display

Documentation that ensures the reader that systematic attention has been devoted to gauging the empirical support for a set of alternative explanations for key findings is part of most of the reporting guidelines developed by many professional associations. Ruling out rival explanations strengthens internal validity (Johnson & Schoonenboom, 2015). While the topic of alternative

TABLE 5.7 Documenting the Systematic Testing of Alternative Explanations from the Hypothetical Collaborative Space Study

Alternative Hypothesis About the Usefulness of Collaborative Spaces	Source of Data		
	Space Usage Data	Structured Observation	Interviews
Students prefer locations that are easy to get to.	X		
Students prefer private spaces.			X
Students prefer spaces that are in the center of traffic flow.		X	
Students prefer spaces with movable furniture.	X	X	X
Students prefer spaces with technical supports that make it possible to project a computer screen.			X

explanations often earns at best a single sentence during reporting, documenting what steps were taken to process competing explanations for key findings can enhance the credibility of an argument and the likelihood that others will find it useful.

Table 5.7 picks up on the hypothetical study of collaborative spaces on a university campus described in an earlier section in the chapter about using qualitative, quantitative, and visual data for case-based analysis. In this case, we are imagining how a visual display or data matrix could be used to document or warrant that alternative explanations about space use were pursued systematically. Several theoretical propositions or hypotheses are listed in the table, along with an indication if there was support from them in any or all of three different sources of data: space usage statics, a structured observation protocol, and individual interviews. Two of the sources of data are quantitative (a structured observation protocol and space usage statistics); while one is conventionally assumed to be qualitative. The theoretical propositions could emerge as categories emerging during the process of coding the qualitative data.

The table illustrates how it is possible to build an argument for credibility of findings through a visual display. Findings from the three sources of data listed only triangulated on one item appearing in the table that is related to the flexible ways a space might be used: Students prefer space with movable furniture. Differences between interview data and the two quantitative indicators suggest that what a student might voice as a preference during an interview is not necessarily reflected in the way they end up acting.

CONCLUSIONS

Whether it emerges from differences of opinion between collaborators or the different angles presented when more than one method is used, a central feature of the experience of executing MM-GTM with a dialectical perspective is that it introduces diverse perspectives. Dissonance, incongruities, unexpected or paradoxical findings simultaneously generate complexity while at the same time reflecting it. Unexpected findings that confound expectations can introduce delays and generate surprise and uncertainty. This has the benefit of forcing the conscientious investigator to avoid foreclosing prematurely on a quick or obvious answer, while at the same time making it difficult to achieve saturation about core constructs. Dissonance is not the exception but the rule in real-world research framed as MM-GTM.

The complexity introduced when findings from the analysis of different sources of data are integrated in interactive ways is one reason for the variability in the way MM-GTM research executed. Referring to it as mixed grounded theory (MGT), Johnson and Walsh (2019) found it challenging to use conventional terminology or a conventional notation system to deconstruct the timing and sequence of articles reporting on MM-GTM. They commented about their variety, writing: "There are perhaps an infinite number of versions of MGT to be explored and 'invented' by practicing researchers in the production of knowledge" (Johnson & Walsh, 2019, p. 523). The variety that is evident in MM-GTM, when an integrated approach is used, resists categorizing them or approaching them in a formulaic way. "Following textbook prescriptions and laying down approved research designs may be a necessary rite of passage but the benefits of mixing flow from creative innovation and conceptualization rather than a pragmatic approach" (Fielding, 2012, p. 126).

Building on the cross-cutting themes

The role of dissonance in MM-GTM is one of the cross-cutting themes that makes an appearance in all of the chapters in this book. The same can be said for case-based analysis. Table 5.8 contributes a final layer to the cross-cutting themes and to building an argument of MM-GTM as a distinct methodology. The table is organized around three clusters of concepts: (a) integrated mixed methods designs, (b) MM-GTM, and (c) complexity and dissonance.

A summary of all findings for all the cross-cutting themes appears in Appendix A.

Looking forward to the next chapter

The final chapter revisits several issues that have been introduced already and introduces some new topics. It reinforces the argument for the variety, if not idiosyncrasy, that is evident

TABLE 5.8 Additions from Chapter 5 to the Architecture of the Cross-Cutting Themes

Themes	Integrated Approaches to Mixed Methods Research	Mixed Method Grounded Theory (MM-GTM)	Complexity and Dissonance
Chapter 5 Leveraging Dissonance for Theoretical and Analytical Insight	A study can be designed to explore divergence, including between theoretical perspectives available in the literature, but more often dissonance is encountered unexpectedly.	Findings can be warranted through joint displays and other types of visual displays.	Integrating qualitative and quantitative data in case studies is one tool to investigate dissonant data and to weigh the level of support for theoretical propositions.

in integrated MM-GTM and the difficulty that creates for attempts to apply conventional mixed methods language and design templates to what are often complex, multi-phase studies. It expands the discussion about gauging quality in MM-GTM that began in this chapter with the introduction of the notion of using visual displays to build and argument for the credibility of findings. It argues for foregrounding some indicators of quality well known to qualitative researchers, including saturation, methodological transparency, reflexivity, originality, and utility.

REVIEW QUESTIONS

1. In what ways can unexpected, counterintuitive, or dissonant findings contribute to theoretical insight?
2. What analytical strategies can used to engage dissonant findings productively?
3. What differences are there in views about the role of dissonance in exceptions among the "schools of thought" surrounding grounded theory?

SUPPLEMENTAL ACTIVITY

1. Consider several examples of reflexive accounts about the experience of using grounded theory in a doctoral dissertation (e.g., Alammar, Intezari, Cardow, & Pauleen, 2018; Nelson, 2017; Nagel, Burns, Tilley, & Aubin, 2015). Analyze these to identify what proved most challenging about using grounded theory for novice researchers.

CHAPTER 6
Highlighting quality through reporting

A specific research design or method is no guarantee that a study is scientific or that the results are credible or useful. This chapter considers different strategies that can be used to gauge the quality of MM-GTM research, including in the ways that research procedures or a final theoretical framework can be visualized effectively in a table or figure. A list of indicators of quality is discussed that extends beyond a singular reliance on transparency about research methods during reporting.

TERMS INTRODUCED IN THE CHAPTER

- Methodological transparency
- Procedural diagram
- Reflexivity

INTRODUCTION

Ian Dey, author of an influential second-generation textbook about grounded theory, underscored the great variety of ways that grounded theory has been adapted in the real world of research practice. Dey was unusually direct in the words he chose to make the point that there is no one codified approach to grounded theory: "There is no such thing as 'grounded theory' if we mean by that a single, unified methodology, tightly defined and clearly specified. Instead, we have different interpretations of grounded theory," Dey wrote (2004, p. 80). The benefit to recognizing the diverse ways grounded theory methods have been applied in research practice is that it signals its potential to meet diverse purposes and to adapt to situation-specific approaches that honor the complexity of real-world problems.

Purpose, contribution, and key points

This chapter brings the book to a close by introducing some ideas about reporting and evaluating quality in MM-GTM, while at the same time pulling together threads from earlier chapters. By focusing on saturation, methodological transparency, reflexivity, utility, and originality as criteria for evaluating the quality of reports about MM-GTM studies and projects, the chapter promotes a set of criteria that apply to other qualitative research methods as well. The chapters adds to the argument about the power of a visual display to both imagine and report a holistic theoretical framework.

Aims of the chapter

The chapter suggests different strategies that can be used not only to gauge the quality of MM-GTM during reporting, but to embed them in the way a project is conceived. Specific aims of the chapter are to:

1 Summarize characteristics of the chapter exemplars and what they tell us about the way mixed methods and grounded theory have been used across the globe.
2 Review the foundations of the methodological rationale for combining mixed methods and grounded theory and the argument that it is a distinct methodology.
3 Acknowledge tensions between MM-GTM and classic or formal grounded theory.
4 Demonstrate ways to visualize a theoretical model developed through MM-GTM.
5 Consider ways that an interactive approach to MM-GTM can be embodied in a procedural diagram.
6 Identify criteria to evaluate the quality of the research methods and theoretical and analytical outputs of MM-GTM.
7 Recognize challenges to conducting MM-GTM.

Key takeaways from the chapter

The following lists principal takeaways from this final chapter:

1 The impressive variety in the ways MM-GTM has been implemented makes it nearly impossible to categorize them.
2 MM-GTM is a distinct but eminently adaptable methodology that has as its foundation a shared set of assumptions about the way knowledge is constructed.
3 The assumptions of an interactive approach to MM-GTM are probably not compatible with a classic or formal approach to grounded theory.
4 A figure that depicts a theoretical or explanatory framework in a parsimonious way may well be the single most important element in the judgment of quality about a manuscript with a theoretical purpose.
5 An expansive view of criteria for weighing the merits of a MM-GTM include indicators related to the research methods (transparency, saturation, reflexivity) and the analytical and conceptual outputs (utility and originality) that apply equally to reporting in many research approaches.

Organization of the chapter

The chapter is organized in three major parts. The rationale for the methodological similarities between mixed methods and grounded theory is re-iterated in the first section of this chapter. This is followed by an exploration of different ways that a grounded theory model developed through mixed methods can be presented, including in conventional and less conventional ways. Then we shift our attention to considering how a generic set of quality criteria can apply to MM-GTM. Finally, the chapter begins to come to a close by identifying challenges researchers face, which are unique to MM-GTM. I end the chapter and the book by recognizing intriguing topics that I was not able tackle within the confines of this book but would be well worth pursuing elsewhere.

CONSIDERING THE VARIETY EVIDENT IN THE CHAPTER EXEMPLARS

In a recent exploration of the use of mixed method grounded theory reported by Johnson and Walsh (2019) illustrates the challenge of trying to catalog and label complex research using the conventional annotation system that has been widely adapted as a shorthand in mixed methods. Johnson and Walsh (2019) set out, much as Walsh (2015) did a few years earlier, to categorize examples of MM-GTM using conventions that distinguish the timing of the phases of the research process and that communicate whether priority is awarded to a qualitative or quantitative logic.

The experience Johnson and Walsh (2019) report illustrates the inherent paradox in trying to catalog and label complex research. They were only able to identify a few commonalities among the six illustrative cases MM-GTM designs they were able to categorize using a standard notation system employed by mixed method researchers (see Table 25.1, p. 525, not included here). Of the six cases featured in Johnson and Walsh's table (2019), an equal number analyzed the qualitative and quantitative strands separately as did those that approached data analysis in an integrated way. Of the cases categorized as integrated, an exploratory stance was carried through in the analysis of both the qualitative and quantitative data. One important similarity between the illustrative cases is that they all gave comparable weight to the quantitative and qualitative phases.

The conclusions Johnson and Walsh (2019) reached after trying to categorize even a small number of MM-GTM articles match observations that Sharlene Hesse-Biber (2018) made about qualitative dominant mixed method designs. Hesse-Biber argued that the emergent quality that is evident in some or all of the phases of the research process makes it difficult to affix a label from a specific mixed method design up-front. "Locking one's mixed methods project into a particular mixed methods design template a priori would be particularly challenging when doing research from a qualitatively driven standpoint," Hesse-Biber wrote (2018, p. 449).

Johnson and Walsh's (2019) analysis led them to conclude that the variety among MM-GTM reports is so notable that it supports Walsh's (2015) earlier conviction that every project is like a specialized ecosystem with its own unique methodology that combines beliefs and practices with a specific combination of methods and techniques. "Each research project may be considered as having a specific methodology," Walsh wrote in the earlier (2015, p. 4).

> Within acceptable limits, methods are reinvented every time they are used to accommodate the real world of research practice.
> (Sandelowski, Voils, Leeman, & Crandell, 2012, p. 320)

That there is no single, formulaic way to implement a MM-GTM study is also evident in the exemplars that are showcased in this book. "Variety" is the single word spotlighted in Chapter 2. There the attention is not to try to categorize the ways the research was conducted but to the ways that MM-GTM can be paired with other qualitative approaches like case study.

A list of the exemplars appears as Table 1.1 and in Appendix A. Both grounded theory and mixed methods are awarded meaningful attention in each of the exemplars. A list of additional examples of MM-GTM appears in Appendix B. By and large, there is less transparency about research methods in the articles listed in Appendix B.

The diversity that is evident in the set of exemplars featured in this textbook extends to disciplinary affiliation, geographical location, and the type of journal where the article appeared. Diversity is manifested in the following ways in the group of exemplars identified in this text:

1 The disciplinary affiliation of the first author of each exemplar extends beyond the fields of education and health where grounded theory is used most widely. Five emerged from authors in health-related field, one from management, one from social work, one from urban affairs, and one from child psychology.
2 The usefulness that has been found for mixed methods across the globe is evident in the institutional affiliation of the first author of each exemplar. Five of the first authors are affiliated with an institution in the United States, two in the United Kingdom, one in Japan, and one in Canada.
3 Most mixed method research is published in disciplinary journals, rather than methodological ones. This is evident in the exemplars as well. Only three of the exemplars featured in this text appeared in specialized, methodologically oriented journals.

Given the admonishment that many doctoral student are given to avoid studies with a complex research design, it is gratifying to realize that three of the exemplars were completed as part of the requirements for a doctoral dissertation (i.e., Catallo, Jack, Ciliska, & MacMillan, 2013; Kawamura, Ivankova, Kohler, Purumean-Chaney, 2009; Shim et al., 2017). Each of these come from the health field where doctoral research is not as individualistic as it often thought to be in other applied fields, particularly education, where research is less likely to occur within the context of a larger team receiving support from external funding. Another unexpected finding is that authors of three of the nine exemplars benefited from the tutelage of a well-recognized expert in mixed methods (i.e., Kawamura et al., 2009; Kaplan & Duchon, 1988;

Shim et al., 2017). With MM-GTM as with any other methodology, there are innumerable benefits to the novice researcher committed to producing cutting edge research to seek out a scholar who is engaged in a contemporary dialog about a research method and willing to share his or her expertise.

ARTICULATING A METHODOLOGICAL RATIONALE FOR MM-GTM

A methodological rationale that supports the compatibility between mixed methods and some approaches to grounded theory was introduced in the first chapter. A figure provided there (Figure 1.2.) highlights paradigmatic assumptions that underlie that two research approaches that are compatible. Areas of compatibility include: (a) the iterative nature of the constant comparative method, (b) abduction as an analytical logic, (c) the adaptability of both approaches to diverse philosophical paradigms, and (d) their ability to accommodate complexity. Another figure in Chapter 1 (see Figure 1.3) adds to the argument about the philosophical and analytical compatibility of the two approaches by highlighting areas where each makes a distinct contribution. Most notably for grounded theory this includes prioritization of an exploratory stance that allows the unexpected to emerge. For mixed methods, this could include a commitment to a dialectical approach to mixed methods (Johnson, 2012) to engage multiple perspectives and viewpoints.

The methodological rationale I advance moves considerably beyond the additive logic long advocated by influence leaders in grounded theory, almost all of whom recognized the potential to use both qualitative and quantitative data with grounded theory. My position extends the idea of MM-GTM as both a methodology by embedding an abductive logic into core grounded theory procedures. This is likely to produce findings that cannot be disaggregated and reported separately in an article about the qualitative methods and another about the quantitative methods. An integrated approach to MM-GTM downplays trivialization of the qualitative component of a MM-GTM study, including by the simplistic assumption that in mixed methods qualitative analysis is primarily accomplished by quantifying qualitative data.

The methodological rationale I have developed downplays the argument often presented in the early days of the development of mixed methods in the 1980s when one of the arguments for its legitimacy was that using more than one method makes it possible to offset the weaknesses of another method (Creamer, 2018a). The methodological rationale I present is more about the value-added of linking different research methods. It is not a critique of the more contentious aspects of grounded theory, most notably about the role of the literature and the potential for a truly inductive approach.

The methodological framework I provide for MM-GTM is not conveniently housed within a single "school of thought" about grounded theory. While my perspective shares qualities with the constructivist approach to grounded theory that Charmaz (2014a) championed, my interest in producing a theoretical model shares and some features of Corbin and Strauss (2008). The emphasis I place on dissonance, paradox, and the messiness of research in the real discloses an affiliation with a postmodern perspective advanced by Clarke (2005).

Tensions between MM-GTM and a classic or formal approach to grounded theory

Critical researchers "pick and choose" from different approaches to grounded theory (Sebastian, 2019, p. 6). The methodological rationale for pairing grounded theory and mixed methods and the description of the way that its procedures can be extended to include a dialectical perspective borrows from more than one approach to grounded theory. It is most at odds with the philosophical assumptions of classic or formal approach to grounded theory. Areas where the position I take about epistemology and methods departs most noticeably from a classic or formal approach to grounded theory include the following:

1. Prioritizing of abduction rather than induction as the principal, if not the only, analytical logic.
2. Endorsing ongoing engagement with relevant literature throughout the research process rather than simply as a sensitizing concept.
3. Reservations about the idea that it is critical for a researcher to "bracket" out his or her own experiences and preconceptions.
4. Valuing both the process and product of grounded theory by recognizing the act of theorizing as Charmaz (2014a) presents it, but also its potential to generate a theoretical framework or paradigm as Strauss and Corbin (1990) referred to in early versions of their textbook.
5. Suggesting that MM-GTM can be used to elaborate or extend theory as well as to generate it.
6. Recognizing that it is very likely that an investigator might launch the coding process with a set of pre-established codes adapted from the literature or from previous phases of the research project.
7. Welcoming the idea that grounded theory can be applied to data collected through diverse means, including through visualizations or from the internet.
8. Describing situations where grounded theory approach can be added unexpectedly to what was planned as a quantitative study to explain unexpected or contradictory findings.
9. Showcasing the potential of dissonance and exceptions as a source of original insight.

Some of the items appearing in the aforementioned list have the potential to enhance the usefulness of MM-GTM in settings beyond nursing and education where grounded theory has been used most widely. The idea that MM-GTM can be used to elaborate an existing theory can extend the likelihood it could prove useful in non-applied disciplinary contexts, like psychology or in health fields, where a researcher is expected to launch each and every project with a well-substantiated theoretical perspective.

Pairing MM-GTM with other qualitative approaches

The rationale that highlights the compatibility between mixed methods and grounded theory can extend to other qualitative traditions, including discourse analysis (Hadley, 2019a, 2019b; Johnson, 2014), case study (Cook & Kamalodeen, 2020), narrative analysis (Floersch, Longhofer, Kranke, & Townsend, 2010), and participatory action research (Ivankova, 2015). This type of three-way pairing of methodologies, like mixed methods plus grounded theory plus case study, is not unusual. Any use of more than one research method is considered an advanced mixed method design. In their systematic review of MM-GTM articles, Guetterman, Babchuck, Howell Smith, and Stevens (2017) calculated that more than 25% of the 61 articles they analyzed were using an advanced mixed method design. These included action research, longitudinal studies, and community-based participatory action research.

The idea of a study that uses an advanced mixed methods design that includes more than one qualitative method is still open for debate. Janice Morse, a long-time editor of the *International Journal of Qualitative Inquiry* who has a long history of engagement with both qualitative and mixed method research, is among those who are comfortable with the position that as long as findings are integrated, two qualitative approaches can be accurately described as mixed methods (Morse, 2010).

MM-GTM can be extended to include findings that emerge from not just one but several qualitative approaches. This might be the case, for example, with inductively driven mixed method case study research (Cook & Kamalodeen, 2020). We saw additional examples of the way that MM-GTM has been paired with more than a single qualitative approach. This includes the three-way pairing of MM-GTM with event analysis in the exemplar by Evans, Coon, and Ume (2011) as well as with the exemplar by Westhues et al. (2008) that paired MM-GTM with community-based participatory action research. Both of these are featured as exemplars in the chapter about variety (Chapter 2). One advantage of mixing findings from multiple qualitative methods is that it is possible to circumvent the ever-present debates about paradigm compatibility by approaching each method from a single paradigm like constructivism.

An example from four US-based authors from social work illustrates how the label "mixed method" can be applied appropriately to the process of integrating findings from more than one qualitative approach. In a study about adolescents' perspectives about psychotropic treatment, Floersch et al. (2010) integrated thematic, grounded theory, and narrative methods. They labeled their approach as "a multi-analytic, mixed, or hybrid approach to qualitative analysis" (p. 15). Floersch et al. (2010) conducted the analysis sequentially, developing core themes in the first phase of analysis using thematic analysis. Turning to line-by-line coding of interview data was done as a second step with the purpose of seeing the connections between key constructs through axial coding. Narrative analysis was used in the third to phase to recognizing temporality in the experience and to understand shifts in views that occurred before, during, and after treatment began. The intent to integrate findings from the different qualitative approaches extended to producing "an integrated conceptual framework" (Floersch et al., 2010, p. 1).

The task of communicating theoretical insight from a MM-GTM study is aided by a graphic or visualization. In the next section, we consider two examples of the use of a composite model to communicate a theoretical framework during reporting. Authors of both of these models further help to communicate their findings by the way they organized their findings sections.

VISUALIZING A THEORETICAL MODEL DEVELOPED WITH MM-GTM

Only a small proportion of investigators that use both grounded theory and mixed methods extend the analytical process to include a visualization or graphic that embodies a theoretical framework. It is much more common to find examples that short-circuit the analytical process after generating a list of categories. Others move it one step closer to a theoretical framework by producing a set of themes (also called theoretical propositions) that link constructs. During analysis, diagrams can help a researcher make sense of relationships that may not have been previously explicit (Buckley & Waring, 2009). In this way, diagramming is an active part of the theory generation.

In addition to their role during analysis, translating a theoretical model into a visual display provides a succinct way for an investigator or group of investigators with a realist orientation to communicate a complex theory (Buckley & Waring, 2009). A realist orientation is one that envisions causality in a qualitative way (Maxwell, 2012). Buckley and Waring (2009) provide several examples of ways that grounded theory models have been depicted. A figure that embodies a theoretical or explanatory framework in a parsimonious way may well be the single most important element in the judgment of quality about a manuscript with a purpose to develop or refine a theoretical theory.

The most common approach in MM-GTM is to generate or refine a theoretical model in a strand of research devoted to a qualitative approach. We saw that, for example, in two MM-GTM exemplars discussed an earlier chapter (i.e., Catallo et al., 2013; Kaplan & Duchon, 1988). In research about an intervention in a medical setting designed to create a safe environment for battered women to speak candidly about their injuries, Catallo et al. (2013) turned to grounded theory to develop a model to explain a non-significant results in what was otherwise a quantitative study. Kaplan and Duchon (1988) also dedicated a phase of the research project to qualitative analysis, again for the purpose of explaining non-significant quantitative findings. In both cases, the theoretical model was built or elaborated through qualitative methods.

Integrated approaches to a grounded theory visualization

Some authors of MM-GTM studies have taken a more unconventional and integrated approach to developing or elaborating a theoretical framework. Two of these (Kawamura et al., 2009; Shim et al., 2017) presented a final grounded theory model that fits the definition of an integrated visual display. Both of these sets of authors depicted their final theoretical model in a way that included constructs and links between constructs that were identified through both qualitative and quantitative procedures. A figure that depicts a final grounded theory that was generated entirely through qualitative procedures is not a joint display.

The final models presented by Kawamura et al. (2009) and Shim et al. (2017) recognize the possibility that findings from qualitative and quantitative analytical procedures do not always cohere to reveal a unified story line. Each of their models includes a notation system to indicate when findings from the analysis of different types of data were consistent or inconsistent. The utility of signaling parts of a theoretical model where findings did not entirely cohere is that it is an invitation for future research.

The integrated composite model presented in the chapter exemplar

The exemplar featured in this chapter is one of several articles authored by Minjung Shim that reported on research that she did for her doctoral dissertation about the impact of a health intervention targeted at ameliorating chronic pain through dance and movement therapy (Shim et al., 2017). I singled out this article for inclusion in this final chapter as an exemplar primarily because of the quality and transparency of reporting, including by providing a figure that visualizes a "grounded theory meta-model" (p. 36). In the first phase of what is described as a three-phase process, Shim was strategic but departed from a classic approach to grounded theory by first developing a preliminary conceptual model based on the literature and interviews with practitioners. The model was revised in the third and final phase of the process.

Box 6.1 uses the customary template to summarize key features of the 2017 article by Shim et al. (2017). It identifies the purpose of the article, features of the way the research was executed, and how integration occurred. It also incorporates information about the way Shim created an integrated joint display to identify inconsistencies between participants and sources of data.

BOX 6.1

Shim et al.'s (2017) MM-GTM Study About a Health Intervention

Purpose: Produced from research Shim's did for her dissertation, this article is one of several she produced to describe the impact of an intervention that was designed to test the impacts of dance or movement therapy on the management of chronic pain.

Design: Shim et al. labeled her research as using a sequential exploratory-confirmatory MM-GTM design, citing a fairly early version of Strauss and Corbin (1998). The procedural diagram included in the article depicts the research as occurring across three phases, each involving some type of mixing. The first phase is described as exploratory where an initial model was developed that combined the literature and the results from the analysis of interview data. In the second experimental phase, standardized survey data and qualitative data from journals and interviews were constructed to test and refine the model. The third phase of the research involved the construction of a final composite model.

Integration: This is a fully integrated, multi-phase mixed methods study. Shim enhanced awareness of the significance of mixing methods through a number of joint displays that compared qualitative and quantitative findings on the same constructs.

Unexpected findings: Shim et al. annotated the final composite model by using an asterisk to indicate when qualitative and quantitative results were consistent. These largely involved the identification of intervening conditions, like peer support, that influenced project outcomes.

128 REPORTING

> ***Theory produced:*** The final composite model embodies the multi-dimensionality that is characteristic of a formal or classic grounded theory. It singles out an underlying social process (referred to as learning new ways of living in the body and being in the world), as well as the personal and clinical conditions that influence it. The authors used an asterisk as a simple but effective way to signal corroboration between the qualitative and quantitative data.

The article by Shim et al. (2017) includes a figure of the theoretical model that some refer to as a formal grounded theory. They developed a graphic to embody a theoretical model (see Figure 4, p. 36) that is based on components from Strauss and Corbin's (1990) conditional matrix. The model identifies a core construct around which all other constructs are linked (learning new ways of living in the body and being in the world), outcomes (both anticipated and unanticipated), intervening conditions (factors that mediated the main therapy process), and other contextual conditions, like evidence of a social support network, that impact the effectiveness of the therapy in achieving its intended outcomes.

A time-ordered process is at the center of Shim et al.'s theoretical model. This is a priority in Charmaz's (2014a) constructivist approach to grounded theory. As is the case with many health-related or educational interventions, the process at the center of this grounded theory model is steps on the journey to behavior change. The model no doubt went through many iterations over the life of the project. Subjecting the theory to multiple revisions contributes to theoretical saturation (Shim, Johnson, Bradt, & Gasson, 2020).

Figure 6.1 reproduces (with copyright permission) the composite grounded theory model that is depicted in Figure 4 (p. 36) from Shim et al. (2017). Shim et al. adapted a similar strategy as Kawamura et al. (2009) in using textual symbols. An asterisk is used to alert readers to elements of the model where findings from qualitative and quantitative data were consistent. The asterisks appearing in the final composite model produced by Shim et al. indicate that both qualitative and quantitative data were collected about the majority of constructs in the model.

Both Kawamura et al. (2009) and Shim et al. (2017) found the truth in Sanscartier's (2018) observation that when multiple sources of data are analyzed and integrated, findings do not always cohere to present a single or coherent view of reality. In the process of exploring complexity, Sanscartier (2018) observed that norm of presenting findings "as unified, singular reality" (p. 3) can mask divergent views and findings. He maintains that the danger in presenting a theoretical model in a visual is the risk over simplifying reality.

An additional reporting feature: addressing inconsistent data through a joint display

In addition to enhancing the quality of reporting by organizing the findings section of the article that appeared in the *European Journal of Integrative Medicine* around key components of a conditional matrix from Strauss and Corbin (1990), Shim et al. (2017) added another layer of

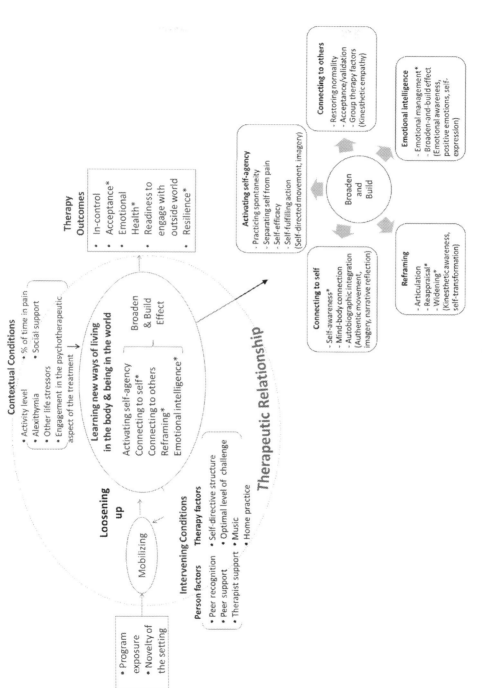

FIGURE 6.1 A Final Composite Grounded Theory Model from Shim et al. (2017)

transparency through a joint display (see Table 6, p. 33; table not shown). The purpose of what they referred to as "a joint display of comparisons" was "to assess to what extent the quantitative and qualitative results converge/diverge" (p. 31). This table provides assurances that the investigators enhanced validity by taking steps to more fully understand discrepant data.

WRESTLING WITH WAYS TO GAUGE QUALITY IN MM-GTM

There is a substantial body of methodological literature devoted to the task of identifying criteria to weigh the quality of empirical research and reporting. This extends to mixed methods where I have questioned the practice of the practice to apply one set of criteria to the qualitative research methods and a second one to the quantitative methods because it totally disregards integration (Creamer, 2018a). The Mixed Method Evaluation Rubric (MMER) that I introduced in my 2018 textbook, *An Introduction to Fully Integrated Mixed Method Research*, is the only one of a cluster of rubrics to include a set of criteria specifically targeting integration. The construct referred to as "interpretive comprehensive" in the MMER is also the only rubric to include items related to validity. It contains items such as recognizing alternative explanations and acknowledging inconsistencies between findings from different sources of data.

I am a proponent of a more generic set of criteria that cross methods and that prioritizes attention to the act of integration that is so central to any definition of mixed methods (Creamer, 2018a). A UK methodologist with expertise in a variety of methods, Stephen Gorard, takes the position that many core criteria of research quality cross methods one step further. He argues that many shared assumptions and practices cross not only methods but academic fields. He writes: "at its core, the nature of scientific inquiry is the same in all fields" (Gorard, 2004, p. 12).

Standards of quality in reporting in mixed methods, such as those published by the National Institute of Health (Creswell, Klassen, Plano Clark, & Clegg Smith, 2011) and the American Psychological Association (Levitt et al., 2018), simplify the task of gauging quality by providing a checklist of items that should be included in a research report. In mixed methods, this includes applying a label to name the research design, specifying the timing of data collection and analysis, and making a comment about the priority awarded to the qualitative and quantitative strands, among other things. While clear-cut and easy to implement, this type of standard for reporting leaves unclear ways to address the quality of the research methods and the way they were executed and if the product generates any new analytical insight. Gorard objects to equating research design with quality. He writes: "A specific design or method does not make a study scientific" (Gorard, 2004, p. 12).

Criteria for weighing the merits of research conducted using MM-GTM extend beyond the expectation for transparency in reporting. An expansive view of criteria for weighing the merits of a MM-GTM include indicators related to the research methods (transparency, saturation, reflexivity) and the analytical and conceptual outputs (utility and originality) that apply equally to reporting in many research approaches. **Methodological transparency** *refers to providing enough detail about the research methods for a reviewer or reader to be able to draw conclusions about its credibility.* From a post-positivist, but not necessarily a constructivist perspective, the expectation for methodological transparency extends to providing sufficient documentation (i.e., warranting) to support conclusions.

A specific design or method does not make a study scientific.

(Gorard, 2004, p. 12)

In MM-GTM, methodological transparency requires identifying how core grounded procedures were implemented and details about how integration occurred and what it accomplished. On the other hand, saturation is a type of quality criterion that is core to procedures used in grounded theory. It is a signal that data collection is sufficient when no new properties of a category emerge that contribute to further analytical insight.

The application of saturation, transparency, reflexivity, utility, and originality as indicators of the quality of reporting we explore further in this final section of Chapter 6.

Saturation

Saturation often appears in lists of the core procedure in grounded theory. In grounded theory, saturation is applied relative to theoretical categories. The most frequent way it is described is as a signal that data collection is sufficient when no new properties of the categories emerge that contribute further analytical insight. According to Charmaz (2014), saturation is accomplished when *no* new properties about a category emerge. Acknowledging the challenge of this task in a complex design, Dey (1999) is more pragmatic. He prefers the term theoretical sufficiency. Eisenhardt similarly sets a less absolute goal for saturation, observing that the process ends when "marginal improvement becomes small" (1989, p. 533).

The ability to achieve a reasonable degree of saturation depends on sampling strategy and sample size. One of the greatest limitations of grounded theory studies is inadequate sample size (Morse & Clark, 2019). Saturation is linked to theoretical sampling and "means more than a one-time check" (Charmaz, 2014a, p. 215). The more multi-dimensional the core construct and complex the model, the less likely that saturation can be achieved without an uncommon amount of data. An expectation to saturate categories and their properties can have an impact on a final composite model. It is very likely to produce a more streamlined or parsimonious final theoretical model or statement.

Methodological transparency

Standards for quality of reporting that have been adapted for mixed methods emphasize methodological transparency about the research procedures, particularly about integration, and the utilization of method-appropriate terminology (e.g., Creswell et al., 2011; Levitt et al., 2018). In MM-GTM the expectation for methodological transparency extends to using appropriate terminology and an explanation about how core grounded theory analytical procedures, like theoretical sampling, were executed. The emphasis on methodological transparency is evident in the first analysis of a body of MM-GTM research articles where quality was assessed by the number of core grounded theory procedures that were identified and explained (e.g., Guetterman et al., 2017), without attending to integration.

Transparency about research methods is strongly related to the utility of the research for other investigators and to understanding how the research was conducted. It is no guarantee that a study is rigorous or that the conclusions are valid or warranted (Maxwell, 2013). In MM-GTM, evaluative criteria extend to finding a way to warrant the conclusions, including key themes or constructs and relationships depicted in a final composite theoretical model. The process of warranting a conclusion refers to documenting the link between data and key findings. In mixed methods, findings are often warranted through a table or figure or table that incorporates qualitative and quantitative data and traces the link between data and themes or hypothesis that are central to the conclusions.

Conventional approaches to reporting mixed method research can camouflage how much interaction there was between the qualitative and quantitative data, methods, or strands of a study. It is a challenge to determine if integration occurred and, if so for what purpose, when the qualitative and quantitative findings are reported in separate manuscripts (Archibald, Radil, Zhang, & Hanson, 2015; Bryman, 2007). Conventional approaches to reporting that divide quantitative and qualitative findings in separate sections can impose a barrier to integrating results (Reeping, Tayler, Knight, & Edwards, 2019). Standard strategies for organizing manuscripts that downplay the contribution of the integration of different sources of data or analytical techniques can be offset by devoting a section to integration and by using visual displays that juxtapose or link data from different sources.

Procedural diagrams

Procedural diagrams are a staple of reporting mixed methods research and part of the expectation for methodological transparency (Creamer, 2020). A **procedural diagram** *is a process-oriented figure like a flowchart that contributes to transparency by clearly describing important steps in the research process.* It is a type of integrated visual display that contributes to transparency by clearly communicating important steps in the research process. One of challenges in reporting introduced by a fully integrated mixed method design is to find innovative ways to summarize key steps in a dynamic, interactive process in a procedural diagram, especially when interaction among team members proves instrumental to the insight drawn (Creamer, 2020). A procedural diagram bolsters the credibility of the research by providing enough documentation for a reader or audience member to reach a judgment about whether procedures were executed in a systematic way.

A procedural diagram often goes through multiple iterations as an investigator or research team moves from an initial proposal to the task of reporting it to a wider audience. The final version of a procedural diagram that appears in a journal article or as part of a research presentation necessarily simplifies the research process. It distills key steps, planned or not, that proved instrumental to the research process. Particularly in complex multi-phase projects, the final version of the procedural diagram very likely differs in substantive ways from an initial conception constructed months, if not years, ahead of time.

REPORTING   133

Business tycoon Warren Buffet is reputed to have said, "The rearview mirror is always clearer than the windshield." What that means in this context is that choosing an appropriate label and designing a procedural diagram that accurately reflects how research unfolded is something that cannot be fully envisioned until it is completed. Conventional templates (see Creswell & Plano, 2011) for depicting a basic design have to be adapted for an advanced design, including in situations where there is a high level of interaction between collaborators or between findings emerging from different sources of data (Creamer, 2020). Conventional approaches to reporting that divide quantitative and qualitative findings in separate sections can prove to be a barrier to integrating results (Reeping & Edwards, 2020).

The procedural diagram provided by the exemplar featured in the preceding chapter by Wesely (2010) about the role of motivation in persistence in a language immersion program, illustrates some techniques that can be used to embody a complex, integrated mixed methods study with a grounded theory component and a mixed priority. The figure is unusual because it does not include both data collection and analysis. It concentrates only on the phases of analysis. It uses a horizontal orientation that is generally used in mixed methods to depict a sequential design. Wesely's figure depicts a research project that was executed in six phases. Curved lines in the figure show the interaction between findings emerging from the qualitative and quantitative strands.

Figure 6.2 reproduces (with copyright permission) the procedural diagram provided by Wesely (2010, p. 302).

Several additional strategies used by Wesely (2010) could be useful to others intent on representing an interactive mixed methods design. Observe, first, that although there was a feedback loop later in the process, that qualitative and quantitative data were first analyzed separately. A footnote to the table notes that different types of shading were used to distinguish qualitative data or analytical procedures, quantitative data or analytical procedures. Particularly of note is that multiple forms of shading were used to indicate when qualitative and quantitative phases were integrated.

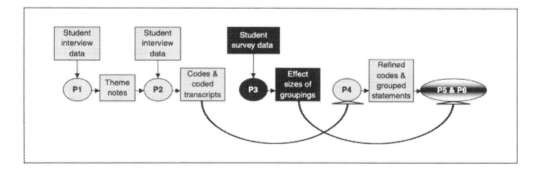

FIGURE 6.2 Wesely's (2010) Procedural Diagram Showing in Interactive Design

Reflexivity

Reflexivity is an additional dimension of quality that is part of the expectation for transparency, particularly in qualitative research. *An expectation that has an effect on both the way research is executed and reported, reflexivity involves considering ways that a lone researcher or, in a team setting, the way that team dynamics, influence the way research was executed and/or its outcomes.* It includes recognizing the ways that the researcher has an effect on the research process (Hall & Callery, 2001). Reflexivity is more challenging in the type of team-based research that is to so common with large scale mixed methods projects. In this setting, reflexivity includes considering the ways that team dynamics influenced the insight that was generated. This extends to acknowledging ways that differences in interpretation informed the research process.

Reflexivity serves multiple purposes. Sometimes referred to as positionality, reflexivity is conventionally thought of as a fixture of reporting that contributes to understanding the research and weighing its credibility. Framed at a time when positivism and, later, post-positivism dominated scientific thinking as a strategy to offset "bias" and bolster "objectivity" by setting aside preconceptions, more contemporary views frame reflexivity as an act that helps a reader or audience member understand how a theoretical perspective, like feminism or critical race theory, informed the choices made in a research project. This type of reflexivity can be seen in an account by Malagon et al. (2009) that explores the use of grounded theory with critical race theory.

There is a place for reflexivity about paradigmatic positioning at the beginning of a research project as well. Describing his journey from thinking he would be forced to choose just one approach to grounded theory during his doctoral research, Irish author James Nelson (2017) recommends reading enough of the methodological literature about grounded theory to grasp the different approaches ("schools of thought") as an important intellectual exercise that sensitizes the researcher to the choices that are available in designing and executing a study. While navigating the different points of view about grounded theory and uncovering some of the more hegemonic elements of its politics, Nelson found it liberating when he came upon Dey's (2004) observation that there is no one single unified grounded theory methodology, but many.

In a complex project where there is a high level of interaction among team members about findings that emerge, the expectation for reflexivity often extends to explaining how diverse approaches to interpreting findings were navigated. Rather than sweeping these kinds of differences under the rug, this can involve a polyvocal approach that acknowledges differences of perspectives (Creamer, 2011). Polyvocality enlivens voice in a text. More importantly, it has implications for social justice as well. It offsets the inclination to allow a single authorial voice to dominate and to erase the contributions of those with less power or authority.

The exemplar written by Bonnie Kaplan and Dennis Duchon (1988) and reported in the preceding chapter about research involving the implementation of an information system provides an example of the type of reflexivity that communicates respect for different perspectives. In some cases, this can be tensions introduced at a point in time or in an academic field where a qualitative research is awarded less regard. In the discussion section of the article, after describing how the qualitative researcher (Kaplan) pushed the quantitative research (Duchon) to re-analyze the quantitative data in light of the grounded theory model she produced from the qualitative data, the authors stressed the value-added of wrestling with these tensions. They pointed to the value-added to producing synthetic insight when they observed in the discussion section that it took "a strong determination to accommodate each approach and to reconcile apparently conflicting data resulted in an interpretation that synthesized the evidence" (Kaplan & Duchon, 1988, p. 582). Overlap in areas of expertise can make it easier to negotiate the kinds of tensions introduced when findings from different sources of data are engaged in meaningful ways (Bryman, 2007).

Utility

Pragmatically oriented researchers have been at the forefront of advocating utility as a key indicator of quality. The pragmatic view is that the key issue is if research produces conceptual and theoretical insight that is useful (Bryant, 2009). This includes scientific usefulness in generating new research as well as utility in practice (Corley & Gioia, 2011). In practice-oriented fields, like management, information systems, nursing and other medical fields, and education, it includes the synergy produced in generating new ideas for evidence-based practice.

Originality

Originality is related to the novelty of the analytical insight or the way it is displayed in a figure or table and the extent it adds to what has previously been known about the phenomenon. The argument for an original contribution is something a researcher generally pursues in the discussion section of a manuscript where authors are expected to re-integrate their findings with the literature, including theories (Morse, 2020). In MM-GTM, a novel contribution might be the addition of a recognition of how contextual factors, like a marginalized status, can interrupt conventional patterns of association. A nuanced yet parsimonious figure that integrates findings from multiple sources of data or research methods is one way to demonstrate originality.

Table 6.1 builds on the idea that indicators of quality include both a contribution to knowledge and to practice. It is informed by two projects where I had the opportunity to serve as an external evaluator for funded grants about the role of an undergraduate research experience in promoting an interest in a career that involves research. One was with a team of collaborators from engineering education. This is the team I referred to in Chapter 3 in a section about using integrated memos as the basis for a case-based analysis (see Lee et al., 2019). The second was a funded project led by two faculty members in geology at Concord College (Allen, Kuehn, & Creamer, 2020). A dissertation completed by a former doctoral student advisee about the undergraduate research experiences by Janice Austin (Austin, 2017) served as an additional source of ideas for Table 6.1.

Table 6.1 is a hypothetical example that offers a template for the task of re-integrating findings with the literature in a succinct way that highlights the contribution. This could help an investigator build the case for the originality and utility of the research. It lists examples of the types of theoretical propositions that might be generated in a grounded theory study, extracts related information from the literature that would normally be accompanied by a reference, and then explicitly identifies what the research adds to existing knowledge and suggests about practice.

TABLE 6.1 Documenting the Contribution of Selected Theoretical Propositions from a Grounded Theory Model: A Hypothetical Example

Theoretical Proposition	Current State of Knowledge*	Contribution to Knowledge	Contributions to Practice
Identity as a researcher is only one of many emerging identities a novice researcher juggles.	As they are making the choice of an academic field to study, developmentally many students are at a stage where they view knowledge as fixed and characterized by a right and wrong.	In engineering, experience with real-world research projects often shake confidence in the idea that there are clear right and wrong answers.	Students benefit from the opportunity to reflect on their ideas about the nature of knowledge and how the way it is constructed differs across academic disciplines.
Peers play as strong a role as a research mentor in shaping an identity as a researcher.	Mentors play a critical role in promoting a student's interest in science or engineering.	The inter-disciplinary and team-based nature of much research challenges ideas that interpersonal skills are unimportant in engineering and the sciences.	It is helpful to provide training about ways to be an effective member of a research team.
Real-world impact is an important motivator for interest in a career in science or engineering.	Students are often motivated to enroll in a science or engineering major by a conviction of their potential to generate social and global benefits.	The routine and repetitive nature of experiments that occur in a controlled laboratory setting can dampen the conviction about the global impact of science and engineering.	It is important for researchers to highlight the real-world implications of research.

* Each of the entries in this column would be supported by a series of references.

CHALLENGES FACED BY INVESTIGATORS USING MM-GTM

Most research in the human and social sciences, including in health-related fields and business management, is complex and multi-phase. It has a habit of sending an investigator down many "rabbit holes." Even though we constantly have an eye on the clock, the calendar, and resources, I would say the type of messiness introduced by unexpected, but substantiated findings, is part of what fuels an interest in research that for many academics extends over the entire course of a career. Professional standards for reporting, professional conventions, and word limits for journal articles add to the challenge of reporting a methodologically nuanced research project.

MM-GTM introduces its own set of challenges, particularly for the novice researcher. These include: (a) juggling the proliferation of terminology that is introduced when two or more research methods are used, (b) establishing a meaningful sample size, and (c) reflecting sensitivity to different approaches to grounded theory by carefully incorporating appropriate references. Each of these is discussed in the following section.

Juggling a surplus of technical language

Using research methods as established as grounded theory and mixed theory introduces the need to navigate the distinct dictionaries of terms associated with each in ways that demonstrate that the researcher has expertise in both methods. This is especially the case when publishing in a methodological journal where a fairly sophisticated level of knowledge is required. In MM-GTM, methodological transparency requires identifying core grounded procedures. The specialized terminology associated with a research method is a shorthand that facilitates communication among the informed but that can simultaneously be alienating to those unfamiliar with it. The challenge is to deploy specialized terminology accurately and in ways that do not overburden the text.

The purpose of the project and the nature of the audience both have something to do with the choice to prioritize the language of one method over another. For example, mixed methods might be downplayed when the submission is made to a qualitative journal. On the other hand, the mixed method component might be highlighted in quantitative journal. A balanced approach that awards the same amount of space to each method in a manuscript could work well when the journal is a methodological one. Regardless of the priority awarded to any one method, knowing enough about each method to be successful at publishing is certainly possible, but challenging in MM-GTM.

Extending the conception of a meaningful sample size

Artificially setting a sample size is a risky venture in both grounded theory and MM-GTM. The expectation for ongoing waves of theoretical sampling, including to pursue exceptions or unexpected findings, is one reason for this. A second is the drive to achieve theoretical saturation/sufficiency with multiple, inter-related constructs. Although classic grounded theorist may be satisfied with a small sample (Charmaz & Thornberg, 2020), a token number of participants can limit the amount of data available to a researcher. Except in certain types of research like biography, it restricts the ability to achieve analytical density, to publish in a reputable venue, and to build an agenda for future research. Morse is blunt in the language she used when she observed: "Small sample studies, although they proliferate, are not usually implementable and do not make a substantial contribution" (Morse, 2020, p. 3). Similarly, a homogenous sample can delude a researcher into thinking saturation has been achieved (Morse, 2020).

On the other hand, the labor-intensive nature of emergent coding procedures, particularly if it involves line-by-line coding, sets practical limits on how much data can be managed in the grounded theory portion of a MM-GTM study. This might be the case, for example, in a study that extracts a large amount of data from social media platforms, YouTube videos, or webpages. In this kind of situation, a reasonable solution is to develop or refine a coding scheme with a systematically selected (not purposeful or convenience) sub-sample of data. In some contexts, text mining approaches can prove useful to confirm properties of a category, to trace steps or transitions in a process, or to verify links between categories suggested by Inaba and Kakai (2019).

Being sensitive to different schools of thought

Authors of a number of reflective accounts reporting on the experience of using grounded theory or MM-GTM for doctoral research, have commented on the challenge of juggling not only of the different points of views of the founders of grounded theory, but also between the second generation of scholars, often their students, who, like Charmaz, followed them but bought an entirely different paradigmatic perspective to the enterprise (e.g., Alammar, Intezari, Cardow, & Pauleen, 2018; Nagel, Burns, Tilley, & Aubin, 2015; Nelson, 2017).

Developing familiarity with the differences in viewpoints between leaders of the different schools of thought about grounded theory is not as daunting a task as it might seem to be at the onset. Although each brings a slightly different stance to it, there is no shortage of summaries that have been published recently that single out key topics where the perspectives differ (e.g., Apramian, Cristancho, Watling, & Lingard, 2017; Reiger, 2018; McCall & Edwards, 2021; Sebastian, 2019). These streamline the task of distinguishing the points of views and can help to increase the likelihood that supporting references are used in an informed way during reporting. Apramian et al. (2017) are among those who insist that differences between the schools of thought associated with grounded theory have been exaggerated and that lines between them are far more permeable than is suggested in some of the literature.

Many investigators approach grounded theory in ways that borrow from more than one school of thought or epistemological perspective. Recognizing these differences through informed use of supporting references adds credibility to research and the expertise of the authors. We see that tensions play out in an example of MM-GTM that is listed with other example in Appendix B, which methodological limitations. Laws et al. (2015) in a MM-GTM reported results from an intervention designed to promote obesity prevention in early life. These authors claim to use "grounded theory principles" (p. 4). Charmaz's 2014a book is the only item related to grounded theory to appear in the reference list. Laws et al. (2015) presented a theoretical model and summarized it using language from Strauss and Corbin's (1990) conditional or consequential matrix (context, strategies, conditions, contextual factors, and outcomes) that is not associated with Charmaz. As I highlighted in the chapter about process (Chapter 3) by using a block quote, Charmaz used explicit language to voice her interest in theorizing and not theory. The type of generic attribution we see in this article is not unusual in reporting about grounded theory studies. It weakens the credibility of the research by communicating only a very narrow familiarity with the methodological literature.

Developing an expansive view of expertise

Many of most well-known academics have dedicated a lifetime to fine-tuning their expertise in a research method and/or substantive content area. While it has long been a point of pride to situate one's identity as *either* a qualitative researcher or a quantitative one, to be a reputable mixed method researcher in these complex times demands expertise that extends beyond this arbitrary distinction. UK researcher and prolific author Tony Onwuegbuzie (2012) was one of the first to articulate that to be a "mixed researcher" requires familiarity with (and no doubt respect for) both qualitative and quantitative research methods. This same call for a more expansive view of expertise extends to engaging what has been published about a phenomenon in more than one academic field or discipline. A more expansive conception of methodological expertise better positions a researcher to choose and to adapt the methods that are most suited to the problem at hand.

Research methods are not frozen in time. Changes in methods are occurring in what senior scholar Janice Morse describes as "breath-taking speed" (2020, p. 2). One implication of this is pressure for researchers to engage not only the classic or cannon about a research method, but also methodological literature and examples from diverse disciplines that reflect more contemporary applications. By and large, textbooks that played a formative role in shaping understanding of a methodology become in a way historical artifacts of the socio-cultural movement at the time and are replaced by a second and third generation of books that reflect more contemporary perspectives. Developing methodological expertise requires reading a breadth of different viewpoints about any method. Increasingly, this can be accomplished at no cost by consulting with videos available through the internet. The expertise to utilize multiple approaches demands that researchers continually engage and re-engage with contemporary viewpoints about qualitative, quantitative, and mixed methods approaches. It often means a reading list that extends into unfamiliar fields and disciplines. Reading broadly means making a point not to read just familiar names from the Western world, but to search out publications by authors writing from within an array of different socio-political contexts.

Advancing methodological training through professional development activities, now readily available online, can promote dialog that bridges disciplinary domains. It builds fluency with a dictionary of the terminology associated with different research methods. It contributes to the ability of researchers to develop the confidence about the potential for creativity and new insight when mixed methods is recognized as a methodology that extends well beyond the initial act of collecting qualitative and quantitative data.

CONCLUSIONS

No methodology is without its detractors. Among those frustrated with how grounded theory is used routinely, there is a concern that it reduced to a mechanical approach to coding, regardless of the context or purpose, at the cost of its most important outcome – an explanatory framework. Others have voiced reservations about that are fundamental to its core methodological assumption, including the possibility, or even desirability, of entering a research project in an "objective" way with no a priori assumptions, or of the feasibility of "discovering" a theory without consulting the literature. Investigators of a postmodern persuasion may well challenge the presentation of composite theoretical models as reductionist and simplistic. Detractors of mixed methods point criticize its apparent receptivity to combining methods that reflect different paradigmatic assumptions. Some question the feasibility of developing expertise in multiple methods. Investigators can be advised that both mixed methods and grounded are too complex, and possibly too ambitious, for the novice researcher.

Certainty is a mirage in a complex, rapidly changing world. I could not disagree more with the advice to novice researchers to avoid advanced mixed methods designs, like those that are used when methods are combined. Both mixed methods and grounded theory can be conducted from grounding in a wide range of paradigmatic positions. Each offers a broad set of guidelines and a palette of procedures to tackle the complexity that is introduced, including in an intervention, when the core constructs, like trauma or identify or caregiving, are multi-dimensional and subject to a multi-layered set of micro- and macro-level contextual conditions.

Innovation is not achieved simply by applying a standardized procedure (Erzberger & Kelle, 2003). Rather than offering the certainty of a simplistic formulaic approach, I have explored MM-GTM as basic scaffolding for an investigator or a set of investigators to customize a range of tools that are suitable to contemporary problems and contexts.

> Truly novel discoveries are never the result of simply applying some standardized procedure.
> (Erzberger & Kelle, 2003, p. 465)

The chapter closes by summarizing the cross-cutting themes and recognizing important topics that have yet to be addressed about MM-GTM.

Cross-cutting themes

I have brought each of the preceding chapters to a close by summarizing the ways that what was discussed in the chapter added to three cross-cutting themes. These are about (a) integrated approaches to mixed methods research as compared to those that by and large keep the qualitative and quantitative strands separate, (b) MM-GTM, and (c) the role of complexity and dissonance in executing research as well as in advancing the analytical insight that is generated.

Appendix C provides the reader a concise overview of the architecture of the book by distilling key points from each chapter about each of the cross-cutting themes. It is organized by chapter and theme. It integrates information from the summaries that have appeared in each chapter. The following further condenses key takeaways from the text about MM-GTM:

1. MM-GTM is an advanced mixed method design that is generally conducted with a multi-phase research design.
2. From a pragmatic or dialectical perspective, areas of overlap in the philosophical foundations of mixed methods and grounded theory include extending the constant comparative method to include different types of data and embedding an abductive logic in core grounded theory procedures, including theoretical coding, theoretical sampling, diagramming, and the construction of analytic memos.
3. The monumental variety in the ways MM-GTM research has been conducted defies classification. The variety includes its pairing with more than one qualitative method, including participatory action research, discourse analysis, and case study to name just a few.
4. MM-GTM can be used to build a conceptual or theoretical framework or to elaborate an existing theoretical framework from the literature.
5. Integrative joint displays and case-based analysis play an instrumental role in advancing analytical and theoretical insight.
6. Dissonance between findings from different methods or evidence of gaps that they suggest can introduce an unexpected element to the analysis that produces explanatory inferences or theoretical propositions.

Topics left unaddressed

I should not, I suppose, be surprised to reach the end of this book to find that there are a number of topics that I have not addressed that could be addressed in a book about mixed methods approaches to grounded theory. Most notable among these is quantitative approaches to grounded theory. With the exception of Walsh (2014), I have not devoted much space to quantitative dominant MM-GTM. These omissions are largely a reflection of my own interests and should not be taken as a statement about their quality or dismissal of the possibility they could be legitimate examples of MM-GTM.

There are some topics that I intended to address but I could not. The main reason for this is largely that, as I did in my first book (Creamer, 2018a), the commentary I have been able to provide has been shaped by the exemplars I located. In a few cases, these are extended by hypothetical examples. This explains, for example, the omission of a discussion about causality in grounded theory that is associated with a realist perspective. This is present in methodological literature but virtually absent in examples of MM-GTM with a genuine qualitative component where claims about prediction and causality are rarely made. Consistent with the research trajectory launched in my early days as a faculty member (see Schneider, 1998), it was my intention to devote a good bit of space to feminist MM-GTM. A constructivist orientation to grounded theory is well adapted to feminist positionality. There are many examples of grounded theory studies conducted from a feminist standpoint and of those that deploy multiple methods. I was not able to locate one that reflected feminist MM-GTM in ways that awarded comparable attention to both mixed methods and grounded theory. For someone interested in building on the topic of this book, there is much more that could be written about MM-GTM with case study and case-based analysis.

REVIEW QUESTIONS

1   What are some of the similarities in the philosophical foundations of mixed methods and grounded theory?
2   In what ways are there important differences in the philosophical assumptions of mixed methods and grounded theory?
3   What are steps an investigator to highlight the quality, originality, and utility of the research that is being reported?
4   How can an investigator communicate through a final, composite model that there is contradictory evidence about some of the findings?

SUPPLEMENTAL ACTIVITY

1   Before fleshing out your ideas about launching a research project, it can be surprisingly liberating to read a critique about grounded theory and one about mixed methods. For mixed methods, I suggest a highly cited article by Guest (2012). An alternative would be

to read the last chapter about controversies by Creamer (2018a). An article by Thomas and James (2006) problematizes three issues about grounded theory, including what is meant by the word "theory," "ground," and "discovery." Reading a critique by someone who is well versed in the history and nuances of a research methodology can be liberating because it assures an investigator that there are many different ways to approach even the most widely used methodologies.

Glossary

(with a notation of the chapter where the term is first introduced)

Abduction. Abduction is one of three approaches to reasoning that include induction (generalizing from the specific to the general) and deduction (generalizing from the general to the specific). It is the process of generating multiple possible explanations for an unexpected or surprising finding and then systematically investigating these. (Chapter 1)

Analytic density. Associated with validity, analytic density refers to envisioning constructs in a multi-dimensional way or to developing or elaborating an explanatory framework in a way that adds conceptual nuance or richness to the findings. (Chapter 1)

Case-based analysis. Qualitative and quantitative data are integrated in a narrative or visualization for further analysis. (Chapter 3)

Concept map. A diagram that is constructed by participants and/or the researcher that serves as visual data in analysis. These often create a network of clustered words or concepts. (Chapter 4)

Conceptual framework. A conceptual framework offers a tentative explanatory framework that is based on a synthesis of related literature and what is known in a practical way about a phenomenon. (Chapter 1)

Constant comparative method. An analytical strategy where data, and eventually emerging constructs and themes, are continuously compared and contrasted as data collection and analysis unfolds. (Chapter 1)

Design. A map or plan about how an empirical study is executed. (Chapter 2)

Formal or classic grounded theory. A formal or classic grounded theory is envisioned in a multi-level way. Stages in the progression through a temporal process are at the center of a visualization of formal or grounded theory. Other elements include references to outcomes (anticipated or not), intervening conditions that mediate the outcome, and contextual factors. (Chapter 2)

Fully integrated mixed method research. A research methodology where the integration of qualitative and quantitative data and/or analytical procedures is embedded through all phases of the research process from the formulation of the research questions, to data collection and sampling, during analysis, and during the process of drawing conclusions. (Chapter 1)

Fully integrated mixed method grounded theory methodology (FIMM-GTM). Uses grounded theory procedures and strategies to integrate different sources of data throughout the research process, including during data analyses, to produce and sometimes test a theoretical framework. (Chapter 1)

Graphic elicitation. A data collection procedure where participants physically create and/or verbally edit a diagram or other visual display. (Chapter 4)

Grounded theory. Often confused with a set of procedures to guide the coding and analysis of qualitative data, grounded theory is first and foremost a methodology that provides a comprehensive approach to generate a theoretical framework inductively from data. (Chapter 1)

Initiation rationale. One of the five principal rationales for integrating data that involves additional rounds of data collection and analysis to further explore unexpected, contradictory, or paradoxical findings. (Chapter 5)

Integrated case-based analysis. A mixed methods analytical strategy that leverages data generated from qualitative and quantitative methods into a narrative or visualizations in ways that inform the analysis. (Chapter 3)

Integrated analytical memo. Integrates data collected with qualitative and quantitative methods to advance theoretical insight. (Chapter 3)

Integrated theoretical coding. A mixed methods analytical strategy that engages findings from more than one type of data to generate theoretical propositions or hypotheses about the relationship among categories. (Chapter 3)

Integrated theoretical sampling. Engages multiple sources of data to advance theoretical insight about categories, concepts, relationships, and themes. (Chapter 3)

Integrative display. A figure or table that integrates data from multiple sources one during analysis for purposes of advancing analytical or theoretical insight. (Chapter 4)

Joint display. A table or figure that arrays and sometimes links qualitative and quantitative data about the same constructs, research questions, or themes. (Chapter 4)

Matrix mapping. An interactive graphic elicitation method that asks participants to, first, enter the intersection of a quantitative score on a scale on the vertical axis and, second, score on a scale on the horizontal axis and then to annotate the point of intersection with a few words that describe it. (Chapter 4)

Methodological dynamism. Refers to how methods evolve and remain viable over time. (Chapter 2)

Methodological transparency. Providing sufficient details about research methods during reporting for a reviewer or a reader to be able to reach a judgment about the credibility of the research. (Chapter 6)

Mixed method research. A systematic approach to data collection and analysis that combines different sources of data and quantitative and qualitative analytical procedures with the intention to engage multiple perspectives in order to more fully understand complex social phenomenon. (Chapter 1)

Mixed method grounded theory methodology (MM-GTM). A methodology that embeds a dialectical logic in the constant comparative method and grounded theory procedures to develop a mid-level theoretical framework or to elaborate an existing one. (Chapter 1)

Multi-method research. Research that incorporates multiple sources of data and/or methods but does not integrate them in a substantive way. (Chapter 1)

Participatory photo mapping. A graphic elicitation method that integrates photography, community mapping, and walk-along interviews to learn about people's experiences in a spatial context (Texiiera, 2014). It can also utilize diagramming. (Chapter 4)

Procedural diagram. A procedural diagram is a process-oriented figure like a flowchart that contributes to transparency by clearly describing important steps in the research process. (Chapter 6)

Quantitizing. A type of data transformation where qualitative data are quantified for purposes of statistical analysis. (Chapter 4)

Reflexivity. An expectation that has an effect on both the way research is executed and reported, reflexivity involves considering ways that a lone researcher or, in a team setting, the way that team dynamics, influence the way research was executed and/or its outcomes. (Chapter 6)

Rupture theorizing. Rupture theorizing occurs when results from the empirical analysis challenges a long-standing measure, instrument, or theoretical framework. (Chapter 5)

Saturation. One of the core procedures in grounded theory. It is a signal that data collection is sufficient when no new properties of a category emerge that contribute to further analytical insight. (Chapter 3)

Theory. A cohesive explanatory framework generated empirically through a systematic set of procedures. (Chapter 1)

Theoretical coding. Theoretical coding generates constructs that conceptualize the relationships between categories. (Chapter 3)

Theoretical sampling. An emergent and purposeful approach to sampling that follows and initial purposeful sampling that is designed to advance theoretical insight by adding to the understanding of concepts, categories, relationships and themes. (Chapter 3)

Theoretical sensitivity. Having sufficient familiarity with relevant bodies of literature to recognize the theoretical implications of findings. (Chapter 5)

Theoretical triangulation. Contributes to internal validity by drawing on multiple theoretical frameworks as a means to explain findings and weigh competing explanations. (Chapter 5)

Timelining. A participatory graphic elicitation method that encourages the construction of rich, time-ordered narratives of peoples' life and experiences that is accomplished through diagramming or sketching combined with an open-ended interview. (Chapter 4)

Verification. Refers to procedures to verify findings that contribute to the rigor of a research study, construct validity, and in some contexts the reliability of findings. (Chapter 5)

Warranting. A type of methodological transparency in reporting that supports the credibility of conclusion, generally through a visual display. (Chapter 5)

Appendices

List of exemplars by chapter

CHAPTER 1: ESTABLISHING LANGUAGE AND PURPOSE

Kawamura, Y., Ivankova, N., Kohler, C., & Purumean-Chaney, S. (2009). Utilizing mixed methods to assess parasocial interaction of an entertainment-education program audience. *International Journal of Multiple Research Approaches, 3*, 88–104.

CHAPTER 2: VARIED APPROACHES TO USING MIXED METHODS WITH THEORETICAL FRAMEWORKS

Catallo, C., Ciliska, D., & MacMillan, H.L. (2012). Minimizing the risk of intrusion: A grounded theory of intimate partner violence disclosure in emergency departments. *Journal of Advanced Nursing, 69*(6), 1366–1376.

Evans, B. C., Coon, D. W., & Ume, E. (2011). Use of theoretical frameworks as a pragmatic guide for mixed methods studies: A methodological necessity. *Journal of Mixed Methods Research, 5*(4), 276–292.

Westhues, A., Ochocka, J., Jacobson, N., Simich, L., Maiter, S., Janzen, R., & Fleras, A. (2008). Developing theory from complexity: Reflections on a collaborative mixed method participatory action research study. *Qualitative Health Research, 18*(5), 701–717.

CHAPTER 3: MIXED METHODS AND THE PROCESS OF THEORIZING

Jones, L., & Kafetsios, K. (2005). Exposure to political violence and psychological well-being in Bosnian adolescents: A mixed method approach. *Clinical Child Psychology and Psychiatry, 10*(2), 157–176.

CHAPTER 5: LEVERAGING DISSONANCE TO ADVANCE THEORETICAL REASONING

Carmona, M. (2015). Re-theorizing contemporary public space: A new narrative and a new normative. *Journal of Urbanism*, 8(4), 373–405.

Kaplan, B., & Duchon, D. (1988, December). Combining qualitative and quantitative methods in information systems research: A case study. *Management Information Systems Quarterly*, 571–586.

Wesely, P. (2010). Language learning motivation in early adolescents: Using mixed methods research to explore contradiction. *Journal of Mixed Methods Research*, 4(4), 295–312.

CHAPTER 6: HIGHLIGHTING QUALITY THROUGH REPORTING

Shim, J., Johnson, R. B., Gasson, S., Goodill, S., Jermyn, R., & Bradt, J. (2017). A model of dance/movement therapy for resilience-building in people living with chronic pain. *European Journal of Integrative Medicine*, 9, 27–40.

APPENDIX B

List of examples of MM-GTM*

Agerfalk, P. J., & Fitzgerald, B. (2008). Outsourcing to an unknown workforce: Exploring open sourcing as a global sourcing strategy. *MIS Quarterly, 32*(2), 385–409.

Alexandre, R., Walsh, I., & Michel, K. (2016). Is SAM still alive? A bibliometric and interpretive mapping of the strategic alignment field. *Journal of Strategic Information Systems, 25*(2), 75–103.

Ball, S. B. (2013). Accelerated baccalaureate nursing students use of emotional intelligence in nursing as "caring for a human being": A mixed methods grounded theory study. *International Journal of Nursing Education Scholarship, 10*(1), 293–300.

Barley, S. R., & Meyerson, D. E. (2011). E-mail as a source and symbol of stress. *Organization Science, 22*(4), 887–906.

Bussing, R., Koro-Ljunberg, M., Gary, F., Mason, D. M., & Garvan, C. W. (2005, March–April). Exploring help-seeking for ADHD symptoms: A mixed methods approach. *Harvard Review of Psychiatry*, 85–101.

*Carmona, M. (2015). Re-theorizing contemporary public space: A new narrative and a new normative. *Journal of Urbanism, 8*(4), 373–405.

*Catallo, C., Ciliska, D., & MacMillan, H.L. (2012). Minimizing the risk of intrusion: A grounded theory of intimate partner violence disclosure in emergency departments. *Journal of Advanced Nursing, 69*(6), 1366–1376.

DeVito Dabbs, A., Hoffman, L. A., Swigart, V., Happ, M. B., Iacona, A.,& Dauber, J. H. (2004). Using conceptual triangulation to develop an integrated model of the symptom experiences of acute rejection after lung transplantation. *Advances in Nursing Science, 27*(2), 138–149.

*Evans, B. C., Coon, D. W., & Ume, E. (2011). Use of theoretical frameworks as a pragmatic guide for mixed methods studies: A methodological necessity. *Journal of Mixed Methods Research, 5*(4), 276–292.

Floersch, J., Longhofer, J. L., Kranke, D., & Townsend, L. (2010). Integrating thematic, grounded theory and narrative analysis. *Qualitative Social Work*. http://qsw.sagepub.com/content/early/2010/02/24/1473325010362330

Forrest, L., Huprich, S., Jacobs, S. C., Elman, N., Veilleux, J., C., & Kaslow, N. J. (2013). Training directors' perceptions of faculty behaviors when dealing with trainee competence problems: A mixed method pilot study. *Training and Education in Professional Psychology, 7*(1), 23–32.

Gallagher, J. A., Hall, E. L., Anderson, T. L., & Del Rosario, K. L. (2013). A mixed-methods exploration of Christian working mothers' personal strivings. *Journal of Psychology Theology, 41*(1), 48–60.

Gasson, S., & Waters, J. (2013). Using a grounded theory approach to study online collaborative behaviors. *European Journal of Information Systems, 22*, 95–118.

Grant, A. M., Berg, J. M., & Cable, D. M. (2014). Job titles as identity badges: How self-reflective titles can reduce emotional exhaustion. *Academy of Management Journal, 57*(4), 1201–1225.

*Refers to articles singled out for discussion as exemplars.

Harms, K., King, J., & Francis, C. (2009). Behavioral changes based on a course in agroecology: A mixed methods study. *Journal of Natural Resources and Life Sciences Education, 38*, 183–194.

Harrison, Y. D., & Murray, V. (2012). Perspectives on the leadership of chairs of nonprofit organization boards of directors: A grounded theory mixed-method study. *Nonprofit Management and Leadership, 22*(4), 411–437.

Hausman, A. (2000). A multi-method investigation of consumer motivations in impulse buying behavior. *Journal of Consumer Marketing, 17*(5), 403–419.

★Jones, L., & Kafetsios, K. (2005). Exposure to political violence and psychological well-being in Bosnian adolescents: A mixed method approach. *Clinical Child Psychology and Psychiatry, 10*(2), 157–176.

★Kaplan, B., & Duchon, D. (1988, December). Combining qualitative and quantitative methods in information systems research: A case study. *Management Information Systems Quarterly*, 571–586.

★Kawamura, Y., Ivankova, N., Kohler, C., & Purumean-Chaney, S. (2009). Utilizing mixed methods to assess parasocial interaction of an entertainment-education program audience. *International Journal of Multiple Research Approaches, 3*, 88–104.

King, K. P. (2010). Advancing educational podcasting and faculty inquiry with a grounded research model: Building on current mixed-methods research across contexts. *The Journal of Continuing Higher Education, 58*, 143–155.

Laws, R., Campbell, K. J., Plight, P., Ball, K., Lynch, J., Russell, G., Taylor, R.,& Denney-Wilson, E. (2015). Obesity prevention in early life: An opportunity to better support the role of maternal and health nurses in Australia. *BMC Nursing, 14*, 26. https://doi.org/10.1186/s12912-015-0077-7

McFerran, K., Roberts, M., & O'Grady, L. (2010). Music therapy with bereaved teenagers: A mixed methods perspective. *Death Studies, 34*, 541–565.

Meschede, T., Thomas, H., Mann, A., Stagg, A., & Shapiro, T. (2016). Wealth mobility of families raising children in the twenty-first century. *Race and Social Problems, 8*, 77–92.

Milford, T. M., & Tippett, C. D. (2013). Preservice teachers's images of scientists: Do prior science experiences make a difference? *Journal of Science Teacher Education, 24*, 745–762.

Morgan, D. G., & Stewart, N. J. (2002). Theory building through mixed-method evaluation of a dementia special care unit. *Research in Nursing and Health, 25*, 479–488.

Nelson, A., Cordova, D., Walters, A., & Szecsy, E. (2016). Storytelling for empowerment for Latino teens: Increasing HIV prevention knowledge and attitudes. *Journal of Adolescent Research, 31*(2), 202–231.

★Shim, M., Johnson, R. B., Gasson, S., Goodill, S., Jermyn, R., & Bradt, J. (2017). A model of dance/movement therapy for resilience-building in people living with chronic pain. *European Journal of Integrative Medicine, 9*, 27–40.

Teixeira, S. (2016). Beyond broken windows: Youth perspectives on housing abandonment and its impact on individual and community well-being. *Child Indicators of Research, 9*(3), 582–607.

Thornberg, R., & Knutsen, S. (2011). Teenagers' explanations of bullying. *Child & Youth Care Forum, 40*(3), 177–192.

Tu, M. (2018). An exploratory study of Internet of Things (IoT) adoption intention in logistics and supply chain management. *The International Journal of Logistics Management, 29*(1), 131–151.

Wall, J. D., & Knapp, J. (2014). Learning computing topics in undergraduate information systems courses: Managing perceived difficulty. *Journal of Information Systems Education, 25*(3), 245–259.

Walsh, I. (2014). A strategic path to study IT use through users' IT culture and IT needs: A mixed-method grounded theory. *The Journal of Strategic Information Systems, 23*, 146–173.

★Westhues, A., Ochocka, J., Jacobson, N., Simich, L., Maiter, S., Janzen, R., & Fleras, A. (2008). Developing theory from complexity: Reflections on a collaborative mixed method participatory action research study. *Qualitative Health Research, 18*(5), 701–717.

Yang, D. Z., Richardson, J. C., French, B. F., & Lehman, J. D. (2011). The development of a content analysis model for assessing students' cognitive learning in asynchronous online discussions. *Educational Technology Research and Development, 59*, 43–70.

APPENDIX C

Summary by chapter and cross-cutting theme

Chapter	Cross-Cutting Themes		
	Integrated Approaches to Mixed Methods Research	Mixed Method Grounded Theory Methodology (MM-GTM)	Complexity and Dissonance
Chapter 1: DEFINITIONS *Establishing Language and Purpose*	Integrated research uses strategies that intentionally promote interdependence between their sources of data, methods, or approaches. The most effective way to become an integrated researcher is to be competent in more than one qualitative and quantitative research method. Fully integrated mixed method grounded theory (FIMM-GT) uses grounded theory procedures with both qualitative and quantitative data and integrates them in substantive ways throughout the research process to produce and sometimes test a theoretical framework. Integration generally serves multiple purposes in this type of study.	Conventional perspectives maintain the independence of the stands and the view the purpose MM-GTM to build theory with qualitative procedures and to test it with quantitative ones. In MM-GTM, the constant comparative method can be applied to quantitative, qualitative, and mixed data.	A dynamic design is needed to adapt to rapidly changing research environments, unexpected results, and to negotiate different perspectives team members bring to research initiatives. A process that is deliberate about engaging the dissonance and paradox that is introduced by abduction is the lynchpin that reaches across mixed methods, grounded theory, and complexity.

154 APPENDICES

Chapter	Cross-Cutting Themes		
	Integrated Approaches to Mixed Methods Research	Mixed Method Grounded Theory Methodology (MM-GTM)	Complexity and Dissonance
Chapter 2: VARIETY *Varied Approaches to Using Mixed Methods with Theoretical Frameworks*	Conceptualizing a problem and research questions in a multi-dimensional way is a foundation for thinking theoretically and advances an integrated approach to mixed methods. Launching a project with a conceptual framework developed during the process of consulting a cross-disciplinary body of literature facilitates integration across research phases.	It is possible to sustain an inductive/exploratory drive in a study that is framed by a theoretical framework from the literature at the onset. MM-GTM has informed research in a wide variety of different ways. It is its adaptability and variety that sustains its continued usefulness. MM-GTM has been paired with a variety of other qualitative research approaches, including participatory action research.	A theoretical framework can provide an explanation for unexpected findings. An expectation for plurality and dialectical exchange is built into the design of a MM-GTM participatory action research.
Chapter 3: PROCESS *Mixed Methods and the Process of Theorizing*	A narrative or visualization that integrates qualitative and quantitative data can be used as the basis for a case-based analysis. Fully integrated mixed method grounded theory (FIMM-GTM) embeds both qualitative and quantitative data in basic grounded theory procedures like theoretical coding, diagramming, analytical memoing, theoretical sampling, and saturation.	The inductive and exploratory component in MM-GTM means that new insight with theoretical implications can emerge even in a study with a purpose to test an existing theory or hypothesis. The constant comparative method is not simply an inductive analytical approach, but one that also engages deduction and abduction.	Dissonance between findings from different methods or evidence of gaps that they suggest can introduce an unexpected element to the analysis that produces explanatory inferences or theoretical propositions. Theoretical sampling can be directed by unexpected findings.
Chapter 4: VISUAL DISPLAYS *Advancing Theoretical Reasoning with Visualizations*	While integrative and joint displays play a critical role during reporting, they can also play an instrumental role in advancing analytical and theoretical insight.	Visual displays have the potential to generate theoretical insight by helping a researcher envision patterns and relationships among constructs.	Joint and integrative displays can reveal diverse perspectives and expose dissonance between findings from different analytical methods.

(Continued)

APPENDICES

Chapter	Cross-Cutting Themes		
	Integrated Approaches to Mixed Methods Research	Mixed Method Grounded Theory Methodology (MM-GTM)	Complexity and Dissonance
	In some fully integrated mixed method (FIMMR) designs, the qualitative and quantitative phases may be difficult to disentangle, while in other cases, the phases are quite distinct. FIMMR designs can be executed in a concurrent or sequential manner. A visual display can be used to structure data collection that simultaneously collects qualitative and quantitative data.	Data generated from timelines, concept maps, matrices, and mapping exercises that combine multiple sources of data can be used as the basis of case-based analysis and facilitate cross-case comparison.	
Chapter 5: DISSONANCE *Leveraging Dissonance for Theoretical and Analytical Insight*	A study can be designed to explore divergence, including between theoretical perspectives previously considered in the literature, but more often dissonance is encountered unexpectedly.	The credibility of findings can be warranted through different types of joint displays.	Integrating data from different analytical procedures for a case-based analysis is one tool to investigate dissonant data and to weigh the level of support for theoretical propositions.
Chapter 6: REPORTING *Highlighting Quality in Reporting*	Qualitative and quantitative findings can be integrated in a composite theoretical model.	Mixed methods and grounded theory share several key epistemological assumptions. MM-GTM is an advanced design that is often executed in more than two phases. There is huge variety in the way that MM-GTM studies have been accomplished.	

References

Agerfalk, P. J. (2014). Insufficient theoretical contribution: A conclusive rationale for rejection? *European Journal of Information Systems*, *23*, 593–599.

Alammar, F. M., Intezari, A., Cardow, A., & Pauleen, D. J. (2018). Grounded theory in practice: Novice researchers' choice between Straussian and Glaserian. *Journal of Management Inquiry*, *28*(2), 225–245.

Allen, J., Kuehn, S., & Creamer, E. G. (2020, May). A boost for the CURE: Improving learning outcomes with curriculum based undergraduate research. *GSA Today*, *30*. https://doi.org/10.1130/GSATG458GW

Apramian, T., Cristancho, S., Watling, C., & Lingard, L. (2017). (Re) grounding grounded theory: A close reading of theory in four schools of thought. *Qualitative Research*, *17*(4), 359–376.

Archibald, M. M., Radil, A. I., Zhang, X., & Hanson, W. E. (2015). Current mixed methods practices in qualitative research: A content analysis of leading journals. *International Journal of Qualitative Methods*, *14*(2), 1–33.

Austin, J. (2017). *Incidents in the undergraduate research experience that contribute to an interest in science, technology, engineering, and math (STEM)* (Unpublished doctoral dissertation). Virginia Polytechnic Institute and State University, Blacksburg, VA.

Bazeley, P. (2018a). *Integrating analyses in mixed methods research*. London, UK: Sage.

Bazeley, P. (2018b). "Mixed methods in my bones": Transcending the qualitative-quantitative divide. *International Journal of Multiple Research Approaches*, *10*(1), 334–341.

Bazeley, P., & Jackson, K. (2013). *Qualitative data analysis with NVIVO* (2nd edition). Thousand Oaks, CA: Sage Publications.

Benoliel, J. Q. (1996). Grounded theory and nursing knowledge. *Qualitative Health Research*, *6*(3), 406–428.

Birks, M.,& Mills, J. (2015). *Grounded theory: A practical guide* (2nd edition). Thousand Oaks, CA: Sage Publications.

Boeije, H., Slagt, M., & van Wesel, F. (2013). The contribution of mixed methods research to the field of childhood trauma: A narrative review focused on integration. *Journal of Mixed Methods Research*, *7*(4), 347–369.

Booth, A., Carroll, C., Ilott, I., Low, L. L., & Cooper, K. (2013). Desperately seeking dissonance: Identifying the disconfirming case in qualitative evidence synthesis. *Qualitative Health Research*, *23*(1), 126–141.

Boychuk Duchscher, J. E., & Morgan, D. (2004). Grounded theory: Reflections on the emergence vs forcing debate. *Methodological Issues in Nursing*, *48*(6), 605–612.

Bravington, A., & King, N. (2018). Putting graphic elicitation into practice: Tools and typologies for the use of participant-led diagrams in qualitative research interviews. *Qualitative Research*, *19*(5), 502–523.

Bruce, C. D. (2007). Questions arising about emergence, data collection, and its interaction with analysis in a grounded theory study. *International Journal of Qualitative Methods*, *6*(1), 1–12.

Bryant, A. (2002). Re-grounding grounded theory. *Journal of Information Technology and Theory and Application*, *4*, 25–42.

Bryant, A. (2009). Grounded theory and pragmatism: The curious case of Anselm Strauss. *FQS: Forum: Qualitative Social Research, 10*(3), Art 2, no page numbers.

Bryant, A. (2017). *Grounded theory and grounded theorizing: Pragmatism in research practice*. New York, NY: Oxford University Press.

Bryant, A., & Charmaz, K. (2019). *The SAGE handbook of current developments in grounded theory*. London, UK: Sage.

Buckley, C., & Waring, M. J. (2009). The evolving nature of grounded theory: Experiential reflections on the potential of the method for analyzing children's attitudes towards physical activity. *International Journal of Social Research Methodology, 12*(4), 317–334.

Buckley, C., & Waring, M. J. (2013). Using diagrams to support the research process: Examples from grounded theory. *Qualitative Research, 13*(2), 148–172.

Burch, P., & Heinrich, C. J. (2017). *Mixed methods for policy research and program evaluation*. Thousand Oaks, CA: Sage Publications.

Bussing, R., Koro-Ljungberg, M. K., Gary, F., Mason, D., & Garvan, C. (2005). Exploring help-seeking for ADHD symptoms: A mixed methods approach. *Harvard Review of Psychiatry, 13*(2), 85–101.

Bussing, R., Koro-Ljungberg, M. K., Noguchi, K., Mason, D., Mayerson, G., & Garvan, C.W. (2012). Willingness to use ADHD treatments: A mixed methods study of perceptions by adolescents, parents, health professionals, and teachers. *Social Science and Medicine, 74*, 92–100.

Bustamante, C. (2017). TPACK and teachers of Spanish: Development of a theory-based joint display in mixed method case study research. *Journal of Mixed Method Research*. https://doi.org/10.1177/1558689817712119

Carmona, M. (2015). Re-theorizing contemporary public space: A new narrative and a new normative. *Journal of Urbanism, 8*(4), 373–405.

Castro, F. G., Kellison, J. G., Boyd, S. J., & Kopak, A. (2010). A methodology for conducting integrative mixed methods research and data analysis. *Journal of Mixed Methods Research, 4*(4), 342–360.

Catallo, C. J., Ciliska, D., & MacMillan, H.L. (2012). Minimizing the risk of intrusion: A grounded theory of intimate partner violence disclosure in emergency departments. *Journal of Advanced Nursing, 69*(6), 1366–1376.

Catallo, C. J., Jack, S. M., Ciliska, D., & MacMillan, H. L. (2013). Mixing a grounded theory approach with a randomized controlled trial related to intimate partner violence: What challenges arise for mixed methods research? *Nursing Research and Practice*, 1–12. doi:10.1155/2013/798213

Chamberlain, K., Cain, T., Sheridan, J., & Dupuis, A. (2011). Pluralism in qualitative research: From multiple methods to integrated methods. *Qualitative Research in Psychology, 8*, 151–169.

Charmaz, K. (2006). *Constructing grounded theory*. Thousand Oaks, CA: Sage Publications.

Charmaz, K. (2014a). *Constructing grounded theory* (2nd edition). Thousand Oaks, CA: Sage Publications.

Charmaz, K. (2014b). Grounded theory in a global perspective: Reviews by international researchers. *Qualitative Inquiry, 20*(9), 1074–1084.

Charmaz, K. (2017a). Special invited paper: Continuities, contradictions, and critical inquiry in grounded theory. *International Journal of Qualitative Methods, 16*, 1–8.

Charmaz, K. (2017b). The power of constructivist grounded theory for critical inquiry. *Qualitative Inquiry, 23*(1), 34–45.

Charmaz, K. (2019). "With constructivist grounded theory you can't hide": Social justice research and critical inquiry in the public sphere. *Qualitative Inquiry, 26*(2), 165–176.

Charmaz, K., & Thornberg, R. (2020). The pursuit of quality in grounded theory. *Qualitative Research in Psychology*. https://doi.org/10.1080/147480887.2020.1780357

Clarke, A. E. (2005). *Situational analysis: Grounded theory after a postmodern term*. Thousand Oaks, CA: Sage Publications.

Clarke, A. E., & Friese, C. (2007). Grounded theorizing using situational analysis. In A. Bryant & K. Charmaz (Eds.), *The SAGE handbook of grounded theory* (pp. 363–397). London, UK: Sage.

Collins, C. S., & Stockton, C. M. (2018). The central role of theory in qualitative research. *International Journal of Qualitative Methods, 17*, 1–10.

Collins, K. M. T., Onwuegbuzie, A. J., & Johnson, R. B. (2012). Securing a place at the table: A review and extension of legitimation criteria for the conduct of mixed research. *American Behavioral Scientist, 56*(6), 849–865.

Conlon, C., Carney, G., Timonen, V., & Scharf, T. (2015). "Emergent reconstruction" in grounded theory: Learning from team-based interview research. *Qualitative Research*, *15*(1), 39–57.

Cook, L. D., & Kamalodeen, K. J. (2020). Combining mixed methods and case study research (MM+CSR) to give mixed methods case study designs. *Caribbean Journal of Mixed Methods Research*, *1*(1), 47–76.

Corbin, J., & Strauss, A. (2008). *Basics of qualitative research: Grounded theory procedures and techniques* (3rd edition). Thousand Oaks, CA: Sage Publications.

Corley, K. G., & Gioia, D. A. (2011). Building theory about theory building: What constitutes a theoretical contribution. *Academy of Management Review*, *36*(1), 12–32.

Creamer, E. G. (2004). Collaborators' attitudes about differences of opinion. *Journal of Higher Education*, *75*(5), 556–571.

Creamer, E. G. (2011). Experimenting with voice and reflexivity to produce multi-voiced texts. In C. Conrad & R. C. Serlin (Eds.), *The SAGE Handbook for Research in Education* (2nd edition, pp. 367–380). Thousand Oaks, CA: Sage.

Creamer, E. G. (2016). A primer about mixed methods in an educational context. *International Journal of Learning, Teaching, and Educational Research*, *15*(8). www.ijlter.org/index.php/ijlter/article/view/700

Creamer, E. G. (2018a). *An introduction to fully integrated mixed methods research*. Thousand Oaks, CA: Sage Publications.

Creamer, E. G. (2018b). Enlarging the conceptualization of mixed method approaches to grounded theory with intervention research. *American Behavioral Scientist*, *62*(7), 919–934. http://journals.sagepub.com/doi/10.1177/0002764218772642

Creamer, E. G. (2018c). Paradigms in play: Using case studies to explore the value-added of divergent findings in mixed methods research. *International Journal of Multiple Research Approaches*, *10*(1), 30–40.

Creamer, E. G. (2018d). Editorial: Striving for methodological integrity in mixed methods research: The difference between mixed methods and mixed up methods. *Journal of Engineering Education*, *107*(4). https://onlinelibrary.wiley.com/doi/pdf/10.1002/jee.20240

Creamer, E. G. (2020). Visualizing dynamic fully integrated mixed method designs. *International Journal of Multiple Research Approaches*, *12*(1), 1–13.

Creamer, E. G. (2021, March). Extending the value-added of mixed methods in sustainability research. In A. Factor & J.P. Ulhoi (Eds.), *Sustainability and small to medium-sized enterprises: Lessons from mixed methods research* (pp. 177–191). Abingdon, UK: Routledge.

Creamer, E. G., & Edwards, C. D. (2019). Embedding the dialogic in mixed method approaches to theory development. *International Journal of Research and Method in Education*, *42*(3), 239–251. https://doi.org/10.1080/1743727X.2019.1598357

Creamer, E. G., Guetterman, T., Govia, I., & Fetters, M. (2020, December). Challenging procedures used in systematic reviews by promoting a case-based approach to the analysis of qualitative methods in nursing trials. *Nursing Inquiry*. Early view. https://doi.org/10.1111/nin.12393

Creamer, E. G., & Schoonenboom, J. L. (2018). Introduction: Inter-method mixing as a gateway to methodological mixing. *American Behavioral Scientist*, *62*(7), 879–886.

Creswell, J. W., Klassen, A. C., Plano Clark, V. L., & Clegg Smith, K. (2011). *Best practices for mixed methods research in health sciences*. Bethesda, MD: Office of Behavioral and Social Science Research, National Institute of Health.

Creswell, J. W., & Plano, C. V. (2011). *Designing and conducting mixed methods research* (3rd edition). Thousand Oaks, CA: Sage Publications.

Creswell, J. W., Shope, R., Plano Clark, V. L., & Green, D. O. (2006). How interpretive qualitative research extends mixed methods research. *Research in Schools*, *13*(1), 1–11.

Cronin, A., Alexander, V. D., Fielding, J., Moran-Ellis, J., & Thomas, H. (2007). The analytic integration of qualitative data sources. In P. Alasuutari, L. Brickman, & J. Brannen (Eds.), *SAGE handbook of social research methods* (pp. 572–584). London, UK: Sage.

Davis, P., & Baulch, B. (2011). Parallel realities: Exploring poverty dynamics using mixed methods in rural Bangladesh. *Journal of Development Studies*, *47*(1), 118–143.

Dey, I. (1993). *Qualitative data analysis*. London, UK: Routledge.

REFERENCES

Dey, I. (1999). *Grounding grounded theory: Guidelines for qualitative inquiry*. London, UK: Academic Press.

Dey, I. (2004). Grounded theory. In C. Seale, G. Gobo, I. Gubrium, & D. Silverman (Eds.), *Qualitative research practice* (pp. 80–93). London, UK: Sage.

Dickinson, W. B. (2010). Visual displays for mixed methods findings. In A. Tashakkori & C. Teddlie (Eds.), *SAGE handbook of social and behavioral research* (2nd edition, pp. 469–504). Thousand Oaks, CA: Sage.

Dunne, C. (2011). The place of the literature review in grounded theory research. *International Journal of Social Research Methodology, 14*(2), 111–124.

Eccles, M., Grimshaw, J., Walker, A., Johnston, M., & Pitts, N. (2005). Changing the behavior of healthcare professionals: The use of theory in promoting the uptake of research findings. *Journal of Clinical Epidemiology, 58*, 107–112.

Edwards, J. R. (2008). To prosper, organization psychology should . . . overcome methodological barriers to progress. *Journal of Organization Behavior, 29*, 469–491.

Eisenhardt, K. M. (1989). Building theories from case study research. *Academy of Management Review, 14*(4), 532–550.

Eisenhardt, K. M., & Graebner, M. (2007). Theory building from cases: Opportunities and challenges. *The Academy of Management Journal, 50*(1), 25–32.

Erzberger, C., & Kelle, U. (2003). Making inferences in mixed methods: The rules of integration. In A. Tashakkori & C. Teddlie (Eds.), *Handbook of mixed methods in social and behavioral research* (pp. 457–490). Thousand Oaks, CA: Sage Publications.

Evans, B. C., Coon, D. W., & Ume, E. (2011). Use of theoretical frameworks as a pragmatic guide for mixed methods studies: A methodological necessity. *Journal of Mixed Methods Research, 5*(4), 276–292.

Evans, B. C., Crogan, N., Belyea, M., & Coon, D. W. (2009). Utility of the life course perspective in research with Mexican American caregivers of older adults. *Journal of Transcultural Nursing, 20*, 5–14.

Faber, C. J., Benson, L. C., Kajfez, R. L., Kennedy, M. S., Less, D. M., McAlister, A. M., & WU, G. (2019). *Dynamics of researcher identity and epistemology: The development of a grounded theory model*. 2019 ASEE Annual Conference and Exposition. Tampa, Florida.

Fielding, N. G. (2009). Going out on a limb: Postmodernism and multiple method research. *Current Sociology, 57*, 427–447.

Fielding, N. G. (2012). Triangulation and mixed method designs: Data integration with new research technologies. *Journal of Mixed Methods Research, 6*(2), 124–136.

Fielding, N. G., & Fielding, J. L. (1986). *Linking data: The articulation of qualitative and quantitative methods in social research*. Beverly Hills, CA: Sage.

Flanagan, P. J., McGrath, M. M., Meyer, E. C., & Coll, C.T. (1995). Adolescent development and transitions to motherhood. *American Academy of Pediatrics, 96*(2), 273–282.

Flick, U. (2017). Mantras and myths: The disenchantment of mixed-methods research and revising triangulation as a perspective. *Qualitative Inquiry, 23*(1), 46–57.

Floersch, J., Longhofer, J. L., Kranke, D., & Townsend, L. (2010). Integrating thematic, grounded theory and narrative analysis. *Qualitative Social Work*. http://qsw.sagepub.com/content/early/2010/02/24/1473325010362330

Freshwater, D. (2007). Reading mixed methods research: Contexts for criticism. *Journal of Mixed Methods Research, 1*(2), 133–146.

Gasson, S. (2009). Employing a grounded theory for MIS research. In D. Yk, L. B. Williams, S. L. Schenberger, & M. Wade (Eds.), *Handbook of research on contemporary theoretical models in information systems* (pp. 34–56). Hershey, PA: IGI Publishing.

Gasson, S., & Waters, J. (2013). Using a grounded theory approach to study online collaborative behaviors. *European Journal of Information Systems, 22*, 95–118.

Gibson, C. B. (2017). Elaboration, generalization, triangulation, and interpretation: On enhancing the value of mixed method research. *Organizational Research Methods, 20*(2), 193–223.

Gioia, D. A., & Pitre, E. (1990). Multiparadigm perspectives on theory building. *Academy of Management Review, 15*(4), 584–602.

Glaser, B. (1978a). *Theoretical sensitivity*. Mill Valley, CA: Sociological Press.

Glaser, B. (1978b). All is data. *Grounded Theory Review: An International Journal, 6*(2), no page numbers.

Glaser, B. (1992). *Emergence vs forcing: Basics of grounded theory analysis*. Mill Valley, CA: Sociology Press.

Glaser, B., & Strauss, A. (1967). *The discovery of grounded theory: Strategies for qualitative research*. New York: Aldine.

Gorard, S. (2004). Sceptical or clerical? Theory as a barrier to the combination of research methods. *Journal of Educational Enquiry, 5*(1), 1–21.

Gorard, S. (2010). Research design, as independent of methods. In A. Tashakkori & C. Teddlie (Eds.), *SAGE handbook of mixed methods in social and behavioral sciences* (2nd edition, pp. 237–251). Thousand Oaks, CA: Sage Publications.

Greckhamer, T., & Koro-Ljungberg, M. (2006). The erosion of a method: Examples from grounded theory. *International Journal of Qualitative Studies in Education, 18*(6), 729–750.

Greene, J. C. (2005). The generative potential of mixed methods inquiry. *Journal of Research & Method in Education, 28*(2), 207–2011.

Greene, J. C. (2007). *Mixed methods in social inquiry*. San Francisco, CA: Wiley Publishers.

Greene, J. C. (2008). Is mixed methods social inquiry a distinctive methodology? *Journal of Mixed Methods Research, 2*(1), 7–22.

Greene, J. C., Caracelli, V. J., & Graham, W. F. (1989). Toward a conceptual framework for mixed-method evaluation designs. *Educational Evaluation and Policy Analysis, 11*(3), 255–274.

Guest, G. (2012). Describing mixed methods research: An alternative to typologies. *Journal of Mixed Methods Research, 7*(2), 141–151.

Guetterman, T. C., Babchuck, W. A., Howell Smith, M. C., & Stevens, J. (2017). Contemporary approaches to mixed methods-grounded theory research: A field-based analysis. *Journal of Mixed Methods Research, 13*(2), 179–195.

Guetterman, T. C., Creswell, J. W., & Kuckartz, U. (2015). Using joint displays and MAXQDA software to represent the results of mixed methods research. In M. T. McCrudden, G. Schraw, & C. W. Buckendahl (Eds.), *In use of visual displays in research and testing: Coding, interpreting, and reporting data* (pp. 145–175). Charlotte, NC: Information Age Publishing.

Guetterman, T. C., & Fetters, M. D. (2018). Two methodological approaches to the integration of mixed methods and case study designs: A systematic review. *American Behavioral Scientist, 62*(7), 900–918.

Guetterman, T. C., Fetters, M. D., & Creswell, J. W. (2015). Integrating quantitative and qualitative results in health science mixed methods research through joint displays. *Annals of Family Medicine, 13*(6), 554–561.

Hadley, G. (2019a). *Grounded theory in applied linguistics research*. London, UK: Routledge.

Hadley, G. (2019b). Critical grounded theory. In A. Bryant & K. Charmaz (Eds.), *The SAGE handbook of current developments in grounded theory* (pp. 564–589). London, UK: Sage.

Hall, K. P. (2010). Advancing educational podcasting and faculty inquiry with a grounded research model: Building on current mixed-methods research across contexts. *The Journal of Continuing Higher Education, 58*, 143–155.

Hall, W. A., & Callery, P. (2001). Enhancing the rigor of grounded theory: Incorporating reflexivity and relationality. *Qualitative Health Research, 11*(2), 257–272.

Happ, M. B., Dabbs, A. D., Tate, J., Hricik, A., & Erlen, J. (2006). Exemplars of mixed methods data combination and analysis. *Nursing Research, 55*(28), 343–349.

Harrison, Y. D., & Murray, V. (2012). Perspectives on the leadership of chairs of nonprofit organization boards of directors: A grounded theory mixed-method study. *Nonprofit Management and Leadership, 22*(4), 411–437.

Hausman, A. (2000). A multi-method investigation of consumer motivations in impulse buying behavior. *Journal of Consumer Marketing, 17*(5), 403–419.

Hay, M. C. (Ed.). (2016). *Methods that matter: Integrating mixed methods for more effective social science research*. Chicago: The University of Chicago Press.

Hesse-Biber, S. N. (2018). Toward an understanding of a qualitatively driven mixed methods data collection and analysis: Moving toward a theoretically centered mixed methods praxis. In U. Flick (Ed.), *The SAGE handbook of qualitative data collection* (pp. 545–563). Thousand Oaks, CA: Sage Publications.

REFERENCES

Hesse-Biber, S. N., & Flowers, H. (2019). Using a feminist grounded theory approach in mixed methods research. In A. Bryant & K. Charmaz (Eds.), *The SAGE handbook of current developments in grounded theory* (pp. 497–516). London, UK: Sage.

Hesse-Biber, S. N., & Leavy, P. (2008). Pushing on the methodological boundaries: The growing need for emergent methods within and across disciplines. In S.N. Hesse-Biber & P. Leavy (Eds.), *Handbook of emergent methods* (pp. 1–16). New York, NY: Guilford Press.

Hiles, D. (2012). *Mixed methods and the problem of the logic of inquiry*. Draft paper presented at the QMiP symposium on "Mixed Methods in Psychology". Annual BPS Conference, London, April 18–20, 2012.

Hites, L. S., Fifolt, M., Beck, H., Su, W., Kerbawy, S., Wakelee, J., & Nassell, A. (2013). A geospatial mixed methods approach to assessing campus safety. *Evaluation Review*, *37*(5), 347–369.

Holton, J. D. (2008). Grounded theory as a general research methodology. *Grounded Theory Review*, *7*(2), 67–93.

Holton, J. D., & Walsh, I. (2017). *Classic grounded theory: Applications with qualitative and quantitative data*. Thousand Oaks, CA: Sage Publications.

Howell Smith, M. C., Babchuk, W. A., Stevens, J., Garrett, A. L., Wang, S. C., & Guetterman, T. C. (2019). Modeling the use of mixed methods-grounded theory: Developing scales a new measurement model. *Journal of Mixed Methods Research*, *14*(2), 184–206.

Hume, C., Salmon, J., & Ball, K. (2005). Children's perceptions of their homes and neighborhood environments, and their association with objectively measured physical activity: A qualitative and quantitative study. *Health Education Research*, *20*(1), 1–13.

Hunter, A., & Brewer, J. (2015). Designing multimethod research. In R. B. Johnson (Ed.), *The Oxford handbook of multimethod and mixed methods research inquiry* (pp. 185–205). Oxford, UK: Oxford University Press.

Hunter, A., Murphy, K., Grealish, A., Casey, D., & Keady, J. (2011). Navigating the grounded theory terrain: Part 1. *Nurse Researcher*, *18*(4), 6–10.

Inaba, M., & Kakai, H. (2019). Grounded text mining approach: A synergy between grounded theory and text mining approaches. In A. Bryant & K. Charmaz (Eds.), *The SAGE handbook of grounded theory* (pp. 332–351). Thousand Oaks, CA: Sage Publications.

Irwin, S. (2008). Data analysis and interpretation: Emergent issues in linking qualitative and quantitative evidence. In S. N. Hesse-Biber & P. Leavy (Eds.), *Handbook of emergent methods* (pp. 415–435). New York, NY: Guilford Press.

Ivankova, I. (2015). *Mixed methods applications in action research*. Thousand Oaks, CA: Sage Publications.

Ivankova, N., & Wingo, N. (2018). Applying mixed methods in action research: Methodological potentials and advantages. In E. G. Creamer & J. L. Schoonenboon (Eds.), *American Behavioral Scientist*, *62*(7), 978–997.

Jaccard, J., & Jacoby, J. (2010). *Theory construction and model-building skills*. New York, NY: Guilford Press.

Jang, E., McDougall, D. E., Herbert, M., & Russell, P. (2008). Integrative data analytic strategies in research in school success in challenging circumstances. *Journal of Mixed Methods Research*, *2*(3), 221–247.

Jick, T. D. (1979). Mixing qualitative and quantitative methods: Triangulation in action. *Administrative Science Quarterly*, *24*, 602–611.

Johnson, L. (2014). Adapting and combining constructivist grounded theory and discourse analysis: A practical guide for research. *International Journal of Multiple Research Approaches*, *8*(1), 117–133.

Johnson, R. B. (2012). Guest editor's editorial: Dialectical pluralism: A metaparadigm whose time has come. *American Behavioral Scientist*, *56*, 751–754.

Johnson, R. B., McGowan, M. W., & Turner, L. A. (2010). Grounded theory in practice: Inherently a mixed method? *Research in the Schools*, *17*(2), 65–78.

Johnson, R. B., Onwuegbuzie, A. J., & Turner, L. A. (2007). Toward a definition of mixed methods research. *Journal of Mixed Methods Research*, *1*(2), 112–133.

Johnson, R. B., & Schoonenboom, J. (2015). Adding qualitative and mixed methods research to health intervention studies: Interacting with differences. *Qualitative Health Research*, *26*(5), 587–602.

REFERENCES

Johnson, R. B., & Walsh, I. (2019). Mixed grounded theory: Merging grounded theory with mixed methods and multimethod research. In A. Bryant & K. Charmaz (Eds.), *The SAGE handbook of current developments in grounded theory* (pp. 517–531). London, UK: Sage.

Johnson, R. E., Grove, A. L., & Clarke, A. (2019). Pillar integration process: A joint display technique to integrate data in mixed methods research. *Journal of Mixed Methods Research, 13*(3), 301–320.

Jones, L., & Kafetsios, K. (2005). Exposure to political violence and psychological well-being in Bosnian adolescents: A mixed method approach. *Clinical and Child Psychiatry, 19*(2), 157–176.

Kajfez, R., Lee, D., Ehlert, K., Faber, C., Benson, L., & Kennedy, M. (2021). A mixed methods approach to understanding researcher identity. *Studies in Engineering Education, 2*(1), 1–15.

Kaplan, B., & Duchon, D. (1988, December). Combining qualitative and quantitative methods in information systems research: A case study. *Management Information Systems Quarterly, 12*(4), 571–586.

Kawamura, Y., Ivankova, N., Kohler, C., & Purumean-Chaney, S. (2009). Utilizing mixed methods to assess parasocial interaction of an entertainment-education program audience. *International Journal of Multiple Research Approaches, 3*, 88–104.

Kearney, W. S., Kelsey, C., & Herrington, D. (2013). Mindful leaders in highly effectives schools: A mixed-method application of Hoy-s M-scale. *Educational Management Administration and Leadership, 41*(3), 316–335.

Keddy, B., Sims, S. L., & Stern, P. N. (1996). Grounded theory as feminist research methodology. *Journal of Advanced Nursing, 23*, 448–453.

Kelle, U. (2001). Sociological explanations between micro and macro and the integration of qualitative and quantitative methods. *Forum: Qualitative Social Research, 2*(1), no page numbers.

Kesby, M. (2000). Participatory diagramming: Deploying qualitative methods through an action research epistemology. *Area, 32*(4), 423–435.

Knigge, L., & Cope, M. (2006). Grounded visualization: Integrating the analysis of qualitative and quantitative data through grounded theory and visualizations. *Environment and Planning, 38*, 2021–2037.

Koopmans, M. (2017). Mixed methods in search of a problem: Perspectives from complexity theory. *Journal of Mixed Methods Research, 11*(1), 16–18.

Kushner, K. E., & Morrow, R. (2003). Grounded theory, feminist theory, critical theory: Toward theoretical triangulation. *Advances in Nursing Science, 26*(1), 30–43.

Kutnak, M. J., Jr. (2017). *The process of design for general classroom facilities in higher education institutions.* Degree: PhD, Higher Education, Virginia Tech. http://hdl.handle.net/10919/77575

Laws, R., Campbell, K. J., Van der Plight, P., Ball, K., Lynch, J., Russell, G., Taylor, R., & Wilson, E. D. (2015). Obesity prevention in early life: An opportunity to better support the role of maternal and child health nurses in Australia. *BMC Nursing, 14*, 26. doi:10.1186/s12912-015-0077-7

Lee, D., McAlister, A., Ehlert, K., Faber, C., Kajfez, R., Creamer, E., & Kennedy, M. (2019). *Enhancing research quality through use of analytical memo writing in a mixed methods grounded theory study implemented by a multi-institution research team.* Proceedings of the IEEE/ASEE Frontiers in Education Conference, October 16–19, Cincinnati, OH.

Leech, N. L., & Onwuegbuzie, A. J. (2009). A typology of mixed methods research designs. *Quality and Quantity, 43*, 265–275.

Lempert, L. B. (2007). Asking questions of the data: Memo writing in the grounded theory tradition. In A. Bryant & K. Charmaz (Eds.), *The SAGE handbook of grounded theory* (pp. 245–264). Thousand Oaks, CA: Sage.

Levina, N., & Vaast, E. (2008). Innovating or doing as told? Status differences and overlapping boundaries in offshore collaboration. *MIS Quarterly, 32*(2), 307–332.

Levitt, H. M., Creswell, J. W., Josselson, R., Bamberg, M., Frost, D. M., & Suarez-Orozco, C. (2018). Journal article reporting standards for qualitative primary, qualitative meta-analytic, and mixed methods research in psychology: The APA publications and communications task force report. *American Psychologist, 73*(1), 26–46.

Locke, K., Golden-Biddle, K., & Feldman, M. S. (2008). Making doubt generative: Rethinking the role of doubt in the research process. *Organization Science, 19*(6), 907–918.

Loo, I. D., & Lowe, A. (2011). Mixed methods research: Don't "just do it". *Qualitative Research in Accounting and Management, 8*(1), 22–38.

Malagon, M. C., Huber, L. P., & Velez, V. N. (2009). Our experiences, our methods: Using grounded theory to inform critical race theory methodology. *Seattle Journal for Social Justice*, 8(1), 253–272.

Mark, J. (2017, March 2). Get out of here: Scientists examines the benefits of forests, birdsong, and running water. *The New York Times Book Review*. www.nytimes.com/2017/03/02/books/review/nature-fix-florence-williams.html (Retrieved March 31, 2020).

Mason, J. (2006). Mixing methods in a qualitatively driven way. *Qualitative Research*, 6(1), 9–25. doi:10.1177/1468794106058866

Maxwell, J. A. (2012). The importance of qualitative research in causal explanation in education. *Qualitative Inquiry*, 18(8), 655–661.

Maxwell, J. A. (2013). *Qualitative research design*. Thousand Oaks, CA: Sage Publications.

Maxwell, J. A., Chmiel, M., & Rogers, S. E. (2015). Designing integration in multimethod and mixed methods research. In S. Hesse-Biber & R. B. Johnson (Eds.), *The Oxford handbook of multimethod and mixed methods research inquiry* (pp. 223–239). Oxford, UK: Sage.

Maxwell, J. A., & Loomis, D. (2003). Mixed method design: An alternative approach. In A. Tashakkori & C. Teddlie (Eds.), *Handbook of mixed methods in social and behavioral analysis* (pp. 241–271). New York, NY: Guilford Press.

Maxwell, J. A., & Mittapalli, K. (2010). Realism as a stance for mixed methods research. In A. Tashakkori & C. Teddlie (Eds.), *Handbook of mixed methods in social and behavioral research* (pp. 145–168). Thousand Oaks, CA: Sage Publications.

McCall, C., & Edwards, C. D. (2021). New perspectives for implementing grounded theory. *Studies in Engineering Education*, 1(2), 93–107.

McCrudden, M. T., Schraw, G., & Buckendahl, C. W. (2015). *Use of visual displays in research and testing*. Charlotte, NC: Information Age Publishing.

McFerran, K., Roberts, M., & O'Grady, L. (2010). Music therapy with bereaved teenagers: A mixed methods perspective. *Death Studies*, 34, 541–565.

McGhee, G., Marland, G. R., & Atkinson, J. (2007). Grounded theory research: Literature reviewing and reflexivity. *Journal of Advanced Nursing*, 60(3), 334–342.

Mendlinger, S., & Cwikel, J. (2008). Spiraling between qualitative and quantitative data on women's health behaviors: A double helix model for mixed methods. *Qualitative Health Research*, 18(2), 280–293.

Merriam, S. B., & Tisdell, E. J. (2016). *Qualitative research: A guide to design and implementation* (4th edition). San Francisco, CA: John Wiley and Sons.

Mertens, D. M. (2015). Mixed methods and wicked problems. *Journal of Mixed Methods Research*, 9(1), 3–6.

Miles, M. B., & Huberman, A. M. (1994). *An expanded sourcebook: Qualitative data analysis* (2nd edition). Thousand Oaks, CA: Sage Publications.

Mills, J., Bonner, A., & Francis, K. (2006). The development of constructivist grounded theory. *International Journal of Qualitative Methods*, 5(1), 25–35.

Moran-Ellis, J., Alexander, V. D., Cronin, A., Dickenson, M., Fielding, J., Sleney, J., & Thomas, H. (2006). Triangulation and integration: Processes, claims, and implications. *Qualitative Research*, 6(1), 45–59.

Morgan, D. G., & Stewart, N. J. (2002). Theory building through mixed-method evaluation of a dementia special care unit. *Research in Nursing and Health*, 25, 479–488.

Morgan, D. L. (2013). Pragmatism as a paradigm for social research. *Qualitative Inquiry*, 20(8), 1045–1053.

Morgan, D. L. (2014). *Integrating qualitative and quantitative methods: A pragmatic approach*. Thousand Oaks, CA: Sage Publications.

Morgan, D. L. (2015). From themes to hypotheses: Following up with quantitative methods. *Qualitative Health Research*, 25(6), 789–793.

Morgan, D. L. (2020). Pragmatism as the basis for grounded theory. *The Qualitative Report*, 25(1), 64–73.

Morse, J. M. (1995). The significance of saturation. *Qualitative Health Research*, 5(2), 147–149.

Morse, J. M. (2010). Simultaneous and sequential qualitative mixed methods designs. *Qualitative Inquiry*, 16(6), 483–491.

Morse, J. M. (2015). Issues in qualitatively driven mixed method designs: Walking through a mixed-method project. In S. Hesse-Biber & B. Johnson (Eds.), *The Oxford handbook of multimethod and mixed methods research inquiry* (pp. 206–222). Thousand Oaks, CA: Sage Publications.

REFERENCES

Morse, J. M. (2020). The challenging face of qualitative inquiry. *International Journal of Qualitative Methods*, 19, 1–7.

Morse, J. M., & Clark, L. (2019). The nuances of grounded theory sampling and the pivotal role of theoretical sampling. In A. Bryant & K. Charmaz (Eds.), *The SAGE handbook of current developments in grounded theory*. London, UK: Sage.

Morse, J. M., & Niehaus, L. (2009). *Mixed method design: Principles and procedures*. Walnut Creek, CA: Left Coast Press.

Morse, J. M., Stern, P. N., Corbin, J., Bowers, B., Charmaz, K., & Clarke, A. E. (2009). *Developing grounded theory: The second generation*. New York, NY: Routledge.

Nagel, D. A., Burns, V. F., Tilley, C., & Aubin, D. (2015). When novice researchers adopt constructivist grounded theory: Navigating less travelled paradigmatic methodological paths in PhD dissertation work. *International Journal of Doctoral Studies*, 20, 365–383.

Nastasi, B. K., Hitchcock, J. H., & Brown, L. M. (2010). An inclusive framework for conceptualizing mixed method design typologies. In A. Tashakkori & C. Teddlie (Eds.), *SAGE handbook of mixed methods in social and behavioral research* (2nd edition, pp. 305–338). Thousand Oaks, CA: Sage Publications.

Nelson, J. (2017). Using conceptual depth criteria: Addressing the challenge of reaching saturation in qualitative research. *Qualitative Research*, 17(5), 554–570.

Nightingale, A. (2003). A feminist in the forest: Situated knowledges and mixed methods in natural research management. *ACME: An International E-Journal for Critical Geographies*, 2(1), 77–90.

Omoquit, M., Tso, P., Varga-Atkins, T., O'Brien, M., & Wheeldon, J. (2013). Diagrammatic elicitation: Defining the use of diagrams in data collection. *The Qualitative Report*, 18(30), 1–12.

Onwuegbuzie, A. J. (2012). Introduction: Putting the MIXED back into quantitative and qualitative research in educational research and beyond: Moving toward the radical middle. *International Journal of Multiple Research Approaches*, 6(3), 192–219.

Onwuegbuzie, A. J., & Dickinson, W. B. (2008). Mixed methods analysis and information visualizations: Graphical display for effective communication of research results. *The Qualitative Report*, 13(2), 204–227.

Onwuegbuzie, A. J., & Leech, N. L. (2019). On qualitizing. *International Journal of Multiple Research Approaches*, 11(2), 98–131.

Onwuegbuzie, A. J., & Teddlie, C. (2003). A framework for analyzing data in mixed methods research. In A. Tashakkori & C. Teddlie (Eds.), *Handbook of mixed methods in social and behavioral research* (pp. 351–383). Thousand Oaks, CA: Sage Publications.

Patton, M. Q. (2002). *Qualitative research and evaluation methods* (3rd edition). Thousand Oaks, CA: Sage Publications.

Pearce, L. D. (2015). Thinking outside of the Q boxes: Further motivating a mixed research perspective. In S. Hesse-Biber & R. B. Johnson (Eds.), *The Oxford handbook of multimethod and mixed methods research inquiry* (pp. 42–56). Oxford, UK: Oxford University Press.

Plano Clark, V. L., & Ivankova, N. V. (2016). *Mixed methods research: A guide to the field*. Mixed Methods Research Series. Thousand Oaks, CA: Sage Publications.

Plano Clark, V. L., & Sanders, K. (2015). The use of visual displays in mixed methods research: Strategies for effectively integrating quantitative and qualitative components of a study. In M. T. McCrudden, G. Schraw, & C. Buckendahl (Eds.), *Use of visual displays in research and testing: Coding, interpreting, and reporting data* (pp. 177–206). Charlotte, NC: Information Age Publishing.

Poth, C. N. (2018a). *Innovation in mixed methods research: A practical guide to integrative thinking with complexity*. Thousand Oaks, CA: Sage Publications.

Poth, C. N. (2018b). The curious case of complexity: Implications for mixed methods practice. *International Journal of Multiple Research Approaches*, 10(1), 1–9.

Poth, C. N. (2020). Confronting complex problems with adaptive mixed methods research practices. *Caribbean Journal of Mixed Methods Research*, 1(1), 29–45.

Prosser, J. (2007). Visual methods and the visual culture of schools. *Visual Studies*, 22(1), 13–30.

Ralph, N., Birks, M., & Chapman, Y. (2015). The methodological dynamism of grounded theory. *International Journal of Qualitative Methods*, 1–6.

REFERENCES

Reeping, D., & Edwards, C. (2020, August). *Exemplars of integration in engineering education's use of mixed methods research*. ASEE 2020 Annual Conference and Exposition. doi:10.18260/1-2-34623

Reeping, D., Tayler, A. R., Knight, D. B., & Edwards, C. (2019). Mixed methods analysis strategies in program evaluation: Beyond "a little quant here, a little qual there". *Journal of Engineering Education*, 108(20), 178–196.

Reicherz, J. (2007). Abduction: The logic of discovery. In A. Bryant & K. Charmaz (Eds.), *The SAGE handbook of grounded theory* (pp. 214–228). Thousand Oaks, CA: Sage Publications.

Rieger, K. L. (2018). Discriminating among grounded theory approaches. *Nursing Inquiry*, 26. https://doi.org/10.1111/nin.12261

Rocheleau, D. (1995). Maps, numbers, text, and context: Mixing methods in feminist political ecology. *Professional Geographer*, 47(4), 458–466.

Rossman, G. B., & Wilson, B. L. (1985). Numbers and words: Combining quantitative and qualitative methods in a single large-scale evaluation study. *Evaluation Review*, 9(5), 627–643.

Rucks-Ahidiana, Z., & Bierbaum, A. H. (2015). Qualitative spaces: Integrating spatial analysis for a mixed methods approach. *International Journal of Qualitative Methods*, 14(2), 92–103.

Rule, P., & John, M. (2015). A necessary dialogue: Theory in case study research. *International Journal of Qualitative Methods*, 14(4), no page numbers. doi:10.1177/1609406915611575

Saint Arnault, D. (2009). Cultural determinants of help seeking: A model of research practice. *Research and Theory for Nursing Practice: An International Journal*, 23(4), 259–278.

Saint Arnault, D., & Fetters, M. D. (2011). RO1 funding for mixed methods research: Lessons learned from the "mixed methods analysis of Japanese depression" project. *Journal of Mixed Methods Research*, 5(4), 309–329.

Saldaña, J. (2009). *The coding manual for qualitative researchers*. Thousand Oaks, CA: Sage Publications.

Sandelowski, M. (1993). Theory unmasked: The uses and guises of theory in qualitative research. *Research in Nursing and Health*, 15, 213–218.

Sandelowski, M. (2014). Unmixing mixed-methods research. *Research in Nursing in Health*, 37, 3–8.

Sandelowski, M., Voils, C. I., & Knafl, G. (2009). On quantitizing. *Journal of Mixed Methods Research*, 3, 208–222.

Sandelowski, M., Voils, C. I., Leeman, J., & Crandell, J. L. (2012). Mapping the mixed methods-mixed research synthesis terrain. *Journal of Mixed Methods Research*, 6(4), 317–331.

Sanscartier, M. D. (2018). The craft attitude: Navigating mess in mixed methods research. *Journal of Mixed Methods Research*, 14(1), 47–62.

Santiago-Brown, I., Jerram, C., Metcalfe, A., & Collins, C. (2014). What does sustainability mean? Knowledge gleaned from applying mixed methods research to wine grape growing. *Journal of Mixed Methods Research*, 9(3), 232–251.

Schneider, A. (1998, September 11). Why don't women publish as much as men? *The Chronicle of Higher Education*, pp. A14–A16.

Schoonenboom, J. (2019). Develop your case! How controversial case, subcases, and moderated can guide you through mixed methods data analysis. *Frontiers in Psychology*, 10, 1–13. doi:10.3389/fpsyg.2019.01369

Sebastian, K. (2019). Distinguishing between the types of grounded theory: Classical, interpretive, and constructivist. *Journal for Social Thought*, 3(1), 1–9.

Seidel, S., & Urquhart, C. (2013). On emergence and forcing in information systems grounded theory studies: The case of Strauss and Corbin. *Journal of Information Technology*, 28, 237–260.

Shannon-Baker, P., & Edwards, C. (2018). The affordances and challenges to incorporating visual methods in mixed methods research. *American Behavioral Scientist*, 62(7), 935–955.

Sheridan, J., Chamberlain, K., & Dupuis, A. (2011). Timelining: Visualizing experience. *Qualitative Research*, 11(5), 552–569.

Shim, J., Johnson, R. B., Gasson, S., Goodill, S., Jermyn, R., & Bradt, J. (2017). A model of dance/movement therapy for resilience-building in people living with chronic pain. *European Journal of Integrative Medicine*, 9, 27–40.

REFERENCES

Shim, M., Johnson, B., Bradt, J., & Gasson, S. (2020). A mixed methods-grounded theory design for producing more refined theoretical models. *Journal of Mixed Methods Research*, *15*(1), 61–86.

Strauss, A., & Corbin, J. (1990). *Basics of qualitative research* (1st edition). Thousand Oaks, CA: Sage Publications.

Strauss, A., & Corbin, J. (1998). *Basics of qualitative research: Techniques and procedures for developing grounded theory* (2nd edition). Thousand Oaks, CA: Sage Publications.

Suddaby, R. (2006). From the editors: What grounded theory is not. *Academy of Management Journal*, *49*(4), 633–642.

Sweeney, S. M., & Von Hagen, L. A. (2015). Middle school students' perceptions of safety: A mixed methods study. *Journal of School Health*, *85*(10), 688–696.

Tashakkori, A., & Teddlie, C. (Eds.). (2003). *SAGE handbook of mixed methods in social and behavioral science research*. Thousand Oaks, CA: Sage Publications.

Tashakkori, A., & Teddlie, C. (2008). Quality of inferences in mixed methods research: Calling for an integrative framework. In M. M. Bergman (Ed.), *Advances in mixed methods research* (pp. 101–119). Thousand Oaks, CA: Sage Publications.

Teixeira, S. (2014). "It seems like no one care": Participatory photo mapping to understand youth perspectives on property vacancy. *Journal of Adolescent Research*, *30*(3), 390–414.

Teixeira, S. (2016). Beyond broken windows: Youth perspectives on housing abandonment and its impact on individual and community well-being. *Child Indicators of Research*, *9*(3), 582–607.

Thomas, G. (2010). Doing case study: Abduction not induction, phronesis not theory. *Qualitative Inquiry*, *16*(7), 575–582.

Thomas, G., & James, J. (2006). Reinventing grounded theory: Some questions about theory, ground, and discovery. *British Educational Research Journal*, *32*(6), 767–795.

Thornberg, R. (2012). Informed grounded theory. *Scandinavian Journal of Educational Research*, *56*(3), 243–259.

Thorne, S., Kirkham, S. R., & O'Flynn-Magee, K. (2004). The analytic challenge in interpretive description. *International Journal of Qualitative Methods*, *3*(1). https://journals.sagepub.com/doi/10.1177/160940690400300101

Tiefenbacher, J. P. (2013). Themes of U.S. wine advertising and the use of geography and place to market wine. *EchoGeo*, *23*. doi:10.4000/echogeo.13378

Timmermans, S., & Tavory, I. (2012). Theory construction in qualitative research: From grounded theory to abductive analysis. *Sociological Theory*, *30*(3), 167–186.

Timonen, V., Foley, G., & Conlon, C. (2018). Challenges when using grounded theory: A pragmatic introduction to doing GT research. *International Journal of Qualitative Methods*, *17*, 1–10.

Urquhart, C. (2007). The evolving nature of grounded theory method: The case of the information systems disciplines. In A. Bryant & K. Charmaz (Eds.), *The SAGE handbook of grounded theory* (pp. 339–351). London, UK: Sage.

Umoquit, M., Tso, P., Varga-Atkins, T., O'Brien, M., & Wheeldon, J. (2013). Diagrammatic elicitation: Defining the use of diagrams in data collection. *The Qualitative Report*, *18*, 1–12.

Urquhart, C., Lehmann, H., & Myers, M. (2010). Putting the "theory" back into grounded theory: Guidelines for grounded theory studies in information systems. *Information Systems*, *20*, 357–381.

Urquhart, K. (2013). *Grounded theory for qualitative research: A practical guide*. London, UK: Sage.

Van Maanen, J., Sorensen, J. B., & Mitchell, T. R. (2007). Introduction to special topic forum: The interplay between theory and method. *Academy of Management Review*, *32*(4), 1145–1154.

Walker, R. E., Block, J., & Kawachi, I. (2012). Do residents of food deserts express different food buying preferences compared to residents of food oases? A mixed-methods analysis. *International Journal of Behavioral Nutrition and Physical Activity*, *9*, 41. https://doi.org/10.1186/1479-5868-9-41

Walsh, I. (2014). A strategic path to study IT use through users' IT culture and IT needs: A mixed-method grounded theory. *Journal of Strategic Information Systems*, *23*, 146–173.

Walsh, I. (2015). Using quantitative data in mixed-design grounded theory studies: An enhanced path formal grounded theory in information systems. *European Journal of Information Systems*, *24*, 531–557.

Wang, C., & Burris, M. A. (1997). Photovoice: Concept, methodology, and use for participatory needs assessment. *Health Education & Behavior, 24*(3), 369–387.

Watson, A. (2019). Methods braiding: A technique for arts-based and mixed methods research. *Sociological Research Online, 25*(1), 66–83.

Weed, M. (2009). Research quality considerations for grounded theory research in sports and exercise psychology. *Psychology of Sports Medicine, 10*, 502–510.

Weick, K. E. (1989). Theory construction as disciplined imagination. *Academy of Management Review, 14*(4), 516–531.

Weick, K. E. (1995). What theory is not, theorizing is. *Administrative Science Quarterly, 40*, 385–290.

Weisner, T. S. (2016). Findings that matter: A commentary. In M. C. Hay (Ed.), *Methods that matter: Integrating mixed methods for more effective social science research* (pp. 391–408). Chicago: The University of Chicago Press.

Weiss, H. B., Kreider, H., Mayer, E., Hencke, R., & Vaughn, M. A. (2005). Working it out: The chronicle of a mixed-method analysis. In *Discovering successful pathways in children's development: Mixed methods and the study of childhood and family life* (pp. 47–64). Baltimore, MD: John D. and Catherine T. MacArthur Foundation Series on Mental Health and Development.

Weiss, H. B., Mayer, E., & Kreider, H. (2003). Making it work: Low-income working mothers' involvement in their children's education. *American Educational Research Journal, 40*(4), 879–901.

Wesely, P. (2010). Language learning motivation in early adolescents: Using mixed methods research to explore contradiction. *Journal of Mixed Methods Research, 4*(4), 295–312.

Westhues, A., Ochocka, J., Jacobson, N., Simich, L., Maiter, S., Janzen, R., & Fleras, A. (2008). Developing theory from complexity: Reflections on a collaborative mixed method participatory action research study. *Qualitative Health Research, 18*(5), 701–717.

Whiteside, M., Mills, J., & McCalman, J. (2012). Using secondary data for grounded theory analysis. *Australian Social Work, 63*(4), 504–516.

Whittemore, R. (2005). Analysis of integration in nursing science and practice. *Journal of Nursing Scholarship, 37*(3), 261–267.

Williams, S., & Keady, J. (2012). Centre stage diagrams: A new method to develop constructivist grounded theory-late-stage Parkinson's disease as a case exemplar. *Qualitative Research, 12*(2), 218–238.

Windsor, L. C. (2013). Using concept mapping in community-based participatory research: A mixed methods approach. *Journal of Mixed Methods Research, 7*(3), 274–293.

Wisdom, J. P., Cavaleri, M. A., Onwuegbuzie, A. J., & Green, C. A. (2012). Methodological reporting in qualitative, quantitative, and mixed methods health services research articles. *Health Services Research, 47*(2), 721–741.

Wuest, J. (1995). Feminist grounded theory: An exploration of the congruency and tensions between two traditions in knowledge discovery. *Qualitative Health Research, 5*(1), 127–137.

Wuest, J., & Hodgins, M. J. (2011). Reflections on methodological approaches and conceptual contributions in a program of caregiving research: Development and testing of Wuest's theory of family caregiving. *Qualitative Health Research, 21*(2), 151–161.

Yang, D. Z., Richardson, J. C., French, B. F., & Lehman, J. D. (2011). The development of a content analysis model for assessing students' cognitive learning in asynchronous online discussions. *Educational Technology Research and Development, 59*, 43–70. doi:10.1007/s11423-010-9166-1

Index

Note: Page numbers in *italics* indicate a figure and page numbers in **bold** indicate a table on the corresponding page.

abduction 17–18; abductive reasoning, as mixed methods approach extension 51; integrated analysis using 48–49
Agerfalk, P. J. 4
Alexander, V. D. 49
analytic density 10
Apramian, T. 47, 97, 138
Austin, J. 135

Babchuck, W. A. 8, 125
Baulch, B. 82–84
Bazeley, P. xx, 63, 78, 113
Benson, L. 64
bi-dimensional approach 30
Birks, M. 74
Bosnian War 68
Boyd, S. J. 88, 115
Brown, L. M. 42
Bryant, A. 48, 53, 122
Buckley, C. 74, 126
Buffet, Warren 133
"burden" theoretical code 60
Bussing, R. 52, 59–62, 66, 82

Caracelli, V. J. 94
Carmona, M. 102, 107–109, 111
case-based approach in MM-GTM 105; exploring dissonance with 105; macro-level perspective 109; meso-level perspective 109; micro-level perspective 109; mixed method case studies 107–109; multiple theoretical frameworks 111–113; providing evidence of originality 109–110; stair-step process *110*; theoretical triangulation 111; visual data in 105–106

case-based timeline 82–84, *83*
case study 124
Castro, F. G. 88, 115
Catallo, C. J. 14, 36, 38–40, 43, 63, 126
causality 61, 96–98
change maps 40
Charmaz, K. xx, 4, 6–7, 28–29, 34, 47–48, 54, 60, 65, 74, 97, **98**, 123–124, 128, 131, 138
Ciliska, D. 38, 63
Clark, A. 30, 87
Classic Glaserian grounded theory **98**
close-ended questions 60
community-based participatory action project (CBPR) 36, 41
complexity 19
composite grounded theory model *129*
comprehensiveness 12
Computer Assisted Qualitative Data Analysis Software (CAQDAS) 40, 80
concept maps 40, **77**
conceptual framework 5
concordance table, triangulating through 113–114
Conlon, C. 52
constant comparative method 16–17; iterative exchange embedded in 16–17; linking to an abductive logic 17
constructivist grounded theory 9, 64, **98**
context 29
Coon, D. W. 125
Cope, M. 75, 80–81, 106
Corbin, J. 40, 65, 74, 123–124, 128, 138
core grounded theory procedures 54–56, **55–56**; coding **55**; constant comparative method **55**; core category **55**; frequency of the use of 57; logic model, conditional matrix, or formal grounded theory model

55; memo writing 55; qualitative and quantitative data in 57–58; saturation 55; social process 55; theoretical coding 55; theoretical sampling 55
Creswell, J. W. 23, 28
Cronin, A. 49, 52–54
cross case analysis 64
cross-cutting themes 24–25, 43–44, 70–71, 90–91, 117, 140
crossover methodology 2–3

data analysis in MM-GTM 49–51
Davis, P. 82–84
Dey, I. 33, 97, 119, 131, 134
diagram **77**
dialectical stance 14
discourse analysis 124
Discovery of Grounded Theory, The 23
dissonance in MM-GTM, leveraging to advance theoretical reasoning 93–118; case-based approach in MM-GTM 105; centrality of dissonance to research process 96–98; contradictory findings, explanation for 103–105; cross-cutting themes, building on 117; designing for 101–102, **101**; discipline of generating multiple explanations 98–99; initiation rationale 94; potential sources of dissonance 98–100; unexpected sources of dissonance 99–100; varying points of view **98**; visual data in a case-based analysis 105–106; *see also* visual displays, warranting inferences through
diversity 122
Duchon, D. 102–103, 111, 126, 134
Dunne, C. 34

ecomaps 77
Edwards, C. 77
Eisenhardt, K. M. 64, 66, 105, 113–114
Erzberger, C. 91, 93
Evans, B. C. 31, 35, 37, 125
evidence-based explanatory models 2

feminist grounded theory 26, 28, 70
Fielding, J. 11, 49, 94
Fielding, N. xxi
final composite model from Kawamura, 11–12, *13*
Flick, U. 26
Floersch, J. 125
Flowers, H. 23
Foley, G. 52
formal grounded theory 40

fully integrated approach to mixed methods (FIMMR) 78–79
fully integrated mixed method grounded theory methodology (FIMM-GTM) 8, 58
fully integrated mixed method research (FIMMR) 8

Gasson, S. 17
Glaser, B. 5–7, 9, 28–29, 34, 47, 66, 128
Gorard, S. 43
Graebner, M. 113
Graham, W. F. 94
grand theories 29, 46
graphic elicitation 72
Greene, J. C. 7, 9, 14, 94
grounded theory 2, 4–6; conceptual framework 5; grounded theory method (GTM) 14, 33–34, **40**; meta-model 127; mixed methods and 6–7; social-psychological processes 6
grounded visualization 75–76
Grove, A. L. 87
Guetterman, T. C. 8, 21, 57, 125

Hadley, G. 97
Herbert, M. 94
Hesse-Biber, S. N. 23, 26, 28, 121
Hiles, D. 50
Hitchcock, J. H. 42
Holton, J. D. 7, 34, 57
Howell Smith, M. C. 8, 125

Inaba, M. 137
inductive–deductive–abductive analytical cycle *50*
initiation rationale 94
integrated analysis using abduction 48–49
integrated analytical memo 62–63
integrated approaches to a grounded theory visualization 126
integrated case-based analysis 63
integrated methodological approaches 2
integrated theoretical coding 59–62; causal pathways produced by Bussing **61**; close-ended questions 60; conceptual model from Bussing et al. *60*; open-ended questions 60
integrated theoretical sampling 66
integrative case-based memo 64–65
integrative display **77**
integrative MMR-GTM *50*
integrative visual displays 74–75; concept map **77**; data analysis **76**; data collection **76**; diagram **77**; drawing

conclusions **76**; integrative display **77**; joint display **77**; mapping **77**; matrix mapping **77**; mixed methods used to generate analytical insight 78–79; participatory photo mapping (PPM) 79; purposes served by **76**; reporting **76**; timelining **77**; types 77
interpretive comprehensive 130
Introduction to Fully Integrated Mixed Method Research, An 130
investigators using MM-GTM 136–139; challenges faced by 136; expansive view of expertise, developing 138–139; meaningful sample size 137; technical language 137
Irwin, S. 31
Ivankova, N. 11

Jang, E. 94
Johnson, B. R. 10
Johnson, L. 9
Johnson, R. B. 9–10, 14, 23, 87, 99, 117, 119, 121
joint displays 74–75, 128–130; addressing inconsistent data through 128–130; to advance analysis **77**, 87–89; of comparisons 130; final composite grounded theory model from Shim et al. *129*; qualitative data **88–89**; quantitative data **88**; to warrant conclusions 114–115
Jones, L. 52, 67, 68, 82

Kafetsios, K. 52, 67, 68, 82
Kakai, H. 137
Kaplan, B. 102–103, 111, 126, 134
Kawamura, Y. 11–12, 126, 128
Keady, J. 85
Kelle, U. 91, 93
Kellison, J. G. 88, 115
Knigge, L. 75, 80–81, 106
Kopak, A. 88, 115
Kreider, H. 94
Kutnak, M. 81

language and purpose, establishing 1–25; multi-method research 2; purpose 2–3; contribution 2–3
Laws, R. 138
Lee, D. 52, 59, 64
Lehman, J. D. 33
Lempert, L. B. 64
leverage dissonance and paradox 13–14

literature review 3, 26, 28–30, 34–35, **35**, *100*; in MM-GTM, 51; methodological 138–139; theoretical coding 58–62, 114
Locke, K. 18

MacMillan, H. L. 38, 63
macro-level constructs 29
Malagon, M. C. 134
mapping **77**
mapping software (ArcGis) 80
Mark, J. 85–86
Mason, J. 11
matrix mapping, integrating data through **77**, 84–85; conducive to MM-GTM 85–87; design of *87*; generating analytical insight from *86*; qualitative software 84
Mayer, E. 94
McCalman, J. 52
McDougall, D. E. 94
Mertens, D. M. xxi
meso-level constructs 29
methodological adaptability of grounded theory 33
methodological dynamism 33
methodological rationale for MM-GTM, articulating 123–125; methodological transparency 131–132; originality 135; procedural diagrams 132–133; quality gauge ways in 130–131; reflexivity 134–135; saturation 131; utility 135; visualizing a theoretical model developed 125–126
methodological transparency 130–132
Mexican American immigrants 31, 35
micro-level constructs 29
middle range theory 46
Mills, J. 52, 74
mixed analysis through integrated case-based memos 62–63
mixed grounded theory (MGT) 117, 119
Mixed Method Evaluation Rubric (MMER) 130
mixed method grounded theory methodology (MM-GTM) 3, 7; analytic logic 15, *20*; analytic procedures 15, *20*; "classic" approach to 9–10; compatibility with multiple paradigms 16; contextual issues 15; contributions of each method 19–20; cross-cutting themes 24–25; an exemplar of 11–13; formal approach to grounded theory versus 124; integrated approaches to,

INDEX 171

distinguishing exemplars of 20–23; as an invitation to leverage dissonance and paradox 13–14; link to complexity 19; as a methodology, conceptualizing 14–16; multiple sources of data in, analyzing **18**; pairing with other qualitative approaches 124–125; prevalence, indications of 8–9; qualitative phase 9; quantitative phase 9; research design 15

mixed methods 6–7, 51; analytic density 10; in building explanatory power 10–11; grounded theory and 6–7; prioritizing the role of 10–11; "radical potential" of 10; research 7; used to generate analytical insight 78–79

mixed methods and the process of theorizing 46–71; abductive reasoning to the constant comparative method 51; core grounded theory procedures 54–56; cross-cutting themes 70–71; integrated analysis using abduction 48–49; integrated case-based memos, analysis through 62–63; integrated theoretical sampling 66; integrative MMR-GTM *50*; interactive approach to data analysis 49–51; saturation 66–68; theoretical coding 58–59; theoretical sampling 65–66; theoretical sampling with a promising lead 68–69

mixed methods with theoretical frameworks 26–45; contribution 27; cross-cutting themes 43–44; "design" word, implications of 28–29; demonstrating variability with a group of exemplars in 35–36; explore counterintuitive findings (**Exemplar 2**) 38–40; formal grounded theory 40; life course perspective 37; macro-level constructs 29; meso-level constructs 29; methodological adaptability 33; micro-level constructs 29; multi-dimensionality in research questions, embedding 30–31; multi-layered social contexts 29; objectives 27; purpose 27; research problem in, conceptualizing 29–30, *30*; study design, theory use (**Exemplar 1**) 36–38; theoretical model as an outcome, developing 41–42; theoretical reasoning, literature contribution to **35**; varied approaches to using 26–45

mixed priority 8, 111, 133
moderating cases 63
Moran-Ellis, J. 49
Morgan, D. G. 16, 97
Morse, J. M. 14, 66, 125, 139
multi-dimensionality 2; framing a research problem in 29–30, *30*; in research questions, embedding 30–31

multi-dimensional theorizing 31–33; conceptual framework 31; exemplar that models 31–33; from Evans *32*; initial visualization 31; qualitative data 32; quantitative data 32
multi-method research 2–3
Myers, M. 33

narrative analysis 124
Nature Fix 85
Nelson, J. 134
Niehaus, L. 14

Onwuegbuzie, A. 138
open-ended questions 60

paradigm(s) 15, 125; feminist 80; multiple 16; philosophical 96, 123
participatory action research (PAR) 2, 41, 124
participatory photo mapping (PPM) 79
Plano, C. V. 28
positivism/postpositivsm 16, 56, 79, 97, 130, 134
Postmodern Clarkeian grounded theory **98**
Poth, C. xxi
pragmatism 16–17, 97
procedural diagrams 132–133

quality: assessing in MM-GTM 130–131; highlighting through reporting 119–141
QUAL+QUAN combination logic 21

radical potential 10–11, 94
randomized controlled trial (RCT) 38
reflexivity 134–135
reporting: conventional approaches to 132–134; highlighting through 119–141; inconsistent data 128–130; integrative visual displays 76; mixed methods 89, 130; on MM-GTM 117, 130, 132; shortcomings in 54; visualization in 74
research design 10, 15; adaptability in 99; complex 19, 122; implications of 28; quality and 130
Rieger, K. L. 97
Rossman, G. B. 94
rupture theorizing 108
Russell, P. 94

Saint Arnault, D. 66
Saldaña, Johnny 58, 61

Sandelowski, M. 4, 30, 35, 48
Sanscartier, M. D. 128
saturation 66–68, 131
Schoonenboom, J. L. 63, 99
Sebastian, K. 97
Seidel, S. 14, 33, 40
Shannon-Baker, P. 77
Shim, J. 10, 126–128
social-psychological process 6
spiraling cycles of ideas and evidence 63
Stevens, J. 8, 125
Strauss, A. 9, 28–29, 40, 47, 65–66, 74, 96, 123–124, 128, 138
Straussian grounded theory **98**
Suddaby, R. 17

Tashakkori, A. 91
Tavory, I. 48
Taylor, R. 64
team-based project 38
Teddlie, C. 91
Teixeira, S. 80, 99, 107
theme *see* cross-cutting themes
theoretical coding 58–62; *see also* integrated theoretical coding
theoretical propositions 126
theoretical reasoning advancing with visualizations 72–92; integrative displays 74–75; joint displays 74–75; literature contribution to **35**; matrix-mapping, integrating data through 84–85; visual methods, grounded theory, and mixed methods, overlap between 75–76; *see also* integrative visual displays; joint displays; timelining as visualization strategy
theoretical sampling 65–66, 68–69
theoretical sensitivity 98
theoretical triangulation 111
theory 3–14; "burden" theoretical code 60; case-based approach in MM-GTM 111–113; Classic Glaserian grounded **98**; composite grounded model *129;* constructivist grounded 9, 64, **98**; defining 3–14; feminist grounded 26, 28, 70; formal grounded 40; fully integrated mixed method research (FIMMR) 8; grand 29, 46; in building explanatory power 10–11; middle range 46; mixed grounded theory (MGT) 117, 119; mixed methods and grounded 6–7; Postmodern Clarkeian grounded **98**; Straussian grounded **98**; *see also specific theories/types*
Thomas, H. 49
Thornberg, R. 4, 34, 97
timelining as visualization strategy **77**, 81–82; case-based analysis and 82–84; in integration of different types of data 81–82; in understanding poverty status 82–84
time-ordered process 128
Timmermans, S. 48
Timonen, V. 52
triangulating through concordance table 113–114

Ume, E. 125
unexpected sources of dissonance 99–100; factors that mitigate 100–101; in MM-GTM study *100*
Urquhart, C. 14, 33, 40
utility 135

variety 122
verification 96
visual data in case-based analysis 105–106
visual displays 2, 75–76, 113
visual displays, warranting inferences through 113–116; documenting support for alternative explanations 115–116; joint display to warrant conclusions from a study 114–115; triangulating through concordance table 113–114

Walsh, I. 7, 10, 16, 17, 23, 57–58, 117, 119, 121–122
Waring, M. J. 74, 126
warranting 50, 83; concordance table, triangulating through 113–114; inferences through visual displays 113–116; joint display use in 114–115
Waters, J. 17
Weed, M. 43
Weiss, H. B. 51, 94
Wesely, P. 102, 111, 133
Westhues, A. 41–42, 125
Whiteside, M. 52, 66
Williams, S. L. 85
Wilson, B. L. 94
Windsor, L. C. 84

Printed in the United States
by Baker & Taylor Publisher Services